Shoot the Conductor

Shoot the Conductor

TOO CLOSE TO MONTEUX, SZELL, AND ORMANDY

ANSHEL BRUSILOW
AND ROBIN UNDERDAHL

Number 7 in the Mayborn Literary Nonfiction Series

University of North Texas Press
Mayborn Graduate Institute of Journalism
Denton, Texas

10 9 8 7 6 5 4

Permissions:
University of North Texas Press
1155 Union Circle #311336
Denton, TX 76203-5017

The paper used in this book meets the minimum requirements of the American National Standard for Permanence of Paper for Printed Library Materials, z39.48.1984. Binding materials have been chosen for durability.

Library of Congress Cataloging-in-Publication Data

Brusilow, Anshel, author.
Shoot the conductor : too close to Monteux, Szell, and Ormandy / Anshel Brusilow and Robin Underdahl. -- First edition.
    pages cm -- (Number 7 in the Mayborn literary nonfiction series)
Includes bibliographical references.
ISBN 978-1-57441-613-8 (cloth : alk. paper) -- ISBN 978-1-57441-629-9 (ebook)
ISBN 978-1-57441-646-6 (pbk)
1. Brusilow, Anshel. 2. Conductors (Music)--United States--Biography.
3. Concertmasters--United States--Biography. 4. Music teachers--United States--Biography. I. Underdahl, Robin, 1953- author. II. Title. III. Series: Mayborn literary nonfiction series ; no. 7.

ML422.B885A3 2015
784.2092--dc23
[B]

2015011488

Shoot the Conductor: Too Close to Monteux, Szell, and Ormandy is Number 7 in the Mayborn Literary Nonfiction Series

The electronic edition of this book was made possible by the support of the Vick Family Foundation.

Contents

Acknowledgments

MY FATHER AND MOTHER, Leon and Dora Brusilow, deserve first mention for their dedication to the musical development of their two sons as well as the love and affection shown to us. I wish to honor Nathan, my brother, a world class clarinetist who was instrumental in putting together the Chamber Symphony of Philadelphia. And my darling wife and confidant, Marilyn, who stood by me every inch of the way and encouraged me when life and career were most bleak. My children David, Jennie, and Melinda also played a role in this memoir, and even our grandchildren, Jessica, Kyle, Stephen, Amy, and Jon David. Our great-granddaughter Madeline Rollins, born September 22, 2014, brought so much joy that I forgive her for distracting me from this work.

I wish to express my deepest appreciation to my dear friends Naomi and Gary Graffman. They met with Robin early in the process and have cheered us on and added detail to memories. Naomi read the manuscript repeatedly and helped in many ways.

I am grateful to Mr. Edwin Fleisher for sending my father and me to Mr. William F. Happich, who gave me my musical foundation. I was thrilled that Mr. Efrem Zimbalist, Sr., took me as a student at the Curtis Institute of Music. It was Dr. Jani Szanto who gave me the understanding of how to say something through the music and to understand the wishes of the composer. He was the teacher who most formed me as a musician.

I thank Joe Barone for introducing me to the Monteuxs. The friends I made in Hancock, Maine—Harold Glick, Earl Murray, and others—were life-long. The Meyer Davis family were kind to me there, and the Sakovich family took me in when I went to San Francisco to study with Maître.

I acknowledge my affection and admiration for Stan Grossman, my "Assistant Concertmaster" and my very best friend while growing up.

I would add Ken Cuthbert for giving me the opportunity to join the North Texas State University, later to become the University of North Texas. My dear friends George Papich and Martin Mailman taught me what teaching at a university means. Clay Couturiaux was first my student and became my invaluable assistant at the College of Music. Now my talented successor at the Richardson Symphony Orchestra, he has been instrumental in the research for this book.

My deepest affection and appreciation go to Robin Underdahl, my coauthor, without whom I could not have told this story. I thank my former student, Irene Mitchell for introducing me to Robin. Irene was determined that my memories and experiences should not be lost and she has been involved in our process from start to finish with everything from reading the manuscript to finding photos to bringing chicken soup.

We also want to thank manuscript readers Bill Marvel, Drema Berkheimer, Julianne McCullagh, Dan McCartney, and many more who read specific chapters. Old friends, colleagues, and students talked with Robin or me during the writing and greatly enriched the broth: Margaret McDermott, Wilfred Rogers, Cliff and Sandy Spohr, Jean Larson Garver, Arturo Ortega, Victor Marshall, Doug Walters, Phil Kelly, Elisabeth Adkins, and others.

I am afraid that I have failed to name many who have played an important role in my life and career. I ask you all for your forgiveness. I couldn't have stayed the ground without your help and encouragement. You are all a part of this memoir.

Prologue

IN 1967, I CONCEIVED THE IDEA for this book. *The Philadelphia Inquirer* reported it,[1] and Alfred Knopf wanted to publish it. But I frustrated them by not writing it. I knew something then about wanting to shoot conductors, since I already had Pierre Monteux, George Szell, and Eugene Ormandy making life more difficult than it needed to be. But no one wanted to shoot me yet, except one lone violinist with a pretty good reason (my successor in the Philadelphia Orchestra).

After 1967, the story got more complicated and sometimes so painful I couldn't imagine telling it to anyone. But in the spirit of keeping commitments, and with the help of my coauthor Robin Underdahl, I now submit it to anyone who wants to read it.

Sorry I'm late.

---

1. *The Philadelphia Inquirer,* May 21, 1967.

Chapter 1

I CAME BY IT HONESTLY

I BELIEVE MY FATHER JUST looked Mr. Fleisher up in the telephone directory and asked if he could bring his son to play violin for him. Edwin A. Fleisher was a great man of music in Philadelphia. In that year, 1933, he published a list of his astounding collection of music from all over the world. He had already deeded the collection to the Free Library of Philadelphia.

Mr. Fleisher always made time for a musical child, even a five-year-old. The Jewish "Hatikvah" sufficed as my audition, and he recommended a teacher for me: William Happich.

So my father took me downtown to Brentano's bookstore on Chestnut Street. But we didn't enter the bookstore. We went in a door a few steps farther down the street, one that opened on a steep flight of stairs. These we climbed, then went around a corner, and climbed more stairs. On the third floor, we entered a room where a portrait of a stern man with wild hair faced us.

"Who's that? I don't like him."

"That's Beethoven," my dad said. "Someday you'll play his wonderful music."

"No, I won't."

A tall man in a dark suit came out of an inner room and shook hands with my father. His precise manners made me feel clumsy. Still, he was an improvement over the man in the portrait.

He led us into the inner room, where I opened my case and removed my treasure. Playing the beautiful "Hatikvah" on my own little violin was an experience all to myself. I listened to what I was playing, and my mind drifted along with the notes, and the other people in the room might have gone down to Brentano's for all I cared.

However, they were still in the room.

"Do you *really* want to play the violin?" Mr. Happich asked me.

"Yes."

"Will you work very hard?"

I had no idea what that meant, but I knew the conversation would go better if I said yes.

"Then I will take you as my student."

I learned to say his name correctly, Mr. "Hoppik," and got used to his formal approach to teaching violin.

"You'll never sound good until you tuck that left elbow in." Did he realize, as he said such things in my father's presence, where I had learned every bad habit in my repertoire?

He showed me how to place my fingers correctly in the first position, at the top of the neck. I was sure I was ready for the second position.

After about a month, Dad opened the door on Chestnut Street one day, and we confronted the stairs.

"I'm tired."

"You're tired. What's anyone supposed to do about that?"

"Can I have a piggyback ride?"

My dad stooped down and I climbed on with my violin case.

It was a good deal during the several weeks it lasted.

The room where we waited for my lesson had a large rug woven in a pattern of squares. Since I wasn't as tired as my dad, I hopped from square to square while we waited.

"Stop it, Anshel. You'll use up your energy," he used to say.

Mr. Happich kept me in first position for three months. He provided the music, finding pieces that required only the notes I could play. I remember a piece called "Melody in F" that did justice to my enormous talent.

But soon he started me on the études Otakar Ševčík wrote for teaching violin in 1880, and they did not do justice to my talent at all. Under the torture of his *School of Violin Technics*, I learned to navigate second through seventh positions, shifting, double-stopping, trilling, and string crossings. The odious études built solid technique for me, just as they long had, and still do, for young violinists the world over.

"What else do you hear?" Mr. Happich asked me this right in the middle of a piece I was rendering oh-so-melodically.

"I hear this song. That long A and then the short Ds."

"But what else?"

Outside, a bus ground its gears on Chestnut Street. Was that what he meant?

"What else?" he insisted. Then he played some notes on the piano. They sounded familiar. "This is what the piano was doing while you were playing your part."

Of course, it was true. He often played some accompaniment for me. As he replayed it, I remembered it.

"You must always listen while you play. Listen to *all* the music, not just your own."

That was a new thought for me, one that would expand. Later I would listen to the other students if we played together in a class, and later yet to the other instruments when I played in an orchestra. It seemed a little thing that day. But it became huge.

Sometimes at the end of a lesson Mr. Happich said, "Maybe next week there will be a new piece in your folder."

The next week he would say, "Let's go over to the file, and see if a new piece has come." He would slide open the drawer and tick his fingers over the file tabs. "There's no file for Anshel. Oh, dear. Wait . . . here's one. Is there anything in it? Yes, there is! And what is it? A concerto? No, not yet. It's a lovely little romance by Svenson. Just right for Anshel."

When I got as far as fourth position, he gave me the Viotti Concerto No. 22 especially because it would give me a problem. That's how he conquered the technical challenges. Not "Play this trill eighty-five times," but "Here is a piece of music you will love."

It just happened to be full of trills.

On Saturdays, Mr. Happich taught group lessons in harmony. He would send us home with a melody line and instructions for the type of harmony we were to write into the score. His demanding tutelage was augmented by my mother's unflagging commitment to my daily practice. The intonation had to be just right, not flat or sharp.

One of the rewards was supposed to be performance. My father arranged for me to play for the Allied Jewish Appeal. My mother sewed a gold satin Russian blouse with a high collar. I practiced "Melody" by Glück and "Orientale" by César Cui. The Cui repeats a pizzicato theme that I found terribly exciting—plucking the strings directly with my fingertips.

I came out onto the stage and found myself behind the enormous, shiny piano. I supposed my mother wanted people to be able to see my nice blouse, but I liked it back there, so I stayed put. The pianist was obliged to get up and push me out into view.

The music I knew first came over with my parents from the old country. Leon and Dora Brusilovsky were musical Jews in the Russian Empire. They loved old and new—Tchaikovsky, Rimsky-Korsakov, Glinka, Rachmaninoff.

My mother played piano, my father violin. They married in 1919 and lived in her village in what is now Ukraine. The demand for music was steady with all the bar mitzvahs, weddings, funerals, and Russian holidays. Besides classical chamber works, my parents performed Yiddish klezmer tunes for dancing and light music, as well as the Hatikvah, which is now the Israeli anthem.

As Lenin ascended in Russia, he voiced tolerance. But he couldn't control every faction. In August 1919, many Jewish properties were seized and communities disbanded. When the Cossacks were coming for a pogrom, a messenger ran from house to house shouting the warning, and my parents would quickly bolt the door and stay inside. One of my uncles was caught in the street and lost an arm to a Cossack sword.

Near the end of 1920, my grandfather bought two large white horses, hitched them to a covered wagon, and headed west through Ukraine, Poland, Germany, and the Netherlands. My mother's entire family of eight came, but my father left all his relatives behind. My brother Nathan was an infant. The white horses brought them to Antwerp, Belgium. A ship called the *Zeeland* carried my forebears to Ellis Island in May of 1922. On Ellis Island, Brusilovsky became Brusilow.

My parents made their way to Philadelphia. People were supposed to love music there, and weddings, funerals, and bar mitzvahs would be plentiful.

But it was not so. Or perhaps my father was not a great violinist. Neither of my parents had formal training.

After a time, with one American dollar in his pocket, my father arrived on the doorstep of his uncle, Max Tarnapol, a furrier in North Philadelphia. The Tarnapols welcomed the Brusilows into their home, employed them in their store, and trained them. My father worked with the furs and my mother sewed the silk linings.

It's true, though, that Philadelphians love music. The city was first settled by Quakers, who revere silence over sound and don't even sing in their worship. However, the Quakers welcomed the hymn-singing Germans, Swedes, Anglicans, and Roman Catholics. By 1703 the Swedes had an organ. The Moravians developed original vocal and instrumental music for worship. Benjamin Franklin's press was printing music by 1729, bringing to Americans the music of Handel, Vivaldi, Corelli, and Scarlatti. In the nineteenth century, the citizens of Philadelphia, now including immigrants from France and Scotland, were regularly treated to operas and orchestral music shortly after their debuts in Europe.

In 1857, Philadelphia distinguished itself by opening the most sumptuous opera house in the United States, modeled after La Scala in Milan. It was named the Academy of Music.

Founded in 1900, the Philadelphia Orchestra inaugurated the twentieth century for the city. It performed in the Academy of Music—as it would for the entire twentieth century. While the Brusilows were making furs, Leopold Stokowski was raising the city's orchestra from mediocrity to international acclaim.

At the same time, another institution was born that would intertwine itself fruitfully with the Philadelphia Orchestra. Mary Louise Curtis inherited the fortune her father had earned publishing the *Saturday Evening Post* and *Ladies Home Journal*. She taught music to underprivileged children and was committed to that mission. But she saw another need that no one was addressing: the need for a separate school for kids who might become great musicians. With her husband Edward Bok, she founded The Curtis Institute of Music in 1924.

In the winter, everyone who could afford it wore fur. My parents borrowed from relatives only slightly better off than they were and opened their own store on Girard Avenue. And then I was born on August 14, 1928. The following year, the Depression arrived. As fewer and fewer people could afford fur coats, my parents' fur store became a lost cause.

My own career has sometimes given me good reason to think back on my father's remarkable decision at that time to step forward rather than retreating. The neighborhood on South 60th Street came to his notice. Shoppers there were still buying luxury goods. He managed, in the middle of the 1930s, to borrow enough money to open a new store in that neighborhood and make a go of it. Soon my parents expanded into more spacious quarters down the block, at 141 South 60th Street. We lived above the store, our main rooms on the middle floor, and the bedrooms the third floor.

It was in the dining room of our apartment that my friend Stan and I joined the Philadelphia Orchestra. After the rest of the players were seated, I crossed the rug to the front of the stage, which the window looking down on 60th Street had become. Speaking into one of my mother's silver cups, I announced the symphony and then the concertmaster and assistant—myself and Stan Grossman—and then the conductor, Eugene Ormandy. I set the "microphone" down and lifted my violin to tune the winds and brass, then the strings. Then we got the 78 spinning on the Philco player, touched needle to shellac, and waited. I could close my eyes and see the players all around me, even closer than they were when my parents took me to concerts at the Academy of Music. Stan and I made our contribution to the great Philadelphia Orchestra. Our violins sang out with the cellos coming behind, or fluttered next to the gliding oboes. If we introduced mistakes into the performance, our fellow players didn't complain and we didn't notice.

Beethoven's *Eroica* Symphony was our first performance because my parents had a recording of it, and Dad had laid out forty cents or so for the first violin part, which Stan and I both played. We hit up my dad again and again for more of the repertoire of the orchestra, both the recordings and the violin parts. When the parts divided, I played the top line, and Stan played the lower one.

Stan loved Sibelius's Second Symphony, but we couldn't find our parts. The only thing to do was get the full score and some blank staff paper and copy out the violin parts. It took several weeks.

My name was odd. When I started school, that was my first lesson. I begged and cried until my father relented, and I became Albert.

Albert knew what mattered in life: baseball. My friends and I played every day after school. The next Joe DiMaggio, that's what I wanted to be. Towards the dinner hour, my parents would send my brother to fetch me. My friends were always on the lookout.

"Here comes Nat!" someone would call when he appeared around the corner of a building. I took off like a jackrabbit.

Nat had longer legs, being eight years older, and every day he caught me by the collar or a sleeve and dragged me home to practice. And not for the Yankees.

Nat practiced, too, on the saxophone and then the clarinet. After high school he entered the all-scholarship Curtis Institute of Music.

Our family's music requirement was not unique in the neighborhood. Mrs. Gomberg stopped in frequently to kvetch to my mother. They were Russian Jews, too, their name even more distorted by the officials at Ellis Island than ours. Her children drove her nuts, sawing at their violins and cellos, squeaking the oboe, bellowing with a trumpet. Worse, her neighbors had the nerve to complain. And not just about the noise—they objected to her boys practicing in the back yard in their underwear!

Those were hot summers, and every breeze came with noise attached. Melodic passages followed us down the sidewalk, and I sighed with childish melodrama over more than one cadenza from a window. The Secons' bakery was across the street, and Morris practiced his French horn by the upstairs window. It paid off. He became principal horn of the Rochester Philharmonic. Also nearby, Sidney Sharp practiced his violin, though he would segue into the music contracting business in Hollywood. Little Hershy Kay practiced his piano and cello like a good boy and eventually found himself orchestrating music for Broadway.

Of the Gombergs, all but one studied at Curtis. In fact, concert violinist Efrem Zimbalist, Sr., had lured the whole family down from Chelsea, Massachusetts, for the free music education Curtis offered. The children made good. Robert Gomberg played violin in the Philadelphia Orchestra. Harold was principal oboe in the New York Philharmonic. Ralph took the position of principal oboe in the Boston Symphony Orchestra. Edith, Leo, and Cela I believe all continued in music too.

When I was eight or nine, Mr. Happich suggested that I visit the Symphony Club. This was another of Edwin A. Fleisher's projects, one that got musicians of all ages playing the music in Mr. Fleisher's collection. Mr. Happich conducted the Symphony Club.

I sat right next to concertmaster Florence Rosensweig, a pretty young woman with dimples. We were playing Tchaikovsky's Sixth Symphony, the *Pathétique*. When we came to the third movement, the violin parts divided and she played the top line.

So did I.

When we came to a stop she whispered, "You're supposed to play the bottom line."

"I want to play the top line."

"But you're supposed to play the bottom line." Now her dimples didn't show.

"I don't want to play the bottom line."

Mr. Happich noticed Florence's displeasure as well as my too-innocent expression.

"Oh, just let him play with you," he told her. It was the easy way out for the grownups.

At home, my mother's regimen never relaxed. I wasn't allowed *not* to practice.

"That's flat, Anshel." From where she sat in the painted wooden chair across from me, she reached over and pinched my bow arm. Intonation was always her focus.

I knew perfectly well it was flat—did I need her to tell me what was flat and what wasn't? She said it anyway and gave the pinch, just as she had when I was little, only now I was big. Of its own accord, it seemed, my fingers transferred the bow to my left hand so my right hand could reach over to slap my mother across the cheek.

She jerked into a stiff posture in her chair. Her cheek was reddening, but she did not touch it. The look on her face subsumed the pain under another emotion—a horror at the kind of child she had given birth to.

My tears started even before she got up and went downstairs to the store, and through to the back room, where she found my father cutting furs.

It can't have been as long as it seemed—an hour—before my father made me stand and face him. His eyes fixed themselves on my face. He said only, "You hit Mom."

I nodded. It seemed certain that he would hit me, though it wasn't the way of our family. What else would he do with such a son?

My father had a better idea. "If you ever do it again, I'll take your violin away and you'll never play again."

There was, then, something more important than music in a Russian immigrant household.

When I was eleven, my father took me to Rittenhouse Square, to the corner building with large, corniced windows, which was the Curtis Institute of Music. I was to audition at 12:30. Mr. Happich did not think I was ready for it. Curtis did always let a few children in, but the normal time to enroll was after high school.

"Let me just take you in to the professors," a sympathetic woman named Miss Hill said. My father stayed in the hall, and I followed her into a room where some grownups were having box lunches handed to them.

"This is Albert Brusilow," Miss Hill said. "And this is Mr. Zimbalist, and this is Mr. Hilsberg, and Madame Luboshutz." She named a few others too. They were the string faculty of the Curtis Institute: Mr. Zimbalist, one of the world's foremost violinists; Mr. Hilsberg, concertmaster of the Philadelphia Orchestra; Madame Luboshutz, a world-class musician too. Of course, I knew little of this.

What I did observe was that the faculty members were quite interested in their lunches. I told my pianist to wait.

"Please start, young man," Mr. Zimbalist said.

"I would rather wait until you've finished your lunch." Having made this announcement, I stepped back out into the hall to join my father.

"What happened?" he asked.

"They're still eating."

A sick look crossed his face.

So I added, "I don't play lunch music."

Who knows how it was that those eminent musicians graciously allowed me to audition? Let alone how I was admitted to the Curtis Institute to become a student of Efrem Zimbalist.

There was still one lesson to be taken from Mr. Happich. And there was the news to be conveyed, the goodbye. My father trusted Mr. Happich's judgment, and to me his words were infallible.

"Mr. Happich, tell me honestly. Do you think—is it possible— that my son might have a concert career ahead of him?"

In this moment of disappointment with our decision, my teacher, who was the soul of kindness, said, "I think Albert is going to be a very good violinist. I don't think he's going to be a soloist."

With a heavy heart I turned my face toward Mr. Zimbalist.

"Hey Al," a friend said one day. "We need a fullback. Wanna play?"

We played football in Cobbs Creek Park. To my parents, I'd toss off a vague explanation about hanging out with my buddies.

This was a life of crime. For weeks, I ran like the blazes for passes or touchdowns. Then I crashed into another body and fell. Pain shot up from my right hand to my elbow. Immediately swelling appeared above the wrist. I ran to the spigot carved from the rock there and held my right arm under cold creek water for an endless ten minutes, with no result.

As I entered our house, I kept my arm out of sight. I got through dinner by eating with my left hand. Violin playing makes you some-what ambidextrous.

"Well, I guess I'll go up to bed early." This comment passed without raising suspicions. Ben Gay was supposed to cure things like this, wasn't it? I spread it on the red swelling and closed myself into my room. My parents were going out somewhere, so it was all good.

Later the front door opened and immediately Dad's voice boomed. "Who's been using the Ben Gay?"

His footsteps made a hopping sound on the stairs.

"You?" He was in Nathan's room.

"You?" His head poked in my door.

I didn't answer. Sound asleep.

Nothing stopped Dad. He switched on the ceiling light. "Let me see."

"What?" I squinted sleepily.

"Show me." He pulled down my covers, saw the bulge, and said, "Get dressed."

Next I heard him on the phone to our neighbor who was a doctor. "Yes, I know it's 10:30. I need to bring him over."

I think it was while I was trying to get the shirt over my head, then the pants pulled up—the things that took two hands—that fear stole through me. It could be that my arm was *really* wrecked. Was I prepared to live an unmusical life?

The doctor pronounced it a bad sprain. I could expect to be playing again after some weeks.

Violin, that was. Not football. It all came clear to me, who I was—musical child of musical parents, Russian Jew of musical heritage. I would even practice.

Chapter 2

My Several Educations

MR. ZIMBALIST TAUGHT ME in his studio, the same room where I had auditioned. He took it for granted that such a lucky boy would make the most of his opportunity. His own commitment to excellence was supreme. I did not know that long ago, in Kiev, he had studied under Otakar Ševčík, author of the hated études. But young Efrem Zimbalist escaped from Mr. Ševčík after just a few months—to relieve his aching hands!

Mr. Zimbalist talked to me about bowing and about interpreting those first moments in a concerto where the audience hears the violin alone.

"You are introducing yourself," he said. "You have to have something to say. Through the music, of course."

He taught me to listen to what kind of sound I was getting out of my instrument and to observe fine distinctions in the quality of sound, not just to play the notes and rhythms correctly. He assigned me a concerto, Max Bruch's first, and taught me how to play a very long note, one that required changing the direction of my bow, from up bow to down bow or the reverse, without breaking the sound.

"You are always pulling the bow along at a tilt so that one edge of the horsehair is meeting the string," he said. "When you get to the end of the bow, you must tilt the bow to the other edge of the horsehair while you are switching directions and the sound will flow continuously."

It was magic.

His playing of the violin concerto by Samuel Barber with the Philadelphia Orchestra was magic too. Barber was teaching madrigal chorus at Curtis then. We students always received free passes to see our teachers perform, but we sat in the peanut gallery. When I remember myself leaning forward from my seat near the ceiling in the Academy of Music, I see my whole relationship with Zimmy, as we referred to him. He taught the high art of violin playing, and I learned, but from far away. Though we shared the Russian heritage, he was never *my teacher* in the way Mr. Happich had been.

We children who were allowed to study at Curtis formed our own little society. In harmony and solfège classes, we sat quietly, awed not only by the professors and the subjects, but by the older students too. We were supposed to be taught basic academics— English and math and history and science. But these were given short shrift and, in any case, I was not interested in them much.

We needed a place where no one could make us practice our instruments, and we found it. The janitor tolerated us in his domain of mops and tools and smelly cleaning agents. In the boiler room, we pitched pennies to see whose would land closest to the wall. Winner take all. And nobody knew where to look for us.

A few blocks away at the Academy of Music, I managed to be just as invisible. The stage door was usually unlocked, and nothing prevented me from sneaking in and watching Maestro Eugene Ormandy rehearse the orchestra.

I liked the best possible view. Whenever the closest proscenium box was unlocked, I sneaked into it.

"Hey, kid—get out of there!" Mr. Betz, the stagehand, would say.

I would wear on my face all the guilt I could scrape together, and it satisfied him. Somehow my expulsion was never his priority. A few players noticed me in the dark box, but I don't think Ormandy ever did.

At Curtis, students were welcome to watch Fritz Reiner rehears-ing the school orchestra several times a week. Leonard Bernstein was one of Reiner's graduate conducting students, and sometimes I watched him conduct. He was remarkable.

Mr. Zimbalist's concert career was escalating. If he was out of town when our lessons were scheduled, his assistant Frederick Vogelgesang filled in for him. My exposure to various composers was left to chance.

"Hey, did he give you any Beethoven?" my father would ask.

"No."

At Curtis, I was no longer unusual because all the students were outstanding. A little ego adjustment is good for the work ethic. I practiced more, though perhaps not enough.

The widowed Mary Louise Curtis Bok, founder of the school, was still occasionally seen by students. (Later she would marry Mr. Zimbalist.) She spent her summers at her home in Rockport, Maine. Since the late 1920s, she had been inviting a few faculty members to come up and bring some of their best students. Madame Lea Luboshutz always came.

No strict schedule was imposed, but music was played con-stantly, mixed with a few outdoor activities. It was not pressure-free. The chosen students knew that if their teachers became dissatisfied with their progress, they would be sent home.

At the end of my third year, Madame Luboshutz spoke to me: "Albert, would you like to come up to Rockport for our summer session?"

I was thrilled to join the ranks of the blessed.

Zimmy had a change in mind for me too, and this thrilled me less. "I haven't had enough time for you," he said. "And next year I'll be traveling even more." He was also taking on the director-ship of Curtis. "Madame Luboshutz will be teaching you now. She's very concerned that you build your repertoire in the basics. Bach, Mozart, Beethoven."

I do not know why this made me unhappy. "Lubo," as we stu-dents referred to her, was a terrific violinist and a most elegant lady, especially when she appeared in black silks for concerts. She was only a little bit scary.

But my parents and I had felt that Mr. Zimbalist was the right teacher for me. His scant attention disappointed us, and yet changing teachers did not feel like the best way forward. Still, we agreed to the plan.

Wearing my usual jacket and tie, I took the train through New York and Boston and along the coast of Maine to Portland. Someone met me and drove me to the Curtis summer colony, and right to the house where I would be staying. I carried my suitcase upstairs to the room I would share with two older boys.

The first night, my roommates began playing strip poker, and I was allowed to join—on their terms. This was surely a privilege. I was to become skilled at poker years later, but on this occasion I had to part with my shoes, socks, shirt, etc., etc. After I had nothing left to surrender, I kept losing. The oldest boy thought of some things beyond clothing that could be demanded of me, still in tune with the themes of sex and humiliation. Both boys held me down on the bed.

As the situation ramped up, I began to panic. There came a point where one boy stood aside, no longer willing to participate in what was certainly no game of poker. And something came to my rescue—adrenalin. I found the strength to kick my aggressor off the bed, made a wild grab for my pants, and ran out the door.

I don't remember putting the pants on, but I must have managed it before I was outside, running at full speed down one of the paths and crying.

I ran for a long time in the darkness, barely able to see the path. Then a man, huge and dark-haired, stood in front of me.

"Vere you going?" He spoke with a deep bass voice in the Russian accent I knew so well.

I didn't know how to answer.

"Vat ees the problem? You must tell me."

"I'm homesick."

Strange music was coming from a house nearby, and he led me there. A woman was playing the bassoon. She was his wife, and he was the world famous cellist, Gregor Piatigorsky.

"Vere do you come from?" he asked. Eventually his questions brought forth my Russian background.

"Can I call your fader?"

He and my dad talked in Russian, which I couldn't understand.

"Now vee must see Madame."

Mr. Piatigorsky walked me to Lubo's house and stayed with me. I had no adequate answers for her questions, so I stuck to the home-sickness claim. I could see that she was upset. I wanted to please her.

"If you go home now," Lubo said, "I will not take you as my student. Is that what you want?"

It was not what I wanted. But I said, "Yes."

Mr. Piatigorsky understood on very scant explanation from me that I was unwilling to return to my room. Most kindly, he took me home with him for my last night in Rockport.

With Europe in the turmoil of war, many musicians fled or drifted to the United States and occasionally would turn up in such out of the way places as Rockport, Maine. I was lucky that Gregor Piatigorsky had come that summer to relax for a few weeks in a safe place with friends.

In the morning, Lubo asked me to play for her before leaving. She lived in a pretty white clapboard house with a picket fence. The large entryway was well suited to lessons, and it was there that I played for her.

Later, I learned that everyone believed I left Curtis because I did not want to study with Madame Luboshutz. I did fear the change of teachers. But I would not have left Curtis for that reason. My sudden departure left a regrettable impression. Those were different times, and some things were not discussed.

Dad turned to Mr. Happich for advice in finding me a new teacher. He was abreast of developments in the city. The Philadelphia

Musical Academy had come up for sale. It had been founded in 1870 by three musicians from the Leipzig Conservatory. Today it is known as the University of the Arts.

An old friend of Mr. Happich's had purchased the academy and had just arrived in Philadelphia to run it. He was Dr. Jani Szanto from Hungary. He and his Jewish wife had lived in Munich until the Nazis drafted their two sons into the army and expelled the parents from Germany.

At the Philadelphia Musical Academy, Dad and I once again faced stairs to a third-floor studio. No piggyback ride was offered.

Dr. Szanto was stocky and no taller than I was. I liked him immediately and wanted to show off, and I played a little of the Bruch concerto for him.

"I'd love to teach you. Tell me what Bach sonatas you know."

"None."

"Hmm. What Mozart sonatas?"

"None."

"Oh. Then Mozart concertos."

"No."

"What études . . . the Kreutzer? You've learned the Rode Caprices? And the Paganini Caprices?"

He sent me out to buy the Rode Caprices, which were more elementary than the Paganini.

"You're going to have to work hard." It was the first lesson. He leaned toward me as if we were telling secrets, though the deficiencies in my technique were not a secret. "You know William Happich and I studied together. We studied with Professor Gruen—who was very, very strict."

Yes, and Zimmy had studied violin with Auer, who shouted at all his students, even Jascha Heifetz. We musical children were used to long lines of teachers stretching back into the past and violently conveying genius down to the present.

"If we made even little mistakes in our lessons," my new teacher said, "Professor Gruen got angry. One boy played his études very badly. 'Give me your violin,' he said to the boy. He put the violin in its case and clamped it shut. Then the professor opened the door and kicked the violin down the stairs. His studio was on the third floor."

Teachers of music clearly existed in a reserved stratum of the universe, on the third floors of selected buildings.

Dr. Szanto added, "I wasn't that boy, and I won't do that to you. But you must practice. No yes. No yes."

I don't know why he always said no and yes together. But I knew what it meant. My fingers addressed themselves to the Rode Caprices.

A wise teacher keeps his student away from the Slough of Despond, so next Dr. Szanto assigned me not a Paganini caprice but a Paganini concerto. Of course he supervised my fingering and bowing meticulously. He was looking ahead to what I would need for soloing and, less than a decade later, I would play that concerto with the Philadelphia Orchestra.

Very soon Dr. Szanto introduced me to Johann Sebastian Bach, through one of his violin sonatas. The difficulty Bach presents to the violinist is remarkable. He wrote music that requires us to play all four strings at once, but the curved neck of the modern violin makes this impossible. During Bach's time a curved bow was designed to assist violinists, though it was soon discarded. Given all these simultaneous notes, the violinist must figure out which note represents the melody line and make it dominant. The Chaconne is an example. It is difficult to play at all; in fact, when hearing a recording, listeners often assume two violinists are playing. In addition to playing notes at the same time on different strings, you must stress one more than the other.

Then there is the difficulty of memorizing Bach. Like all composers, he repeats a motif. But it is not quite the same, always a little changed in some unpredictable way. Also he introduces frequent harmonic changes. Your brain cannot make sense of the patterns, so you must rely on your ear and fingers. You do always know when it's perfect.

"Now, Albert," Dr. Szanto said one day, "it's time for Mozart. Let's learn the Violin Concerto in D Major."

Mozart's notes, seen on the page, aren't so very intimidating. His concertos are less flamboyant than many others. But they present a different challenge from anyone else's music. You can't just dig into a Mozart concerto and give it everything you've got and hit all the notes right. That would be like eating a banana with the peel on. You have to strip the music down to its perfect essence. Dr. Szanto showed me what I could and could not do. The delicacy of the music requires space and lightness. Every note is so perfectly arranged that the slightest mistake will clang in the listener's ear. Combining the right style and approach and sound is a complicated task.

The orchestral instrumentation must also accommodate Mozart's style. It's not just a matter of sending the trombones backstage. Everything is trimmed down for balance, even the strings.

At Curtis the focus had been on technical aspects of music, and I needed that then. Now Dr. Szanto brought me into a room full of people and personalities.

"Mozart is not part of the name of a piece of music!" he said. "Mozart was a young man who would have a feeling on a given day and turn it into a musical idea." Dr. Szanto wanted me to seek the music in the composer's mind and give it full expression, not read some marks on paper. The interpretation of great sonatas and concertos was not *reading*. It was making a deep connection with another mind, understanding how the composer approached the writing of music. It's like reading great literature.

"It's a conversation," he said. "You and Herr Bach get yourselves on the same page, no yes. And then when you step out onto the stage, you're talking to the audience about this particular music, how you want to give it to them. Every composer has the same notes available for arranging, but each uses them to bring listeners into a completely different world. The places we go with Brahms aren't the same places we go with Beethoven."

My lessons with Dr. Szanto became the high point of my week. The stairs themselves elevated me into that privileged third-floor space of sound. I was driven to master every trick of the instrument.

Once my dad had gotten me a ticket for a recital by violin virtuoso Jascha Heifetz. My seat was right on the stage. On a violin, fast notes are played most easily with a back and forth motion of the bow. But Heifetz was a master of staccato—a technique that bounces the bow along in the same direction and sounds almost like stuttering. Beautiful stuttering, that is. It's difficult either way, but extremely difficult when playing down bow, starting at the frog end of the bow, near your hand, and pulling the bow down until you are using the far end of it, where it is hardest to apply pressure. Watching Heifetz do this was fascinating to me, and I stared at his bow hold throughout the recital and tried to figure out what he was doing. His bow was very tight on the string as he began the staccato, and then it would bump along almost by itself.

I went to bed thinking about it. The next day, when Mom and Dad went down to the shop to work, I started trying to figure it out, copying Heifetz's bow hold as I remembered it. I failed, I tried again. Hours passed.

Then I got it.

"Dad! Mom!" I shouted down the stairs.

Dad came running through the fur shop, shears in hand. "What's wrong?" He looked up the stairs, alarmed.

I played a gorgeous staccato, all down bow. "I did it! I can do it both ways!" And I gave him an up bow version.

"Great," he said. "Can I go back to this mink?"

Dr. Szanto was more impressed with my staccato. "I'll buy it," he said. "How much do you want for it?"

He also taught me performance skills, offering his own experience.

"Professor Gruen sat in a chair down in front. Separate, where everyone could see him. After he was seated, the student could come out on stage. I did that," he said, "and I began to play my recital piece. After two minutes, Professor Gruen stood up from his chair and walked out of the hall, in sight of everyone."

To prevent my suffering such shame, Dr. Szanto gave me precise instruction in each element of a performance. Better yet, when I was ready, he arranged a recital for me in New York at Town Hall. Then he took me into his own quartet as second violinist.

When I played in Dr. Szanto's quartet, or with other students at the Philadelphia Musical Academy, I listened to the other instruments. Violin made a good sound. But it wasn't the whole. I was just getting a little bit, and I wanted more. This affliction is known as *conductoritis*, and it had not escaped Dr. Szanto's observation. He established a course for winds and brass and appointed me as conductor for them. He chose symphonies that were particularly difficult for the wind and brass players, like Brahms's First and Second, and Tchaikovsky's Fourth. For me to learn those parts, to see those symphonies from a non-violin perspective, was rich. It was like a completely new repertoire for me to learn and control, even though the symphonies were familiar to me.

At the Philadelphia Musical Academy, I felt at home. I got to know Gordon Staples, William Steck, whom I would much later employ, and others. When you make friends in a musical context, there is the talking friendship, and then there is the music. Both connect you.

My parents monitored closely the uppermost track of my musical education, which ran through Curtis and then the Philadelphia Musical Academy. They tolerated the orchestral studies Stan and I continued to pursue in our dining room with the Philadelphia Orchestra. But my parents regretted the "lower" track, which I heard on the radio—big band and jazz.

Benny Goodman was coming to town!

"We put you where you hear the best music in the world," my dad said. "And you want to hear that other stuff?"

He dropped me off at the Earl Theater. Standing-room-only was no deterrent to me if I could hear Benny Goodman with Gene

Krupa on drums, Harry James on trumpet, and Lionel Hampton on xylophone or marimba.

With World War II calling, I gave some thought to those brass instruments. It couldn't be that hard, I thought, blowing into your instrument to get music out. Musicians of draft age were enlisting in the Marine and Navy bands stationed in Washington. Any young musician whose learning curve was interrupted by the standard four-year tour of duty in Europe, the Pacific, or North Africa, assuming he lived, could kiss goodbye to a concert career.

In order to join a military band, I needed to learn a different instrument. My friend Jimmy Chambers got me a French horn. "Fool around with it. See what sounds you can get," he said. Later, he became principal horn of the New York Philharmonic.

I worked at it in my bedroom, pursing my lips the way I'd seen him do and filling my lungs with air to push through that mouthpiece.

Dad came running upstairs and banged open my door. "Anshel! It sounds like you're killing a horse up here!"

The advantage of keeping my parents on edge about my musical tastes was that they made sure I got to see plenty of classical performances. When Dad made his trips to the New York fur district to bargain for skins, I went along. Over the course of a day, the car would fill with black seal, sheared beaver, and the Persian karakul used for Russian hats. Mink we bought on consignment, considering its high price. After the long day's work, we'd go to a concert in New York.

Once a young violinist was playing a Paganini violin concerto at Town Hall. I was learning the same one at the time.

He did poorly.

"When did Paganini die?" my father asked after the brief applause.

"Just now."

I never planned for things like that to come out of my mouth. They just did. In that case, several rows of the audience enjoyed it, but sometimes I wasn't so lucky.

The things that came out of my mouth in another setting, public school, often got me in trouble. My parents had noticed that I needed regular, academic education, too, so they put me on a streetcar headed toward the school.

Rather quickly, I got to know the administration. Miss Loux, assistant principal: "What, Albert—you're being sent to me again? Didn't you come to school yesterday?"

"I did. I checked in at homeroom."

"But it seems you didn't stay for your classes."

Some days I didn't even check in at homeroom. Stan and I took the streetcar to school together. "Where are we going?" he'd say when we passed the school.

"Stay on. Let's see what the Stanton's playing."

No matter what was playing, we went to the movie at the Stanton Theater.

What the school got out of tolerating my enrollment was a little violin music at assemblies. What I got out of it was less than an education, except in history, which I read on my own.

My geometry teacher understood better what I did and didn't know. "Ask him what an isosceles triangle is."

Some girl would respond to his egging on and expose my ignorance.

"But he can play thirty-second notes. And sixty-fourth notes," the teacher said. "Twenty of them in a row. That's math."

I did love Miss Blanchë, my Latin teacher. One day I knew all the answers. I raised my hand on her first question and read my answer out fluently.

"Can I see your book?"

I was caught. She looked at the teacher's answer book I'd picked up in some used bookshop. "That's just terrible," she said.

In the next assembly I dedicated my Mozart to Miss Blanchë. Since music is a conversation, I figured it could say, "I'm sorry."

Eventually the school approached my parents with a plan. They suggested I take the basic subjects in the morning and go home at noon so that I would have time to practice. Philadelphia is a city that loves its music.

I piled up countless afternoons and evenings of practice. I wanted to store them up so when I was a grownup I could get away without practicing. It worked pretty well.

"You must win contests," Dr. Szanto said, and he prepared me.

Most appropriately, it was with a Russian piece that I won the Philadelphia Orchestra Youth Contest when I was sixteen. The prize was the privilege of performing with the Philadelphia Orchestra. I was to play the Glazunov Violin Concerto. For this, Dr. Szanto made me an appointment in New York with Rembert Wurlitzer, purveyor of fine violins. He also lent them out, which was more to the point in my case. I borrowed a fine instrument and played my concerto with the Philadelphia Orchestra.

Afterwards, in my heady state, I approached Eugene Ormandy to shake his hand. "I'm also a conductor," I said. I did not learn that braggadocio from Dr. Szanto, who was a model of humility. Also of tact. I should have paid more attention.

It was a long time before Dr. Szanto let me play my beloved Tchaikovsky. He did not want to see me frustrated before I had the technical skills to do it justice. Or else he wanted to protect Tchaikovsky from death at my hands.

When the time came, he held me to a high standard. More than any other concerto, I played Tchaikovsky's throughout my violin career.

The young conductors' contest was one I was determined to enter. The first level was held at the Ormandys' apartment in the Bellevue-Stratford Hotel. Vladimir Sokoloff played a Beethoven symphony on their piano while I conducted him. For the final competition I had to conduct the Philadelphia Orchestra, sight reading part of the Shostakovich Ninth Symphony.

As second-place winner, I conducted the Philadelphia Orchestra playing Borodin's Polovtsian Dances for a school audience. The orchestra played half a dozen children's concerts every year, conducted by a contest winner or the assistant conductor, and the principal players had to play in just one of these. Two particularly renowned principals, oboist Marcel Tabuteau and flutist William Kincaid, chose this children's concert because Ormandy was conducting the rest of it. I should have been intimidated.

I was listening to the flute and got an idea in my head of another way to phrase it.

"Mr. Kincaid," I said, "would you mind phrasing it like this?" And I sang the bars the way I wanted them to go.

The player next to him erupted in laughter. It was Marcel Tabuteau. The two had a long-term rivalry going, which I had fueled.

Instead of taking my phrasing suggestion, Mr. Kincaid took a dislike to the arrogant kid who was conducting.

Then Mr. Ormandy kindly arranged for me to conduct another concert for young people, which included the overture to *The Magic Flute*. What I can never forget is mounting the podium of Eugene Ormandy, standing up straight, and giving the initial downbeat.

A long and terrifying silence followed. My arms froze in midair.

Finally, the orchestra came in. I had to regroup and catch up with them.

At a break in the rehearsal, a kind-looking trumpet player smiled at me. I gathered my nerve and asked him, "Why didn't you start? I thought I gave a good downbeat."

"Oh!" He laughed. "It's hard to explain. I guess we see the first downbeat, but then we don't actually play till we smell it." Sam Kraus was doing as well as anyone could to explain the Philadelphia Orchestra's usual delayed downbeat.

A lot of my conducting was less glorious, like on the day I was "conducting" in the office of the Philadelphia Musical Academy. My imaginary orchestra was deep into Beethoven's First Symphony, and I was singing along. At the top of my lungs. The kind secretary served as audience, and anyone entering the school could both see and hear me, through the glass wall.

Someone did come in, a distinguished-looking man with a moustache and heavy eyebrows. I'd seen him around the school. He watched through the glass and then entered the office.

"Do you really want to conduct?" he asked me.

I nodded, thinking, *What a dumb question.*

"Do you know who Pierre Monteux is?"

"Sure."

"He's the conductor of the San Francisco Symphony," the man said, just as if I had admitted the truth, that I didn't know. "He'll be teaching conducting in Maine this summer. Would you like to come?"

He seemed to think a kid like me could really study conducting. He was Joseph Barone, director of the Bryn Mawr Conservatory of Music, and he was helping Monteux organize a conducting summer camp.

You'd better believe I was on the bus on the right day with my bags packed and my modest little violin under my arm. Soon I found myself in Hancock, Maine, at a house on a hillside. Five other students were there, but this was no "school" as the Curtis summer program had been because there were no boys—except for me. These were men in their twenties and older.

We formed a line as we were directed into the studio, and we remained in line. I was relieved to find myself behind, and obscured by, a broad-shouldered and extremely tall man named Sam Antek.

Pierre Monteux entered, rotund, with a fluffy moustache parted in the middle and sweeping down over both corners of his mouth. His cheeks rose when he smiled. As we fanned out into a semicircle around him, I kept myself behind Sam.

"Maître," as the others called him, began at one end and shook our hands, one by one. Maître wanted to know where each student had conducted before, what repertoire we had conducted. Sylvio

Lacharité had his own orchestra in Canada. My bodyguard Sam Antek was playing violin under Toscanini in the NBC Symphony.

Suddenly Sam betrayed me by moving aside. I had to take the large hand offered me and say my name to Maître.

"Hah, Albaire! And how old are you?"

"Sixteen."

"You will come back," he said most kindly. "In two, three years. You cannot have the background you must need."

So I had been invited by mistake! "Please," I said. "I came all the way up from Philadelphia. Just let me have one lesson. Then you can send me home, and I will have something to tell my father about."

Full of grace, Maître said, "Well, I suppose one."

He didn't bother extracting the details of my experience. That was saved for dramatic demonstration the following day, in the lesson I had begged for. I stood in front of a music stand and he faced me in a canvas chair. My understanding was that he would sing all the parts of my chosen symphony, Beethoven's First again, and I would conduct. I suppose I thought he had a plethora of voices in that bulky body of his.

"Where is your score?" He indicated my empty music stand.

"Oh, I know it by heart."

His eyebrows went up. "You have memorized it."

"Yes," I confirmed.

"Very good." He pushed himself up from the flimsy chair with some effort. "I will be right back."

I wasn't pleased to lose precious minutes of my lesson. Soon he returned with some papers in hand, which he passed to me.

It was blank staff paper.

"Just write out the first page of the symphony, please, since you know it all, and I will be back in fifteen minutes."

Those were slow minutes. I was not busy writing musical notation on the paper. I sweated and squirmed.

"You don't know it so well? Maybe then we can use this." He set the score on my music stand. "Let's conduct."

I began and quickly figured out that *I* was to sing the melodic line and he would represent other parts. He was able to sing only a single note at a time, so he would switch from one instrument's part to another, whatever he felt was most important after the melodic line. He could not see the score from where he sat, I humbly observed to myself, and yet he knew what to sing.

"Stop!" He waved his hand in front of his face as though a fly were bothering him. "What are you doing?"

Was I in the wrong symphony? No. I was trying to follow the score on my stand.

"Start over."

We began again.

"Stop!"

My arms stopped in whatever awkward position I had thrown them into.

"That's all wrong. It's not in four. It's in eight."

What I wanted right then was for the wooden floor to open up and let me drop down into some cool, secret cellar. The whole world of music had risen out of my reach anyway.

Maître let me stay. I was the youngest by ten years or more, but it didn't seem to matter. Harold Glick became my best friend there. He would later supervise the music for the Rodgers and Hammerstein organization, besides conducting for orchestra, ballet, and opera.

Sometimes Maître gathered us for a group lesson. That first year, he put Leon Fleisher and Vera Franceschi at pianos, and their four hands represented the orchestra, to whatever degree they could manage. The rest of us all conducted, receiving his corrections as he saw the need.

I learned who Pierre Monteux really was because the other students pestered him to tell about the infamous events of 1913—those several debut performances of Stravinsky's *The Rite of Spring* with Diaghilev's ballet company dancing Nijinsky's daring choreography. Our Maître took on heroic proportions as we envisioned the Paris audience acting like hooligans. Soon after the high, convoluted bassoon solo that opens *The Rite of Spring,* the dancers began to shock the audience. Where was the graceful ballerina in this pigeon-toed stomping? Hoots and insulting whistles arose from the crowd. Others shushed the whistlers, which only increased the noise.

Stravinsky sometimes sat behind Monteux in the front of the audience, but he also kept running backstage to check on things. He would stand in the wings and shout, "Keep going!" to Monteux.

Monteux could not allow his eyes to stray from his musicians—especially since much of the time the noise drowned out the orchestra. Somewhere behind him, he heard his friends Claude Debussy and Maurice Ravel shouting at each other from adjacent boxes. It escalated to spitting. Ravel was disgusted with Stravinsky's music and the ballet, and Debussy was transported. Monteux always laughed at that point in his story—"Claude! Yes, *he* was the one who loved it, not Maurice."

In hopes of calming the audience, the house manager brought the lights up. But now audience members could see their opponents. They left their seats to exchange blows or, in some cases, to exchange name cards so that duels could be scheduled. The performance swept away the film of manners that contained class tensions in Paris. People in the balconies shouted toward the expensive seats below, "Down with the Sixteenth-District bitches!"

Pierre Monteux waved his baton toward the raised flutes, then the weaving bows of the strings, presumably all producing sound. Nothing stopped him. His baton waved on and, with all the noise, he might as well have been conducting the riot. Many hecklers were forcibly escorted out by the police, and little by little most of the audience left.

Monteux began to hear his orchestra again. Diaghilev, the impresario, was also signaling him to keep going. He carried through to the last bar of *The Rite of Spring,* the moment when, on stage, the sacrificial maiden is lifted toward the gods. The musicians looked up from their music stands after the final chord and confronted an empty house.

The notes Stravinsky wrote later about the performance do not center on Nijinsky's dramatic ballet, but on an erect back—Monteux's back, dressed in black tails. He said it was "impervious and nerveless as a crocodile."[1] The Maître was my earliest example of a conductor just doing his job, as best he can, whether appreciated or under attack.

Madame Monteux, formerly Doris Hodgkins of Hancock, Maine, hadn't known him in those days. But now she was never far from him and managed logistics so that he could give all his time to music. We called her Mum. She was large, too, with immovable white hair often curled into circles across her forehead above eyebrows as wide as thumbs. Her presence was at least as commanding as his. We complied with Maître in order to please, and with Mum in order to stay this side of trouble. A gifted voice coach, she took on students of her own during their summers in Hancock and hoped to launch a truly great artist who would bring glory to the state of Maine. Every aspect of her voice students' lives was of interest to Mum, and she pressed them to conform their lifestyles to the demands of their careers.

The Monteuxs' son and his wife operated a French restaurant down the road from the school and fed the students breakfast, lunch, and dinner.

Their daughter-in-law Mano was added to the family in an unusual way. Some twenty years before this time, the Monteuxs happened upon the medieval town of Les Baux in southern France. At their hotel, Mum noticed a girl knitting in a corner. She wore long dark braids like a Native American and turned out to be the owner's daughter, Mano. The Monteuxs began taking Mano and her grandmother on excursions with them. At parting, the girl

---

1. Igor Stravinsky and Robert Craft, *Conversations with Igor Stravinsky* (New York: Doubleday, 1959), 47.

clung tearfully to Mum. Among other words of comfort, Mum made her an extraordinary promise—that she would see to it that Mano would marry their son.[2] Not everyone could keep such a promise.

When Mum died, her obituary didn't mention her skill at fostering romances. Samuel Lipman, however, wrote a response to her obituary in *The New Criterion*[3] and named her a "marriage broker."

At the end of the month, *L'École Monteux*, as it was first called (also the Domaine School), gave a free concert, and Mum took her moment in the sun as emcee. I was thrilled to be allowed to open by conducting "The Star Spangled Banner."

The conducting I studied in the summers colored my study of violin the rest of the year under Dr. Szanto. Often as soon as I learned the violin part I was assigned, I would lay my hands on a copy of the full score and look at what everybody else was doing. So it happened that when my brother came home for a visit, I was studying the score of Tchaikovsky's *Francesca da Rimini*.

Nat had landed the principal clarinet position in the Kansas City Orchestra, and he was practicing the beautiful clarinet solo in *Francesca*. I had some ideas about it.

"Hey, Nat. Can I conduct you in that solo?

"I guess so."

Both of us working from memory, I sang the notes of other instruments as the solo came near, gave Nat his cue, and he started playing.

"Hold that note," I told him at one point.

"It's only an eighth note."

"I know, but do it anyway."

---

2. As reported by John Canarina in *Pierre Monteux: Maître* (Pompton Plains, NJ, and Cambridge, U.K.: Amadeus Press, 2003), 119, sourced in Doris Monteux's private journals.

3. Samuel Lipman, "Mme Pierre Monteux," *The New Criterion*, May 1984, 88.

He held the note. Something else wasn't the way I wanted it. After several times through the solo, I finally found the right way to express my musical thoughts with my hands. And it still didn't work.

"You messed it up."

"Anshel, I have to breathe somewhere in there! It's not exactly optional. Conductors understand that—in fact they tell us where to breathe."

"I was going to let you after that phrase." That wasn't strictly true, as I hadn't thought about breathing at first. But now I had a plan. It just required a lot of playing before he got some air.

Nat took a big breath and we tried again. After five or six attempts, he was winded.

After school the next day, Nat grabbed me. "We have to do *Francesca* again!"

We did, and this time he was able to play right through until I wanted him to breathe. What a sense of accomplishment we both felt at the control of his breathing! After that, I worked with Nat on Rimsky-Korsakov's *Scheherazade* and all sorts of other pieces.

A few years later when Nat was principal clarinetist in the Houston Symphony, Sir Thomas Beecham was guest conducting *Francesca da Rimini* with them. At the first rehearsal, after Nat played the solo, Beecham stopped the rehearsal.

"Mr. Brusilow, I have never heard that solo played so beautifully," he said.

On the phone that night, Nat and I indulged in a little brotherly gloating.

The fraternal assists went both ways. Nat discovered another family with our name, except spelled Brusiloff. The Brusiloff family also had a Nat, and Nat Brusiloff directed a big band. My brother bragged to our new relatives about my violin playing. Pretty soon I had to show my stuff to the big band leader.

"Hey!" he said. "You really *are* good. A guy like you should be playing in Carnegie Hall."

I think I was wordless.

"You want to? I could make that happen."

I was a teenager, when magic things are possible. The Brusiloffs reserved a date and found a pianist to accompany me. I was listed in the usual places as playing at Carnegie Hall on such and such a date. Dr. Szanto was beside himself with excitement and bought his ticket as soon as they were available. Of course I was a complete unknown and would be lucky to have a small clump of listeners at the front.

The day came and I walked out onto the stage. I looked out at the vast hall and made out, in spite of the bright stage lights, faces. Not only in the parquet seats on the floor, but in both tiers, in the dress circle, even the balcony. The hall was packed. Who on earth were these people?

I played my fiddle and they clapped. The reviews were great, but one reviewer noted how surprising it was that a violinist no one had heard of should fill the hall to capacity.

As my brother got to know the Brusiloffs better, he learned how Nat Brusiloff had made it happen at Carnegie Hall. They had found a benefactor to back the concert, a Mr. Sobel with a robust brush business outdone only by the Fuller Brush Company. And Mr. Sobel had required every employee of his brush company to purchase at least two tickets for the concert of Albert Brusilow. Attendance was mandatory, and each guest had to sign in.

I always wondered if the applause was mandatory too.

None of this interrupted the real work of my life, which went forward with Dr. Szanto. I could feel my music blossoming under his guidance.

One day he was curt. I began to think my playing displeased him. "Would you like me to try that again? I think I could get it smoother," I said.

He looked up, a little surprised, as if he had forgotten I was there. "I lost my son," he said. "On the Russian front."

"I'm sorry. We can stop for today," I said. Of course he could not teach. I knew he was always worried about his two sons in the German army.

"Let's go on, Albert."

His other son was in Normandy, and some time later the Szantos were to receive news of his death also. Again, he gave me the bare news, simply laid out in words, "My son is dead, the younger one too." I didn't know what to do with the words or with his expressionless face that so thinly covered a deep pit of grief. There was only music, the notes that we played in those lessons, notes given us by Bach and Mozart that would tear at anyone's heart.

Of course, the war was like a gray cloud we lived in. Somehow, our family lost no one in combat. President Roosevelt was managing the war for all of us, and then on April 12 in 1945 he died. I had not imagined such a thing could happen.

The minute school ended that day, I hurried home and through the fur store and up the twenty-three steps to the apartment. There was the record cabinet, there were the Bs, there was Beethoven. I set the *Eroica* Symphony on the Philco player and lowered the needle. The funeral march in the second movement of the *Eroica*—that was what I had to hear.

That summer I went up to Maine again, traveling on my birthday. I was used to my birthday's playing second fiddle to my musical advancement.

My mother had packed me off with a lunch, but I was still glad to get off the bus and walk around when it finally stopped for a break at a little town in southern Maine. The strange thing was that people seemed to be surging out of their houses, hugging one another, some laughing, some crying, and all of them filling the street and making more noise than a bad orchestra. We bus passengers stood watching.

"It's over!" someone yelled. "The Japs surrendered!"

Even a kid knew that was enormous. My birthday played third fiddle. I thought of how I had played once for wounded soldiers in Atlantic City. Irving Berlin was performing after me and patted my head as I walked off the stage.

A privilege awaited me in Hancock. Two log cabins were on the Monteuxs' property, and I was given the nicer one to live in—distinguished by the presence of a rug, whose cleanliness I never probed. The bulb that hung from the ceiling discouraged reading, but I was having too much fun to miss books. I was master of my own one-room house at seventeen and every year thereafter in Hancock.

The conducting students mostly were taken in by town families. On any given day in August, students could be seen walking along the Hancock road with scores in hand, conducting imaginary orchestras, and singing like they were nuts. It seemed as if the people of that small town realized what a great privilege it was to host Pierre Monteux and persons under his tutelage. We all benefited from the welcoming atmosphere.

When we wanted a movie or a restaurant, we drove twenty miles to Ellsworth. Once I went there to eat dinner with Harold Glick and Earl Murray, a trumpet player in Monteux's San Francisco Symphony. We settled into a booth, and Earl chose "Dance of the Snow Maidens" on the jukebox. The fast instrumental music tempted me to show off a skill I had developed with my tongue. I mimicked singing, moving my tongue loosely and making word-like musical sounds.

"What is that?" Earl asked.

"Just talent."

"What are you doing? How can you do that?"

We played the song again and I kept it up. Earl couldn't even figure out what I was doing, and Harold started laughing. So we had to play the song again. Many times. That restaurant manager was glad to see the back of us.

It was a skill I was to make use of in the future.

Later, like almost everyone, I loved the Rodgers and Hammerstein musicals Harold was putting his stamp on. In their funniest moments, I always sensed Harold enjoying himself. When Ado Annie sings, "I'm Just a Girl Who Cain't Say No" in *Oklahoma*, I think of a particular girl who should have said no to Harold's plans.

She was the Monteuxs' housekeeper, and Harold arranged a date with her for me, the only teenager at the conducting school. When he picked me up—Harold was chauffeuring—the front seat was already filled with four conducting students. The girl was in the back seat. Waiting for me.

Well, waiting was not a concept she understood. The minute the car hit the road she began inappropriate explorations and, in less than a minute, had rendered me unfit to appear in public.

Unfortunately, I was already in public, with the four of them in the front seat attending to nothing but the events in the backseat. Harold was so taken in a fit of laughter that the car left the road and entered a grove of trees, which he navigated among, somehow, while the four of them continued to roar at my expense. It was not an event I could live down in the following years.

"Albert! How's it going? Working on that self-control?"

"Albert! I just heard about a new technique to slow things down: make yourself think about clouds."

Year after year I went to conducting school in the summer. I loved it—a kid like me, making music with Leon Fleisher and Isadore Freed and Tossy Spivakovsky! Maître was a demanding teacher. The tendency when learning to conduct is to monitor most closely your own kind, the instrument you also play. But when he saw a violinist giving too much direction to the violins, he would say, "No! You must pick on the tuba or the clarinet. Not just on what you know."

A dozen or so of the students had their own orchestras, and each of them invited me to come and solo with them, which I did.

The Monteux School grew from year to year. In addition to conducting students, auditors were admitted. Everyone played at least one instrument, so we were able more closely to approximate an orchestra. The pianists among us could fill in various missing parts. Now there was something for students to conduct.

It surprised me to realize that I was becoming a favorite, along with Leon Fleisher. I was concertmaster and, in spite of my youth, I was always given a movement to conduct at the final concert.

They were family people, Mum and Maître. One year they invited my parents up for a visit. Another year I stayed on an extra week with Mum's sister's family, who lived nearby.

The year Fifi joined us, she quickly usurped my place as Mum's favorite. Fifi was a poodle. No one ever kicked her while Mum was watching, so she never knew how we viewed her pet. In 1962, Fifi would publish a book containing her observations of Maître.

One day there was a knock on the door of my cabin. A new student named Dick stood there with some staff paper in his hand.

"So, you play violin pretty well, I saw, and I wondered if I could ask you to look at this." He held out the staff paper, covered with music written in pencil. "I'm writing a piece for violin, but I don't actually play violin."

It looked like Bach, stacks of notes. "No," I said, "you can't play that on the violin."

Disappointment settled over his face. He was twenty-eight and was staying with a family up the road. Richard Yardumian was his name. He was tall and had a shock of dark hair that fell over part of his forehead.

We met again after class, and Dick explained that he tried his compositions out on the piano as he went along. He set his music on a table and asked why it wouldn't work for the violin.

"Because you wrote notes that happen at the same time on the same string."

I got out my violin, and we worked together so Dick could see what the violin could and couldn't do. It got to be fun.

When I got back to Philadelphia, I borrowed Dad's car every so often to go see Dick and his wife in Bryn Athyn, where they lived.

"I'm working on a new piece," he said one winter day. "It's for violin alone, so I'm calling it 'Monologue.'"

"Let me see."

"I haven't written it down, but I'll play it."

He played it on the piano. I played it back to him on the violin and suggested changes to make it more violinistic.

He was getting good at composing for strings, and we worked on that piece together every time I visited. Dick had a very original way of working out harmonization, and I came to understand the ways of playing it. In the future, I would perform "Monologue" many times.

Everyone who knew Dick and his wife and children saw their deep faith and their commitment to the Swedenborgian Church. Dick played the organ and led the choir in worship services. I was not terribly surprised when his minister dropped in one day while we were working on some music.

"Do you mind if I listen while you put this piece together?" he asked.

Dick made sure the Reverend was comfortable, and we continued working on "Monologue." Reverend Theo Pitcairn had energetic white hair and a nice, religious beard. He always wore a black, clerical-looking suit with a white shirt. I never saw him *not* wearing a suit, even if sometimes it was a little rumpled.

During a break, the Reverend asked me if I liked music from the Baroque period.

"Well, a lot of it was written for ancient instruments and I don't play any of those. But Bach wrote some good stuff for violin. My favorite is the Chaconne."

"What does it sound like?"

What a question. I still cannot answer it to my satisfaction. How can one piece of music, less than a quarter of an hour long, find and sing so many moods? Dr. Szanto had taught me to treat the Chaconne's parts separately. "Here comes Bach the organist," he would say, "and you must play your violin like an organ for these bars." Another part would be frantic joy.

The Chaconne is littered with chords—three and four notes stacked—as if the violin were constructed like a keyboard. Of course, the curved bridge of modern violins limits playing so many simultaneous notes. A violinist can play two notes together for a long time, but adding more to the chord requires rolling the bow to catch a new note while letting a previous one trail off. So violinists arpeggiate Bach's chords, and choose which notes to lean into and which to deemphasize. When we turn a chord into an arpeggio, we affect the rhythm, too.

I loved playing the Chaconne. I loved the particular way I heard its melodies and the freedom the piece gave me to choose notes out of chords to weave into a melodic line.

I played it for the Reverend, and it pleased him.

He came to watch us work a number of times, and soon I was included in one of the dinner invitations that were a normal pattern for the Yardumian family.

"You need to wear a jacket and tie to the Pitcairns', you know," Dick said.

Dinner at the Reverend's required one person to use more pieces of flatware than my family set out for all of us. In fact, so did lunch. I was to eat with the Pitcairns very frequently. After dinner we adjourned to the solarium, passing a Rembrandt in the hall and sitting under an El Greco. While devotion to God was Reverend Pitcairn's first calling by far, devotion to the arts was a consistent subtheme. For him, the two meshed nicely. He loved the Impressionists and had a villa in France. He loved being a patron of the arts, which was possible because he had inherited a third of the fortune generated by his grandfather's Pittsburgh Plate Glass Company and their investments in railroads.

Dick Yardumian had personally stimulated his minister's interest in music. Reverend Pitcairn had a box at the Philadelphia Orchestra, and on Friday afternoons Dick often accompanied the Pitcairns to concerts.

In the summer of 1946 or 1947, I was invited to solo at the Robin Hood Dell in Philadelphia. I would be playing Édouard Lalo's *Symphonie espagnole* with Vladimir Golschmann conducting.

Dr. Szanto was lending me a fine violin, a Ruggieri, on a long-term basis, but he got the idea of doing something really exceptional for this concert.

The Stradivari family did their best work in the 1720s, and their surviving violins from that era have by now earned individual names. In Philadelphia, violinist Iso Briselli owned the Kochansky Stradivarius.

Dr. Szanto went to Mr. Briselli and asked him to lend me the Kochansky Strad for my Dell concert.

I went to look at it. I touched it, and played it. Then I walked out of Mr. Briselli's house carrying it! My father waited at home, trembling with excitement.

I closed my bedroom door and began to practice. Of course it felt different. Every violin has its own feel. No matter. I had played plenty of violins and could adjust to changes. The chinrest felt unusual. I knew I could get past that, so I kept going with *Symphonie espagnole*. I played the way I always played.

But I wasn't getting anywhere. Just when I'd forgotten the instrument and my head was fully in the music, a note would break. Just for an instant, the tone would disintegrate.

The fault had to be my own, not the violin's. I started the phrase over and tried to adapt to the way the Kochansky Strad had to be handled.

I was glad no one was counting how many times I started over . . . or was someone counting?

"Dad!"

I think he was standing outside my door. "I have to take it back."

Please, he begged, keep trying. I did, and I did, and I did. For several more days. You never saw such a disappointed dad, and such a disappointed boy.

The one who understood best was Iso Briselli. "You're the violinist," he said. "You have to be in charge. It often takes more than a couple of days to forge an alliance with an instrument, especially a Strad."

Time I did not have. One day I would find my way among the work of the luthiers of Cremona, but on that day I thought it would never be possible for me.

At my graduation from the Philadelphia Musical Academy, I was asked to solo. Paul Hindemith was awarded an honorary doctorate at the ceremony.

I did not leave Dr. Szanto behind. He was my teacher forever. He had taken me to that ledge every artist must approach and step off. Because of Dr. Szanto, I could now master my instrument and learn new music on my own. Whenever and wherever I would play the violin in the future, a thank you to him would stir within me.

We still met simply because we were close. When the French violinist Jacques Thibaud came to Philadelphia that year, Dr. Szanto arranged for me to play for him.

Mr. Thibaud said, "You must come to Paris! You are a natural for our contest." He meant the Marguerite Long–Jacques Thibaud International Competition.

I thanked him with a smile that hid my sinking feeling. My parents were already sacrificing all they could. It's not as if I was contributing to the family income; my "work" was practicing.

And yet, when the time came, there I was in the beautiful springtime of Paris, a boy of nineteen. Mouchka, the mother of Mrs. Pitcairn, picked me up from the airport. There was another passenger, her granddaughter, the lovely Brigitte. Brigitte was all of thirteen, and I was obliged to humor her. After all, Mouchka had taken my Paris lodging in hand. Brigitte immediately climbed onto my lap.

"Get off!" her grandmother suggested. Or at least Brigitte took it as a mere suggestion.

She stayed put and kissed me over and over during our two-hour car ride to Mouchka's house.

Mouchka drove me back to Paris the next day to install me in a boarding house, where I would live for a month. I wonder if she was aware that it was actually an international finishing school for girls. I didn't mind.

It was Jacques Thibaud himself who had found the funding for my trip, after Dr. Szanto told him I couldn't come. Mr. Thibaud approached a consortium of singers, including Lawrence Tibbett, who generously underwrote competition costs for young musicians like me.

The venue for the preliminaries right through the finals was the Salle Gaveau, as lovely a place as I have ever performed. I played Lalo again, four movements from the *Symphonie espagnole*. The first experience of a large audience's wild enthusiasm is a lot for a young person to keep in perspective. Christian Ferras was the other finalist, and his playing was superb.

Now it was time for the judges to rule. We all hung around backstage, and the audience also waited. A quarter hour passed, and another, and another. After two hours Mr. Thibaud came looking for me and led me into a small room.

"They don't want to give it to you." Tears stood in his eyes. "An American won last time, too, and they think it should move around. So you'll share the prize. You'll get the money, and Christian Ferras will get the contract."

The contract would provide the French boy with a manager and a recording arrangement, all to begin with a performance with the Paris Orchestra. It was the manager that mattered most.

Jacques Thibaud himself had shared a first-place prize when he was young. He was studying at the Paris Conservatoire in 1896 and shared its violin competition prize with Pierre Monteux.[4]

Four years later a plane would crash into the French Alps, taking Mr. Thibaud out of this world, along with his 1720 Stradivarius.

The prize money was generous, but it had to stay in France. I bought gifts for everyone I could think of and enjoyed my Paris spring to the fullest. Then I boarded the TWA Constellation and flew to New York.

When I got home, I stood outside our house. A month earlier, I had stood there with my parents waiting for the taxi to the airport. The familiar bulk of the yellow cab came up the street, and I had turned to kiss my mother. But she suddenly screamed, "NO! NO!"

A large mangy dog was peeing freely on my violin case.

---

4. Obituary, "Pierre Monteux," *The Musical Times*, August 1964, 610.

Chapter 3

I'll Do As I Please

"ALBAIRE," MAÎTRE SAID. "We think you should come to San Francisco this winter. You could help me with my orchestra and refine your conducting. Besides, I like the way you play."

Yes, I would go. I was twenty-one, and all was right with the world. The violin felt natural, like the part of my body that connected my chin to my hands.

Maître and Mum Monteux lived at the Fairmont Hotel in San Francisco. I stayed with a Russian family friendly to the symphony, Bill and Moussya Sakovich.

I was immediately taken with the three Sakovich boys, especially two-year-old Nicky. It was not surprising that the Monteuxs would find such a family for me.

Each day I showed up at the War Memorial Opera House to function as Maître's assistant conductor. Oddly, there were no duties. I learned by observation, but Monteux left it at that.

For concerts, I entered that impressive venue in the retinue of Madame Monteux. If she was Mum in Hancock, she was the grande dame in San Francisco, and she dressed every inch of it. Her hair was sprayed into a halo. We processed to the conductor's box, which accommodated six people. She invited close friends and major donors to sit with her, and relatives of visiting conductors or soloists. I was usually the only young person in the box.

The others enjoyed the good view, but to me it *mattered*. Maître was an outstanding stick technician, equal to the tempo complexities of the most exacting composers. Few could do such justice to Stravinsky. And Maître could also give the necessary freedom to Impressionist music. French music was his forte, though he did everything well.

When guest conductors came, Maître sat in the proscenium, off to the side of the stage, so he would be out of sight of the audience and not a distraction. I sat there with him. Leopold Stokowski came—a consummate performer in contrast to Maître's modest style. It didn't necessarily improve the music.

Stokowski liked to rearrange the orchestra players after his own quirky preferences. For this performance, he made the unusual choice of placing the percussion section on high risers in the back. Joe Siani, a short man, played the cymbals and raised them at a climactic moment for a perfect clang. He arched his back for maximum uplift. He curved backwards. And continued to curve. Then, he disappeared completely from the riser. Some of us thought we heard a thud, but the wonderful metallic din continued for as long as any good cymbalist could want.

After the performance, we walked backstage, and found Joe, unhurt, though his suit was a little dusty. Monteux asked him, "How come you never do that at my concerts?"

The previous summer in Maine, Maître had begun to watch—really watch—when I played. He spoke to me about it: "We have to get you out more. I mean, if you're going to play *like that*, then people must hear it. I'm going to see what I can do."

So it surprised me, when I came to San Francisco, that he immediately urged me to take additional violin lessons. Dr. Szanto had recognized when we reached the point at which I was my own teacher.

"Ah, yes, but my concertmaster Naoum Blinder," Maître said. "You must study with him. Just a few lessons. He has another pupil who is already doing superbly—Isaac Stern."

Because the Monteuxs insisted, Naoum Blinder and I scheduled some lessons, neither of us willing to offend them. It went like this: I would play something for Naoum, and he would say, "Show me how you did that!" We liked each other, and pretty much goofed around together with our instruments during the lessons.

I was having a great time seeing old friends too. A couple of the San Francisco Symphony players regularly came to Maine with the Monteuxs—violinist David Sheinfeld and trumpeter Earl Murray.

After my first rehearsal, Earl invited me to dinner. His wife Gloria had invited a friend of hers, Marilyn Dow, so we were four. Marilyn was nice-looking in a kelly green suit with a matching hat, but no friendlier than necessary. After dinner, we went for a ride in the Murrays' car, this being back when riding in a car was considered an entertainment in itself. We drove through Golden Gate Park and decided to go to the amusement park on the beach.

"Oh, I love that whirling ride!" Marilyn said, and we all got on. When we were strapped into our places, Marilyn and I looked over at Earl and Gloria.

"Does Gloria like stuff like this?" I asked.

Marilyn didn't know.

Then the machine geared up, and we both knew. The Murrays grabbed fierce hold of each other and the nearest firm bars and their faces went white. Watching them through the ride, we laughed to the point of tears.

The Murrays needed every possible comfort after that, so we went to Pastene's, which offered a fireplace, soft chairs, and nightcaps.

"May I see you again?" I asked.

"Oh." The awkward look told it all. "My flight schedule is so tight this winter. I hardly have time for anything else."

We had talked a little at dinner about what it was like to be a stewardess for United. I'd noticed the graceful walk, the perfect posture, the manicured hands—all things required by the profession at that time. And the legs.

I asked Earl to invite us both to dinner again.

No invitation came.

What I didn't know was that Marilyn Dow had been going with Gloria to the Friday afternoon concerts for some time. When the symphony chartered a United flight for a tour, she worked it and got to know quite a few of the players. She had dated several and just broken up with the last, with the emphasis on *last*. She was done with musicians. *Finis*.

"Earl," I said. "Can't you set something up? I want to see her again."

He and Gloria invited me to a New Year's Eve party at his parents' house, and I went, in hopes that no transcontinental flight had interfered. Luck was on my side, and somehow she had become prettier in the month that had passed, though I hadn't actually observed any room for improvement.

There was still the problem of her indifference.

I worked it. Confidence was the major key with the occasional minor in modesty, little compliments as grace notes, plenty of syncopated humor. She invited me back to her apartment for a drink and told me about her roommates, George and Phil, which gave me pause. Remember, this was just a few minutes beyond the 1940s.

The apartment turned out to be near the Sakoviches, and the roommates turned out to be Georgene and Phyllis, also stewardesses. And the beautiful one, Marilyn, was now amenable to an occasional date.

The first time I took her to the symphony there was a guest conductor, and on this occasion Maître sat with Mum and the rest of us in the conductor's box. It was perfectly acceptable for me to bring dates to orchestra events, but Marilyn suddenly brought out his playful side.

"Is she for me?" he said.

What a promising beginning!

One day while we were driving along the ocean, Marilyn said, "You don't look like an Albert."

That comment didn't have an easy answer. I remembered raising a ruckus to acquire the nice, normal name.

"I don't even like that name," she added.

Suddenly the answer was obvious. "It's not really my name. Shall we start over? Hello, Marilyn. I'm Anshel."

"It's the perfect name for a musician!"

Beginning in early 1950, my performances were under my real name. My parents were pleased.

I had killed two birds with a stone already in my back pocket.

Arthur Fiedler, conductor of the Boston Pops, came to San Francisco that spring to conduct a series of concerts with the San Francisco Symphony, which was becoming an annual tradition. Short of money as always, I accepted an invitation to play with the orchestra for the series and took my assigned place in the sixth stand of first violins. My previous orchestra experience consisted of childhood visits to the Symphony Club in Philadelphia. Other than that, I had only soloed with orchestras. I found it pleasant to play with others.

My first performance as a member of a large orchestra was in the enormous San Francisco Cow Palace. There was room for a buffalo stampede. We were playing well, and Fiedler exuded joy. The piece just before intermission involved a complicated ending, with the orchestra repeatedly playing and stopping.

It required concentration. Which, after the first stop, I suddenly lost. I heard my violin when all else was silence. I moved my bow in some highly original way as if I were trying to play and stop playing at the same time, and my instrument responded with a sound I'd never heard a violin emit, a god-awful sound that should be impossible to make. It was like a primal scream from the spruce tree that had been sacrificed for the violin.

Fiedler stopped conducting—it was that bad. That confused the players, and many stopped. The others tapered off until silence filled the entire Cow Palace and, unbelievably, persisted as if not only the conductor but the thousands of listeners were in shock that such a sound could assault their ears from the San Francisco Symphony.

Fiedler stepped off the podium and walked toward the violin section. "Who did that!" he hissed.

No one answered.

The audience, at this point, concluded that the composer had written a terrible ending for the piece and so began a polite applause.

Fiedler didn't drop it. He walked among the strings, coming toward me. "Who did that?"

I looked behind me as if the culprit were back there.

A week later I soloed with Arthur Fiedler, playing Lalo's *Symphonie espagnole*. I played my heart out and felt I was making it up to Fiedler though, of course, he didn't know. Marilyn came, and seated at her table was the actress Corinne Calvet, the second most beautiful woman in the room.

Back in Philadelphia, Richard Yardumian was imagining his way through a violin concerto. As soon as I got home for the summer in 1950, he enlisted me. Every day I drove up to his house in Bryn Athyn. He played his musical thoughts on the piano, and I gave them back to him violinistically. This was a privilege only Dick could give me—intimate participation in the process of making up brand new music.

I drifted through that pleasant summer, receiving three letters a week from Marilyn and dining often with Yardumians and the Pitcairns. Theo was always interested in how the composing was going and sometimes stopped in to watch. Usually he sat quietly and didn't talk to us much.

Sometimes he said, "Could you play the Chaconne again?"

I always did.

In August I went to Maine and again joined my conducting friends. We all played instruments too. All paths to the podium led through the music stand, one way or another.

This time in Maine, I missed Marilyn.

In the fall of 1950, I continued to learn from Monteux. I took the initiative to question him about everything he did and how he controlled the sounds of the orchestra.

He was zealous about arranging solo performances for me. Maître and Mum together were putting me on the concertizing track. In December I played the Tchaikovsky violin concerto in Houston with Efrem Kurtz conducting and, best of all, my brother Nat playing first clarinet.

Dick's concerto was ready. In March 1951, I played the debut of the Yardumian Violin Concerto with the Philadelphia Orchestra. Playing under Ormandy in the Academy of Music was always magic to me. My parents could come.

Five of Dick's kids were in the proscenium box for that performance. Of course I knew them all. Aram, one of my favorites, was a tease. He stood up during my performance and held his nose. I wasn't sure if he was blaming me or his dad for the stinky music.

In April I played the Tchaikovsky Violin Concerto at the War Memorial Opera House, with Monteux and the San Francisco Symphony. Often people don't like to sit too close to the stage, and the pit seats remain empty. That's how it was that night, except for one elderly woman right in front of me. There came a moment when I played something badly and said in a whisper, "Oh, shit!" I looked out and caught her grinning in the front row.

More people should choose the pit seats.

I noticed that all my reviews identified me as "a student of Naoum Blinder, who also taught Isaac Stern." Blinder's profile as a teacher was important to someone. Eventually I realized that it was more Isaac Stern's concern than Monteux's, to get my name associated with Blinder as a teacher. I didn't care, except that if anyone was to be praised for my training, it should be Dr. Szanto.

By this time, I always wanted to be with Marilyn, and every time a symphony event allowed for guests, I brought her. Maître and Mum were just cordial. A general nervousness surfaced in those closest to us. Earl and Gloria Murray anticipated possible conflict over Marilyn. It was clear that I had been anointed by the Monteuxs. I wasn't sure what that might mean for my personal life. Mum had engineered the marriage of sweet little Mano to her son. She was a matchmaker at heart.

Maybe not for me, though. And yet, why shouldn't I have Marilyn? Was I supposed to be auctioned off to some heiress with symphony connections around the world?

I was willing to face whatever risk might come. However, I didn't want any of my friends in range of stray arrows. Without a word spoken, Marilyn and I drifted apart from the Murrays.

"I want to marry you," I told her.

"Oh, you want to marry me all right. At the moment. But do you really *like* me?"

At least I had gotten her past the initial indifference. I was clear about what I wanted. She was the one.

Also, the three little Sakovich boys bounced into the room every day when I came home. I would pick up Nicky and tease him. I wanted all of that, a life with children.

At last, I persuaded Marilyn to say yes. We told the Sheinfelds.

"Absolutely," David said. "Follow your own heart. Don't listen to anyone else."

Marilyn's parents were pleased.

As for telling my own parents, I wanted a little more time.

One spring day Mum asked me to come and see her at their apartment in the Fairmont Hotel. She was home alone, and I sat in their comfortable living room. They never went in for elaborate décor.

"Are you getting involved with this girl?"

"Yes. I really, really am."

Fifi panted near me, her breath foul. I resisted the urge to push the fluffy black nuisance away with my foot.

"You must know it would be the end. Maître would have nothing more to do with you. I suggest you get out of it now." Her great buxom front puffed itself toward me as she waited for my inevitable surrender. Was any woman ever so satisfied with herself as Mum? Only an idiot would hold out.

"All the solo performances Maître has arranged for you will be canceled," she added.

"I'm sorry," the idiot said.

I walked out of the Fairmont into sunshine and turned onto the side street where I'd parked Marilyn's car, which we now shared. I sensed someone turning the same way behind me and looked back, but it was just some guy I didn't know. I stopped to put the key in the car door, and the guy slowed down. He was looking at the license plate.

"Are you following me?"

He stopped, surprised. "Well . . . yeah. Mrs. Monteux told me to. I work for the Fairmont, so I can't exactly refuse to do something for *them*. She wanted to know about the car you're driving."

At least he was a crummy detective. I let him copy down the license plate.

Several painful realities were screaming in my face. One was that the Monteuxs had not brought me to San Francisco to develop my conducting career. It was to launch my violin concertizing career. Another was that their enthusiasm for family life applied mainly to themselves.

I would not be the only musician to stumble over that second issue. A few years later, Doris Monteux would take on the promising Freda Gray-Masse as a voice student. The only obstacle was the husband and children, and Mum would suggest the obvious solution: divorce the husband and hand over custody to him. Mrs. Gray-Masse would decline and find herself dropped by the Monteuxs.[1]

Mum's next discussion of my personal life was informal: she pulled me aside. "Your parents are very displeased that you're throwing everything away for this girl. *Everything*."

1. John Canarina, *Pierre Monteux: Maître* (Pompton Plains, NJ, and Cambridge, U.K.: Amadeus Press, 2003), 220.

I hadn't told them yet. However, Mum was correct about their reaction—and it was a reaction to *her* version of my present and future life. She had laid it all out before them in a letter: how their son could step into the glory of world fame or crawl into some obscure apartment with his pretty little minx. My father called Mum to get more information and then sent my brother to San Francisco.

Nat drove wildly up Mount Tamalpais to find me and yell things like, "What do you think you're doing? After all Mom and Dad have done for you!"

Nat had already tried to make lifestyle choices for himself. During the war, he served by playing in a military band based in Georgia. He sent his paychecks home to my parents to save for him. Along came a girl, and he married her. Dad, when he found out, froze Nat's assets, to be released only upon annulment of the marriage. He even traveled to Georgia and made things happen.

Nat was always the more compliant son.

In June I went home. It would be a long summer, though at least it offered a break from Maître and Mum. They had arranged some performances, but I expected to hear that they were canceled.

As a substitute for the warmth and laughter of Marilyn's company, I got soured parenting. I lived for my three letters a week.

Suddenly Marilyn stopped writing. Long-distance phone calls were an emergency measure in those days, but this qualified.

"What do you mean?" she said. "I am too still writing!"

She was writing letters, and they were being delivered to our house.

My parents had sacrificed much for me. I asked myself: do they own me forever? I decided they did not.

My parents admitted to taking Marilyn's letters, and I asked for them.

"We didn't keep them."

I called Dr. Szanto and invited him out to lunch. We were very close, but I knew he would feel honor bound to respect my parents, too. I told him all that had happened and that I could not imagine life without Marilyn.

Dr. Szanto knew what it was to love, and he had suffered so much in his life, especially losing both sons in the war. "You must do what your heart tells you to do," he said. "You can have her send letters to my house, no yes. I will keep them for you."

He was more than a teacher to me.

My scheduled performances were not canceled. On July 12, I played the Tchaikovsky violin concerto with the Chicago Symphony at Ravinia Park, Maître conducting. He was professional toward me, and the concert went well. Marilyn had her choice of routes with United, so she arranged to be at the concert, and to work the overnight flight I took home. We planned a September wedding and told a handful of close friends, and her family.

Maître had also arranged for me to play at Lewisohn Stadium when he was guest conducting the New York Philharmonic. He was, as ever, a marvelous accompanist. Only Ormandy could outdo him in bringing the whole orchestra along with the soloist. I was never the easiest violinist to follow. Maître told the New York Philharmonic, "Be careful in the third movement. Anshel likes to play it very fast." As an encore, I used Yardumian's "Monologue."

When I got back to Philadelphia, I picked up a letter at Dr. Szanto's house. "I don't think I can do this," Marilyn began. She didn't absolutely dump me, but any firm commitment was rescinded.

What I didn't know was that my parents had written her an intimidating letter. Marilyn was no pushover. Becoming a stewardess in the 1940s took ambition. Airplanes themselves seemed miraculous, and airlines had their pick of the best for positions. Yes, you had to be attractive. But the nonnegotiable was ensuring passenger safety. Marilyn had to display the leadership skills to force order onto chaos in a crisis.

Even so, the letter laying out all the ways in which a marriage between us would damage my career unsettled her. The Monteuxs were eager to launch me. But the commitment required for a concertizing career was total. My love must be all for the violin and my audiences, my parents said.

I went to Maine as always in August, but my memories of it are hazy. All I knew was that some sort of bulldozer had turned the path to the altar into rough terrain. I was living for a September wedding, and not sure that it would happen. I passed the time with good old Harold Glick.

Marilyn had replied to my parents that she would never want to impede my career. But she also wrote, "This is not a decision you can make for Anshel."

When I returned to San Francisco, I pressed that point—that this was *our* decision. A glorious life of fame without her was something I couldn't bear to think of. She was persuaded again.

On Labor Day weekend, her father had a heart attack that kept him in the hospital for two months. We were grateful for her parents' blessing on our marriage and wanted them both there. We waited.

It was no longer comfortable for me to show up at rehearsals of the San Francisco Symphony, so I kept away. The Monteuxs knew by now that we were engaged. Their interest in me was at an end. It is not easy in the world of classical performance to chart one's own course professionally and also shape one's own life personally. When I was twenty-three, I made my own choice.

Marilyn handwrote the invitations and mailed them to her relatives and friends and to those of our musical friends for whom attendance would not damage their careers. The Sheinfelds signed our certificate. On December 23, 1951, we were married in a church full of poinsettias at no cost to us, Marilyn catching all eyes in an ivory suit from I. Magnin.

After the usual celebrations, we retired to the ground-level apartment we had rented through an ad posted in the orchestra building. Twelve days later, we flew to Boston. I was to play the Tchaikovsky violin concerto with the Boston Symphony Orchestra under guest conductor Ernest Ansermet, on January 4 and 5, another engagement Monteux had arranged. Fortunately, he would not be present.

The Tchaikovsky, by this time, was like a comfortable old song to me. And being on stage never caused me much anxiety. So I played the third movement pretty fast again at the Friday performance. Of course, it's the soloist's prerogative to set the pace. On Saturday I guess I was feeling my oats because I upped the pace a little.

Ansermet shot me an irritated look. He thought it was too fast.

I considered slowing down, but decided not to. The orchestra was doing a great job and I liked playing fast.

Now the orchestra was playing a few measures that were easy for them, and I noticed that Ansermet took the opportunity to push a little, to move them to an even faster tempo. That's when it dawned on me that he was thinking ahead. The third movement would be coming, and the third movement of that concerto is about as fast as music gets. He was nudging me out onto a limb where I would be forced into an impossible speed. *He* would show *me* how I should have paced myself.

We got to the third movement, all of us racing along together, and I couldn't resist upping it even more. I pushed into all-out breakneck speed, the orchestra keeping up and even Ansermet looking pleased. The audience went nuts. I remember the performance with joy.

I was asked to return a week later to play with the Boston Symphony Orchestra again with Ansermet in New Haven, Connecticut.

We came out ahead on the expenses for that weekend. Marilyn had free passes from United and we stayed with a friend of mine she didn't know, bassist Willis Page.

Marilyn refers to that trip as "our so-called honeymoon."

Maître had scheduled a performance for me in mid-January of 1952. I was to play the Glazunov concerto with the San Francisco Symphony in Richmond, California, while he conducted. These things cannot be gracefully undone, or he surely would have managed that.

I had not seen Monteux since getting married, and we decided that Marilyn should be backstage with me, where I would meet Maître. In the semi-darkness, I saw him—and Mum with him. She never traveled to concerts with him. I had the sense that she was the guard, present to make sure he followed through on their policy towards me.

I was waiting for the cue from him to walk on stage. Protocol dictated that I go first and the conductor follow. The soloist bows to the audience. The conductor mounts his podium, and takes his own pre-concert bow. I had learned all of this early, and Maître himself had reinforced it and emphasized the necessity of protocol. It is what the audience expects and what ensures a smooth performance.

When it was time for my solo, I left Marilyn in the dressing room and walked toward the the stage entrance. Maître stood there, waiting for me I thought. He didn't say hello or anything, but I walked toward him, and just before I got there, he turned abruptly and walked on stage ahead of me, as if this performance included no soloist.

I trotted along after him. The audience offered some confused applause. I gave an abbreviated bow and took up my position. By this time I had caught on that we were going to be less than polite.

I tuned my violin and looked at him to signal that I was ready. But he wasn't watching. In fact, he started conducting immediately, whether or not I was ready. Most concertos begin with quite a few measures for the orchestra before the soloist begins to play. The Glazunov Violin Concerto is unusual. After just a few notes— exactly two seconds—the soloist plays. Monteux had begun so suddenly that, just as I heard the orchestra playing, I realized they were already on the very note that coincided with my entrance. He was not going to so much as turn his head my way. It was all the same to him if I actually failed to come in, ensuring the breakdown of my performance. Few soloists can recover from a disastrous beginning.

My bow hit the A natural on the G string after a delay no one perceived except myself, Monteux, and the shocked orchestra members. Fortunately, then Glazunov filled my mind and I was able to play the concerto just as I wanted it to sound.

I always stayed till the end of concerts. I had never left after my own performance, when more was on the program. Marilyn and I made an exception that night.

Pierre Monteux was known for his peaceable nature. He was not a proud person, not a bully, not contentious. I do not know why he felt that it was his right to forbid my marriage. I can more easily fathom it in Doris Monteux. Yet it was Maître who abandoned protocol on stage, possibly for the only time in his life. It grieves me still to have been the musician who impelled him to that.

Anyway, I got the girl.

Since married women were not eligible to be stewardesses, United gave Marilyn a job at the ticket counter. That got us through 1952, along with my earnings from odd jobs. But as I looked toward the future. . . .

Actually, Marilyn was the one who looked toward the future. I looked as far as the next performance. By the fall, she noticed that my career, absent the Monteuxs, would evolve on the East Coast, if at all.

"You're right!" I said. "We have to move back."

"And live on what? Who's going to give me a job now that I'm pregnant?"

I was always in touch with Dick Yardumian, and he suggested that Ormandy might have some office work or something for me. In the next letter from Dick, I was delighted to learn that there was work for me in the orchestra library. Not only that, but Theo Pitcairn was offering a rent-free place for us to live in Bryn Athyn, Pennsylvania.

On December 1, Marilyn quit her job and we moved.

Theo had broken away from the main Swedenborgians and formed The Lord's New Church, Swedenborgian. The chapel where they worshipped was across the driveway from his house in Bryn Athyn and had a couple of basement rooms dubbed the Catacombs. We moved into those rooms.

The Pitcairns were like family to us at a time when family was something we were short on. For lunch and dinner, we joined them, all dressed up. We also attended the services upstairs and tried to read some of their religious literature, though it was hard going. An easier way for me to show my appreciation was to include Bach's Chaconne, at least as an encore, whenever Theo happened to be in the audience.

Theo Pitcairn believed in the value of the arts and took joy in supporting a young violinist, just as he did in supporting an august orchestra. That the Philadelphia Orchestra played the music of Richard Yardumian was an added blessing for Theo. Yardumian was to continue composing hymns and baroque-style choral preludes for his church right along with music for orchestras all his life. The Swedenborgian hymnal is filled with his work.

On Fridays, I sometimes went with the Pitcairns and Dick Yardumian to the orchestra performances. I can still see Theo entering the Academy of Music from the street—gaunt in his black overcoat, walking with his hands clasped behind his back, like Ichabod Crane dropped into the twentieth century.

Dick gradually decided that Ormandy should know about Theo's devotion to the Philadelphia Orchestra. So he arranged a meeting between his minister and Eugene Ormandy. After that, Theo was motivated to give even more generously.

After two months in the Catacombs, our friends the Salverians offered us a bedroom in their apartment.

"Go ahead and take the bed with you," Mrs. Pitcairn offered. The bed in the Catacombs was a loveseat-sized sofa-bed, a bit larger than a twin bed. Marilyn was six months pregnant and I counted myself lucky to be given any space at all on it.

The Salverians were also Swedenborgian, and we continued attending services.

By now it was February of 1953, and we needed income if it meant taking in laundry. I knew Ormandy had noticed my presence in the Pitcairn box at some of the Friday performances. Yet he hadn't called with information about my library job. One day I drove down into Philly to the Academy of Music. The orchestra was rehearsing, and I waited backstage until Ormandy was free.

"Alb—oh, I've got to get used to Anshel."

"Makes me feel like a little kid again."

He smiled. "It's a good name. And your real one."

"Yes. I'm ready to start any time."

"Start what?"

"Work in the library." There was a pause. I began to feel uncomfortable.

"Today? We don't have any openings. I thought you meant some time later."

Now I really did feel like a little kid. I couldn't figure out how I had misunderstood Dick Yardumian so completely.

The moment was awkward for Ormandy too. "I'll see what I can do, . . . Anshel."

Marilyn was dumbfounded. "How could he go back on it?"

"I really don't think he was aware of any agreement. He's going to see what he can do."

"Oh, that's a comfort."

Somewhere between Dick Yardumian and Ormandy and me, communication had gone awry. I flopped down on the couch, in no mood for practicing anything that had no wages attached to it.

A few days later the phone rang.

"Arthur Judson here." He was the manager of many top-level musicians. "I'm putting together an all-Gershwin touring orchestra for next spring and I haven't got a concertmaster yet. Eugene Ormandy called and said you might be available."

With that happy prospect to begin in six months, Marilyn and I rented a small apartment in Hatboro and excused ourselves from the Lord's New Church. I was sorry to disappoint the Pitcairns in this, but we hadn't turned into Swedenborgians.

Sometimes when you put something off and keep putting it off, all of a sudden it throttles you and you give in. That's how it was, having the rift with my parents. One day I put my violin in the case, changed into a clean shirt, and set my face toward home. It would be an hour's drive, time enough to plan what to say.

Marilyn was scrubbing the kitchen floor. She was wearing what young pregnant housewives wore in 1953 to scrub kitchen floors. She had styled her hair in whatever way was suitable for that task.

"Let's go, Mar."

"Where?"

"Philly."

"I'm busy."

"Come on. I just have to break the ice with my parents. A quick visit."

"Are you nuts? Do you see what I look like?"

"Gorgeous."

I needed her support just to go near their house. It had been almost two years. I worked on her, promising she could wait in the car and they'd never know she was around. The moment was now, the keys jangled in my hand, it had to happen. Somehow I got her into the car, just as she was.

I parked on a side street near the fur store. It was a beautiful day, the trees just leafing out, and Marilyn rolled down the windows as I walked around the corner.

My father was overjoyed to see me. He kissed me and called my mother down from upstairs. We all cried and then caught up on family news.

"I've got dinner started," Mom said. "You have to stay."

"I can't."

If she hadn't looked so hurt, I never would have told her. But a lesser excuse wouldn't do. "Marilyn's in the car."

"What? We've been talking for half an hour, and you just left her out there?" my father said. "Bring her in this minute!"

The look on Marilyn's face, when I extended the invitation through the car window, would make Goliath quiver. "As I said before," she said quietly, "I'm not dressed for going into town. Let alone for meeting your parents. *Let alone for eating with them!*"

My parents greeted her warmly—the bulging presence of their next grandchild wasn't lost on them. We were folded into the family and my prodigal status faded away.

By that time, I was soloing with the Philadelphia Orchestra every year. My upcoming performance was the Paganini Violin Concerto No. 1, using the Wilhelmj transcription. I incorporated Sauret's cadenza for it as well. My parents were always in the audience, and for the first time I played for an audience that included them and my wife.

Marilyn gave birth to our son David Eugene on May 29, 1953. When I told Ormandy his name a few weeks later, he was thrilled. It was the nicest thing anybody could do, he said. (I don't want to know if he changed his mind about that. David himself has always been ambivalent.) Ormandy sent us a sterling silver baby cup with a lightly gilded interior. His engraved signature runs below "David Eugene Brusilow."

Not only was I a dad, my adult status was further confirmed in the form of paychecks. The Gershwin Orchestra was still months away, but I was hired for the summer by St. John Terrell's Music Circus in Lambertville, New Jersey. Our small pit orchestra sounded fine under the direction of Oscar Kosarin, and he made sure we had just as much fun as the audience. I used to tear up every time I played the sentimental violin solo, "You'll Never Walk Alone" in *Carousel*. Oscar would stage-whisper, "Are you all right?" to get all the actors and musicians laughing at me.

I didn't realize how much I was learning. Later, when I would conduct singers with an orchestra, I always thought back to the way Oscar did it.

One hot day I went into New York hoping to get a manager for my concerts. I got together with a new friend, Willy Kapell. A young pianist, Willy was stunning audiences the world over. He had attended my Paganini concerto performance and we became friends afterwards. He wanted to do some concerts together.

"A manager is essential," he agreed. "We need someone to help you get one. How about if I arrange for you to play for Heifetz? I'll accompany you on piano."

Jascha Heifetz. No one holding a violin stood on a higher pinnacle. I would love that.

"I go on tour next week," Willy said. "So we'll do it as soon as I get back."

He played thirty-seven concerts in Australia and then flew back to the United States. His plane hit Kings Mountain just south of San Francisco on October 29, 1953, and the world lost a dear person and decades of magnificent piano playing.

The Gershwin tour was pure fun. I had to desert the orchestra briefly to play the Tchaikovsky violin concerto with the Baltimore Symphony. Then I jumped on a plane to rejoin my tour in New Orleans.

The woman next to me on the plane was very pregnant. Partway through the flight she got nervous, so I decided to be friendly.

"When's your baby due?"

"Soon. I hope I can get back to my husband."

"We'll be there in a couple hours."

"It might be coming right now." She was panicked.

There was no doctor on board. We Jews think *chutzpah* is a good thing. Maybe you can have too much of it, though. Somehow I ended up lending my hands to the messy and important business of new life. I tied off the umbilical cord with a new E string.

"Doctor," the mother said, "I want to name him after you. What's your name?"

"Anshel."

Her eyes widened in alarm and then closed.

I didn't get a namesake, but I had fun describing the gory details to my friends in the Gershwin orchestra.

When our tour ended, I had to go straight to Philadelphia to record a new version of the Yardumian Violin Concerto with the Philadelphia Orchestra. Dick had been busy revising it.

"Let's listen to the playback," Ormandy said after the recording session.

"No thanks," I said. "You listen. I'm going back to my family."

I drove faster than I should have. Then I was kissing Marilyn and heading for David's crib. What I dreaded was that he wouldn't remember me. He was not a year old yet, and I had missed one-fourth of his life.

He stood up and raised his arms. I picked him up and never wanted to let him go again.

In the summer of 1954, Alexander Hilsberg called me. He had known me as a kid at Curtis, and he was concertmaster when I began soloing at sixteen with the Philadelphia Orchestra. Under Ormandy, Hilsberg's taste for conducting grew, and he managed to get on the right side of orchestra board president Orville Bullitt and the former president, Judge Curtis Bok. Which was of course the wrong side of Ormandy. Hilsberg made a bid for the conductor's position and by most accounts had a real chance.

Ormandy kept an eye out for usurpers. Other board members alerted him, and he deftly moved Hilsberg out of the way. In fact, he helped Hilsberg land the position as conductor of the New Orleans Philharmonic.

"I need a concertmaster," Hilsberg said to me that summer's day.

"I'd love to!"

"We do a lot of children's concerts here in New Orleans—more than thirty a year—and it's just too much, all the scheduling, programming, and conducting. Would you like to be an assistant conductor, too?"

It was everything I wanted all wrapped up in one package. In New Orleans I began to harvest the benefits of all the violin parts my dad had bought long ago for Stan and me to play in our dining room, pretending to be in the Philadelphia Orchestra. My working knowledge of so many pieces made it easy for me to keep my eyes on Hilsberg's baton and not have my nose in my music stand. Conductors appreciate that.

A wonderful conductor, Hilsberg gave the city of New Orleans more than its money's worth as he upgraded the orchestra and brought classical music into the schools. Many of his players went on to play in stellar American or European orchestras.

Programming was a challenge for me at first. But Hilsberg's guidance has benefited me throughout my career.

"Never do more than eighty-five minutes of music." That was his first rule. "Start with a loud work, followed by a soft work, followed by a loud work. Then intermission. After that soft, then loud." All rules must sometimes be broken, but I still usually follow Hilsberg's. Programming for children was really no different from programming for adults, except that you have to keep the pieces accessible. Our children's concerts were broadcast throughout Louisiana.

Leopold Stokowski came to New Orleans to guest conduct the Shostakovich Tenth Symphony, which had only premiered a year earlier. It is a gigantic work, and I was in awe of Stokowski's magnificent guidance of our playing throughout the rehearsal.

For the performance, I arrived early enough to get dressed, to get out my violin and tune it, and to be in the right frame of mind. A concertmaster is expected to assist the conductor in controlling the orchestra, and I was feeling the privilege of playing that role under Stokowski.

"The Maestro wants to see you," one of the players said the minute I arrived. I hurried to his dressing room, ready to help solve whatever last-minute problem had arisen.

He handed me a little piece of paper covered with handwriting. It said things like, "Slow the oboe down at letter B in the score. At letter D, the second violins must play louder. " Et cetera. Nine or ten different specific directives to be delivered to nine or ten different players or principals.

I set out to find the oboe. He wasn't in his dressing room, nor in the men's room. He was at the poker table. I delivered the instruction, and he looked at me like I was nuts. His music was out on stage on his stand. The audience was coming into the hall already, so he couldn't go out there. Even if he remembered it until he got out onstage, no pencil would be available.

Next, the principal second violin. I'd passed him somewhere. I rushed around till I found him and told him where his section should play louder.

He wrinkled his face at me and scratched his head. Then he turned his attention back to his cufflinks.

I looked down at my brown pants and remembered the white shirt and black coat and pants waiting for me in my dressing room. The buttons. It couldn't be done that quickly. Also, part of why I arrived when I did was to be in the right frame of mind for performance. I stuck the list in the pocket of my brown pants and figured Marilyn could take it out when she did the wash.

In the end, I just went out and played the concert, following Stokowski's conducting, and all was well.

I was to play under him many times in future years. That's just the way Stokowski was. He never stopped thinking about the music and making changes.

In those days, I was devoted to my violin. An approaching solo appearance on my calendar would bring out all my dedication, in the front room of our shotgun apartment. And it brought out the toddler we shared quarters with, little David. What a fine ear he seemed to have, listening to my playing, sometimes humming bits of melody.

But I resisted distraction and tried to shut out everything but whatever concerto I was preparing. My focus was intense and every mistake I made irritated me.

At the dinner table one night, after an afternoon's hard practice, some soup got spilled and David said, "Oh, shit!"

"He didn't learn it from me," his mother said.

I would have to make fewer mistakes in practicing, I decided.

One of my solos with the New Orleans Philharmonic was the Glazunov concerto. I loved the venue: a huge civic center in Lafayette, Louisiana, all decked out for the rodeo. We were sandwiched between rodeo performances and lucky to be raised up on a stage, several feet above the floor, which was entirely covered in sawdust. I have nothing to say about the acoustics.

Until it was time for my concerto, which was second on the program, I stood next to the stage in the sawdust. Suddenly my E string broke. There was time enough to fetch another one from my dressing room, which was also a horse stall, as anyone equipped with a nose could tell. I pulled the broken string out, tossed it aside, and rushed to the dressing room—and then noticed that the wooden peg that holds the E string had fallen out. Somewhere in those shavings between the stage and the horse stall, was a small peg, without which I could not offer Glazunov or anything else.

Then I heard applause. This meant it was my turn.

"What are you doing?" Hilsberg stood over me. The next minute we were both hunched on the floor running our hands through the mess. Other players saw us and wanted to help, but more feet trampling through the stuff was the last thing we needed.

Just in time, I spotted it. One thing I've always been thankful for: performing doesn't make me nervous, even if I have to stick the pieces of my instrument together as I walk on stage.

For out-of-town performances like that one, oboist John Mack and I usually drove together from New Orleans. We had a routine for our late-night returns. Marilyn and David would be asleep, and John would come into the kitchen with me in the dark. I fetched a large knife for each of us. John stationed himself at the pantry door, and I manned the light switch. On the count of three the light blazed and we hacked down as many giant cockroaches as we could before they had all scuttled out of sight. Every climate has its sport.

In the spring of 1955, George Szell, conductor of the Cleveland Orchestra, telephoned in search of a new assistant concertmaster. He and Ormandy were friends, and I guessed correctly how I'd been recommended, though Szell didn't mention it.

"Thank you. But since I'm concertmaster here in New Orleans, I don't think I'll audition."

"This is a major orchestra. With a lot more prestige."

He did have an enormous reputation, Dr. Szell. In fact, my initial dismissal of his invitation could be called sassy.

"And a longer season," he added.

That was a material point. It meant more money.

"So come to Cleveland and play for me. I'd love to hear you."

"Right now I'm so busy I don't know right from left."

A week later he called again. And I'd been thinking—much more sensibly.

"We'll pay all your expenses. Josef Gingold wants to hear you too." That was his concertmaster, whose assistant I would be.

A month later I had two days between concerts and squeezed in a trip to Cleveland. I rushed to Severance Hall where Szell and Joe Gingold were waiting. Szell was most cordial; he always did have manners available when he wanted them. His face alternated between a polite smile and a distant, impassive look, as if music were playing in his head. It was, most likely.

Joe Gingold's face was equally impassive whenever it was in Szell's line of vision. Otherwise, it could be anything—amused, uncomfortable, eyes rolling in sarcasm, disgusted, friendly.

We walked out onto the stage, the only lit part of the dark hall.

"Would you like to warm up?" This was gracious of Szell, and Joe looked surprised and pleased.

"No, I don't need to."

Joe shook his head. They went out to sit in the auditorium, and I began the Sibelius Violin Concerto.

"Wonderful," Szell said after a page. "How about some Bach?"

I began the Chaconne but stopped after four notes.

Szell was startled. "What's wrong?"

"You weren't listening. I'll wait till you're ready."

Joe closed his eyes. I had the impression he was trying to unhear what he had heard me say. Szell shrugged and they came up on stage. He started leafing through a huge portfolio and stopped when he came to *Don Juan* by Richard Strauss.

"Keep turning," I said. "Everyone plays that at auditions."

Behind Szell, Joe mouthed *No! No!*

"He's right," Szell said. "Everyone knows that."

I was quite relieved since I'd never played it.

Joe's face now wore a hopeless look. For some reason, he was already on my side and disappointed that I would have no chance.

Next came Wagner's *Lohengrin*, and Szell turned to a specific page. "I use two solo violins here instead of the entire string section. Play the bottom line for me, please."

"I don't play the bottom line." Joe was looking sick, and I was beginning to have fun.

"Please," Szell said. "Joe plays the top line. I want you to play the bottom line."

I cooperated, and a few minutes later he made me an offer.

"Yes" was the right answer, and after a few weeks I gave it.

I told Hilsberg before a concert. After it, he and the manager locked me into the office.

"You have to stay! Sign that contract."

It is hard on an orchestra to switch concertmasters frequently, and I was sad to leave such a fine conductor and amiable man after only one year. Of course he understood that Cleveland was an opportunity of a whole new magnitude.

But it was a long hour before he let me out of the office.

On a beautiful April day in New Orleans, our daughter Jennie was born. I was dutifully practicing the Brahms concerto for a performance with the Philadelphia Orchestra, with David toddling around. Marilyn would still be in the hospital when I went to Philadelphia, but we had a housekeeper who agreed to stay with David until Marilyn got home.

That was a goodbye I couldn't say. David was two and would have no idea why both his parents had left him. I stuffed some things in a suitcase for him, and we left together, David clutching his blanket.

Weather intervened, and our plane landed in Washington, D.C., instead of Philadelphia. It was already late at night when I told David that we were now going to take a train. He gave me a beatific smile that propelled me into a gift shop near the station, where I got him a foot-long Greyhound bus.

Now to find our train. I carried David, my violin, two suitcases, and the toy bus. David helped by carrying his blanket. Together we faced thirty steps descending into the nether realms, and somewhere down there was a train headed for Philly. I couldn't carry it all.

I set my boy down. "So David. You carry the bus and the blanket. And stay right behind my feet."

Every ten steps I turned around to check. He was still there.

"It's not your job to clean the stairs." I wadded up his blanket. Over and over.

The train was packed, but someone made room for us to sit, no doubt on the assumption that the child needed to sleep. But David didn't want to miss anything and just smiled at all the exhausted grownups whose travel plans were set askew. My parents met us at 2:30 a.m.

After the morning rehearsal, Ormandy kindly sent me home for a nap.

My parents met Ormandy that night for the first time, good manners all around.

Chapter 4

SZELLIAN PERFECTION

ONE OCTOBER DAY IN THE FALL OF 1955, I drove to Severance Hall for my first rehearsal with the Cleveland Orchestra. I parked in the lot, fetched my violin from the passenger seat, and strolled to the door, enjoying the pleasant weather. My mind was open to whatever came through, possibly that back in New Orleans the air was still hot and muggy and we were lucky to be out of it.

That carefree crossing of the parking lot was a moment I would remember with nostalgia. The players in the Cleveland Orchestra quickly shared the common store of warnings with newcomers.

"His office overlooks the parking lot," someone said.

"Always carry some music out with you," another musician said. "He'll think you don't practice and single you out, if he sees you walking to your car without a folder."

So the sense of his power began not on the stage—though his entrance did inspire dead silence—but actually as you turned from the street into the parking lot. His eye was on you as you got out of your car. No wonder he was called Dr. Cyclops.

Still, it was marvelous that I, the boy who was always climbing to third floors in Philadelphia to learn to play the violin, should actually be in the orchestra of George Szell, one of the world's great conductors. I couldn't remember when I had learned his name, as if it had always been in my head.

Szell had the ultimate classical music pedigree: born in Hungary, the cradle of musicians, *and* raised in Vienna, their legendary training ground. From age eleven, he performed throughout Europe as a pianist and composer. But when he lifted the conductor's baton, he found his form. Richard Strauss took the teenaged Szell on as assistant conductor and imparted to him an impeccable conducting technique. Later, Strauss said he could die happy since Szell was there to do justice to his compositions.

In the 1940s, Szell took over the Cleveland Orchestra. He helped it to recover from World War II, to grow in size, and to become one of the finest American orchestras. Of course such a rapid rise in quality usually requires liberal usage of sharp pruning shears. Many decent musicians lost their jobs while superb ones were hired. Szell immediately replaced the concertmaster, and then replaced him again after only a year, by attracting Josef Gingold away from the Detroit Symphony. Few could play the violin like Joe, and somehow Szell seemed to realize that a warm, kind concertmaster was going to be needed. Joe was the man.

The 1955–56 season was seminal for Szell as his tenth anniversary year and the twenty-fifth anniversary of the construction of Cleveland's Severance Hall. Igor Stravinsky guest conducted two of his own works, *Petrouchka* and *Le baiser de la fée*, and other renowned conductors also visited. We served up plenty of Mozart since it was also his 200th birthday.

I expected to work harder than in New Orleans, and I did. Instead of one concert a week, we played two or three. Our season was several weeks longer, which of course kept food on the table.

I had refused Szell when he first offered me a job because it was a step down: to assistant concertmaster. The best counter to my refusal, though Szell didn't know it, would have been this: You are going to have the privilege of working with Joe Gingold. I do love privileges, but having fun is even better. Actually, given the atmosphere in the Cleveland Orchestra, a little fun on the side was as necessary as air.

It should be thrilling to work under celebrated wielders of the baton. But in the Cleveland Orchestra, we sweated our shirts out daily under George Szell. Every note had to meet his exact specification for duration and volume as if he were playing the instruments for us. If anything ever pleased Dr. Szell, he made sure no musician in his orchestra knew.

It was like this: We're playing along, every player knows the music, every note is right. We're all watching the baton and producing a sound that would make most conductors relax and smile. But annoyance crosses his face like a mosquito. He glares at the principal flutist.

"Too short!"

The flutist nods anxiously and we take the measure again, the flutist extending the note by one 128th.

Now the tympanist has not rumbled long enough. He gets the glare and the furious whipping of the baton in his direction. And then a cellist will be too loud and a trumpet too soft. Each musician is tense, knowing the baton may prick him next.

Szell had an assistant conductor, as most conductors do, and one might think he could occasionally soften the atmosphere. But Szell had inherited poor Rudolph Ringwald along with the orchestra, and he wasn't much help. Occasionally Szell had him conduct us, but Ringwald had a penchant for looking at the ceiling while conducting. One by one, we would follow his gaze. It made a compelling case for there being some goings on of interest up there among the lights and cables.

One day during rehearsal, Szell heard some sounds. Universities have soundproof practice rooms, but orchestra halls don't. Mostly we practiced down in the dressing rooms and tuned each other out.

That was far enough away from the stage not to be heard. But if you were excused from a portion of rehearsal, you had to be nearby so you could trot back in when called, wagging your tail.

What Szell heard was our oldest player, a violist. As this man's technique had slipped, he also slipped back a few chairs in the section. We were playing something that called for a smaller orchestra, I think a Mozart symphony, and the violist was among those excused. Being nervous about a piece we were to begin working on soon, he had decided to start learning it. In hearing distance of the stage. It was a poor decision, though not that unusual.

His viola let out sounds that were not particularly musical. The orchestra's big sound easily overcame the distant noise, and we all thought nothing of it.

"Who's doing that?" Szell jerked his head in the direction of the squeaking.

Any string player could have named the culprit, but we were reluctant to. He seemed more to be pitied than strung up. Joe and I sat there hoping no one else would speak up. No one did.

Szell glowered at us all. In each of his temples, a vein meandered from above his ear to above his eyebrow. This was one of those moments when the two veins pulsed.

"I want to know who it is! Somebody go tell him this is not the place!"

We were astonished at this statement. Severance Hall not for music?

No one moved. We knew Szell would not wait long, but fortunately the noise ceased. "Whoever it is, I'm firing him!"

Protected by our conspiracy of silence, the violist survived until he chose to retire.

Szell promised me a solo every year—a very generous deal for an assistant concertmaster. In most orchestras only the principal players soloed, but Szell liked to demonstrate publicly that the Cleveland Orchestra had quality below the surface.

The first year, he suggested the Sibelius Violin Concerto. I supposed either he or Joe had heard the broadcast of my performance of it with the Philadelphia Orchestra a few months earlier. (Szell was generous about approving my absences from Cleveland for soloing.) The first rehearsal loomed darkly over me because, where most conductors give a soloist free rein, Szell usually jettisoned that bit of etiquette and delivered minute instructions to the soloist.

Maybe he was in a good mood. He didn't correct me at rehearsals or the performance, and he asked me to play it again the next week at Oberlin College.

In February the orchestra undertook its annual tour through various towns in Ohio and New York, stopping at Ithaca, at Troy's little hall with the best sound anywhere, and then in New York City.

Wherever we performed, Joe Gingold and I were right at the foot of the conducting podium, Joe on the audience side and I on his left. We had a common experience. Those who sat farther back might not know that when Szell spat a word like *stupid* at the players, actual saliva came with the hiss.

The leadership required of a concertmaster was familiar to me. He is responsible for keeping the orchestra in tune and, equally important, his playing must inspire theirs. His intensity should be contagious. Other musicians will tend to follow his mood. Joe's task in Cleveland took the job to a new level. He had to support the morale of men who are shouted at, insulted, and threatened.

That honestly describes our experience in the beautiful eclectic structure that was Severance Hall. Its Greek revival front has a pediment supported by Ionic columns. High above the entrance, two sculpted figures crouch in the triangle of the pediment. Female and male musicians, each nude, with an arm draped over a stringed instrument, and with head bowed as if pressed down by the upper edge of the pediment. They look uncomfortable. They look put upon. Every day as each of us approached Severance Hall, the Greek musicians continued to suffer their endless musical lives.

Some days, the effort of straining to catch every nuance of criticism that Szell spat our way built into a collective pressure that had to find release. A good concertmaster accepts it as his responsibility to maintain the morale of the players.

Joe Gingold was an exceptional concertmater. He signaled that he had a question, and Szell would stop and turn to him. Which meant everyone stopped and watched. Rapid sounds would come from Joe's mouth, including lots of consonants. You would recognize a technical term in the middle—*up bow* or *pizzicato*. A sentence might end with a common phrase like *do it*. Joe's face conveyed energized sincerity.

"What?" Szell would ask.

A hint of impatience would tug at Joe's eyebrows. With a sigh, he might say, "Dannim phalima deepo we'll do alum," at breakneck speed, all of us trembling with the effort to suppress laughter.

"Well, I think you can use your own judgment there," Szell might answer. Then he would resume conducting with his confidence slightly shaken. And we would play with lightened hearts.

Doubletalk, Joe called it, and I had some experience too, as I had demonstrated back in Maine with the jukebox. We began to play off each other, asking for responses from Szell, and both feeding the "conversation."

A violinist holds his instrument out to the left from his chin, of course. In Joe's case, his violin stuck way out. When it got too close to my head, I shoved it away.

Joe was always quick to apologize. "Sorry!"

His sibilants were mild compared to Szell's, but the temptation was too much. I sometimes wiped my face as if he had spit on me. I always got a second apology.

The goof-off part of the musical life always did give me pleasure but the biggest benefit of my years of partnering with Joe was still the music. I have never worked off another musician so well, and I think for Joe it was a rare experience, too.

Every musician is an individual artist, and while the conductor is able to corral them into a collective sound, each is still, in some sense, playing his own music. The concertmaster leads the whole orchestra in many ways and the string section more particularly. For the first and second violins, Joe was expected to choose ways of playing notes (on which string), bowings (where to start, when to reverse), and sometimes even personal interpretations. Usually the assistant concertmaster's main responsibility, besides playing well, is knowing all these details sufficiently to fill in if the concertmaster gets sick.

It wasn't like that with Joe. He liked to work as a team, and we figured out together what fingering to use and how to bow each passage. He always wanted to hear my interpretation of a piece and sometimes chose it over his own. The upshot was something extremely unusual in a first violin stand—we actually sounded like one violin. It was an exhilarating experience to connect with another artist in that way. For me, that deep aesthetic communication has always been one of the greatest joys of the musical life.

Joe's parents, like mine, had left Russia after the Revolution. He was little Josef Gingold, eleven, when he arrived in New York City, where he would study violin with Vladimir Graffman, the father of pianist Gary Graffman.

"You have to teach, too, Anshel." Joe loved teaching violin and was good at it. "It's just part of what you do. Plus good money!"

He made me accept two students at the Settlement Music School.

I opened the door to the waiting room to greet my first student. His mother clearly was going to have trouble getting through the door, but she meant to try. I walked away to grant her privacy. She succeeded and installed herself in a corner of the classroom.

"How long have you been playing?" I asked the kid.

"Two years."

His mother nodded.

"Who did you study with before?" I didn't know the teachers in Cleveland. I was just making conversation.

He rattled off four names, and his mother nodded.

"Why so many? What happened to them?"

"They died."

His mother nodded.

"If anybody's going to die," I said, "it won't be me."

This little boy played his fiddle with his tongue sticking out the left side of his mouth. Once I pushed it in with my finger, but it just came out the other side.

A little girl also attempted to prosper under my tutelage, but she couldn't tune her violin and had no one who could help her.

These are not adequate reasons for abandoning the task of teaching. It is a noble art, and where would I have been without Mr. Happich and Mr. Zimbalist and Dr. Szanto? But those who teach best are those who learned to play by breaking down the task into small steps, analyzing each challenge, and finding the solution. For me playing came naturally, but the words to describe what I was doing, and why, did not.

One day near the end of my first season in Cleveland, the phone rang at home and I answered it.

"This is George Szell."

"Oh come on," I said. "Who is this?"

"Anshel, this is George Szell."

"Bullshit."

After he identified himself the third time, his voice finally sounded familiar.

"Oh! I'm so sorry, Dr. Szell!"

But he was charming and wanted to discuss my next solo. "I'd like you to do Mozart."

"Great. I'll do the Concerto No. 4 in D Major."

When I told Joe the next day, he looked stunned. "Of course you told him no." Joe was twenty years my senior and quite sensible when he wasn't using doubletalk.

"I said I'd love to."

"Anshel! He'll eat you alive and suck your bones."

"Dr. Szanto taught me Mozart's style. We worked through that whole concerto."

"No. Szell will make your life miserable. It'll all happen in front of the orchestra."

I never was much given to performance anxiety, and in any case I had until the following spring to work up a proper sweat. First on the horizon was a nice long summer.

Szell went to Europe as usual to guest conduct. He also played a Mozart concerto in August, on piano, with the Vienna Philharmonic in Salzburg's Mozarteum.

My Mozart rested in the drawer all summer. I did reflect on something Dr. Szanto said: "No one undresses the imperfect musician as quickly as Mozart does." I thought of Szell in Vienna and wondered if he felt naked.

Occasionally, Szell offered a conductors' workshop, and he did so in the fall of 1956. Knowing of my time with Monteux, he kindly invited me to participate. I felt quite honored, as I was the only orchestra member invited to do this. He assigned me two works, the prelude to Wagner's *Parsifal*, and Strauss's *Till Eulenspiegel's Merry Pranks*. I quickly got both scores and a recording of the Strauss work with Serge Koussevitzky conducting the Boston Symphony. I was excited especially about his choice of the Strauss for me, knowing that early in his career Szell had apprenticed with Richard Strauss. The tone poem *Till Eulenspiegel* is a much-loved piece that captures the mordant wit of a medieval bad boy.

By now I had watched Szell for a year. No one took apart a score and broke it into its component parts the way he did. Some conductors didn't take apart the music at all, but intuited their way along. This, I had noticed, was a dangerous path. Other conductors did take the score apart. But they couldn't put Humpty together again. George Szell had the whole package down. Every painstaking detail. There was much to be learned by watching that.

While each workshop participant conducted, Szell watched from one of the front rows in the house, along with some of the participants. Afterwards, he came up on stage and commented on the conductor's choices and technique.

My turn came and I was satisfied with how it went. At the end, Szell appeared behind me. He did not offer comments but instead asked me to see him in his office. A happy thought sprang to mind—was he going to ask me to replace Rudolph Ringwald as his assistant conductor?

A different invitation, equally surprising, was forthcoming: "I'd like you to come to my house for dinner tonight," Szell said. "I'm cooking."

"Thank you!"

"You can bring your wife."

The days of Maître and Mum were behind us, when Marilyn would be shunned. I was grateful for that.

Joe Gingold saw me a few minutes later. He had attended for my sake, to watch me conduct for Szell.

"He's having us over for dinner!" I said.

Joe looked worried. "Didn't you notice him behind you?"

"I never saw him."

"He stood right there during the *Parsifal*." He pointed to a spot on the stage that was exactly behind the podium, so of course I hadn't seen him. "As soon as you started *Till Eulenspiegel*, he started pacing," Joe said. "Striding back and forth behind you, downstage, all pent up like a caged lion. I've never seen him like that."

I'm an optimist. I can spin anything upward. Marilyn and I found a babysitter on short notice and got ourselves there on time.

Helena Szell answered the door and immediately—confidentially—blurted out, "Don't eat the meat! George doesn't buy from a reputable butcher."

Szell rushed over. "Don't listen to *her*!"

We ate the meat, which was distributed throughout an excellent goulash. When we finished dessert, he said to Marilyn and Helena, "Ladies, would you excuse us?" Yes, he could be a gentleman.

"How was dinner?" he asked on the way upstairs.

I offered the required compliments.

In his studio, he motioned me to sit at his own desk. Then he got something out of a music cupboard and came back. He slammed the score of *Till Eulenspiegel* down in front of me. "I don't know where you think you got that god-awful interpretation today, but *this* is how Strauss wanted it to go!"

I was sitting at Szell's desk. Had he motioned me there so that I would feel trapped? It worked. And I bethought myself—this man learned about *Till Eulenspiegel* from Strauss himself. I will take in every word. I opened the score to the beginning.

Szell sat at the piano and proceeded to play through the piece from memory, commenting as he played. "And this part speeds up right here—you were way too slow! It's the clarinet sounding like Till's laughter because he's goofing off and thinks all is dandy. He has no idea he's going to be hanged. That's the melodic line here. You can't just let every other instrument play loud during solos. You've got to emphasize his impish charm, his lollygagging in the busy marketplace.

"The change of atmosphere when the people get upset because he's overturned baskets and carts—you totally missed that. The percussionist playing the ratchet didn't get enough guidance from you. His part is central. That's how we know Till really irritates everyone.

"You did okay with the clergy coming in, the pretentious viola passage. But you messed up with the violin solo. That's Till at his most blasphemous. And he's climbing the steeple. The tempo has to be like this to get him all the way up. The whole town sees him and points up there. The tempo changes—which you missed—and why do you think Strauss changes the tempo? Then the long glissando. Don't you hear it? That's when Till turns around and pees!

"Now the French horn has the melody. It's the voice of Till again, still sassy but this time he's nervous. Phrase it like this. Maybe he's in trouble, but maybe he'll get out of it. But you let the cellos take over. It was all wrong.

"And the bassoons in this part. They're the academics, obviously! We have to hear them over the strings.

"Then you rushed the death scene! Slow the tubas down. Give the audience time to take it in, to mourn as Till dies. Especially that rest—they have to feel the silence. That gets the audience ready for the happy surprise when Till's spirit comes back. Catch the amusement in that trill at the end."

He had a comment about my *Parsifal* too.

"You can't drop the baton when there's a rest in Wagner. You have to keep conducting, so the players know where they are and will be ready to come back in."

"But they're Cleveland!"

"Forget that. Any orchestra needs the beat with Wagner."

It was a long hour. Some lessons are sweet and some are sour. Here was a huge helping of the rich Germanic music tradition he had imbibed, flavored with vinegar.

When our regular rehearsals began that fall, Joe sent me to see Szell. "He has something to tell you."

Szell opened his office door with a big smile on his face. "Come in, come in, Anshel." He motioned me to one of the several chairs facing his desk, and took his own seat behind it. "I have something special to tell you."

That much I knew.

Finally he said, "You are now the *associate* concertmaster of the Cleveland Orchestra!"

I said, "That's wonderful," which was an acceptable response to Szell. I should have stopped there, but instead I said, "Does that mean more money?"

He slammed his palm on the wooden desktop. "Money! What's money?" It came out of his mouth with a grimace, reminding me of the old term *filthy lucre*. "You're ASSOCIATE CONCERTMASTER OF ONE OF THE WORLD'S GREAT ORCHESTRAS!"

I said, "Thank you. I appreciate it." Landing on that note allowed me to take leave of the conductor of one of the world's great orchestras.

We did need our escape hatches in Cleveland. The poker began, I think, at rehearsals during breaks, or before rehearsals that got started late. We played High-Low, where the players with the best and worst hands split the pot. A pitiful hand could win as much as aces and kings. A game of poker was pretty much always in progress on the table backstage.

It was in the card games that I became friends with David Arben. He joined the violins in Cleveland at the same time as I did. He was a Polish Jew with a number tattooed on his arm.

When the great Efrem Zimbalist played Warsaw, little David heard him and said, "I want to play like that." He'd been well along the path to it when his family was confined in the Warsaw Ghetto. Then they were all killed, except for David, who was sent from camp to camp. At Budzyn, he persuaded Jewish camp manager Noah Stockman to let him show what he could do on a violin. That got him better rations and some clothing, until Stockman disappeared.

David Arben survived seven camps before he was freed. Eventually, with the help of Leonard Bernstein's Hebrew Immigrant Aid Society, he came to the United States. The Curtis Institute welcomed him, and he continued his violin studies with Zimmy himself.

And now he was letting off steam at the card table with the rest of us in the Cleveland Orchestra. Rather often, David and I were the last two in a hand of High-Low. We had amicable ways of landing. "Shall we split it?" we might say, as the others began to drop out.

People who come to concerts often assume that the experience of playing your instrument before so many people must be all-consuming. They forget we have pasts, some of them terrible, and also present-day lives besides music. Backstage, they think, the musician sweats it out, studying the music again. And some players do suffer terrible anxiety. But we poker buddies were all about the cards in our hands and the small winnings we amassed. We were always being tapped and summoned by the other musicians, the ones who paid attention to the dimming of the lights in the hall—"Let's go!" At intermission, we would count the seconds till we could decently amble off the stage out of sight, and then dash back to the table. The dealer—no one ever forgot whose turn it was—somehow got there first and was shuffling and dealing. Applause is all very nice, even standing ovations, but there were times when some of us wished they would quit already so we could get back to the important thing in life.

Musicians long before our time had figured out this method of survival. Szell said that sometimes Richard Strauss seemed bored with whatever he was conducting in rehearsal, as if he were "just serving time earning his fee and waiting for the card game that came after the performance."[1]

Most conductors searched hard for the best concertmaster and the best principal players they could get. Assuming every player was competent, those leaders should be able to keep the standard high. But Szell also paid close attention to the filling of assistant positions. He looked for young players headed for solo or principal musician careers. Berl Senofsky preceded me as assistant concertmaster and went on to a brilliant career of concertizing. Before Berl, the assistant concertmaster in Cleveland was Jacob Krachmalnik, who now sat in the coveted concertmaster's seat in Philadelphia under Eugene Ormandy. After me, Arnold Steinhardt got a good start in Cleveland under Szell and later became first violinist in the Guarneri String Quartet. We all benefited from Szell's perfectionism.

---

1. Michael Charry, *George Szell: A Life of Music* (University of Illinois Press: 2011), 14.

It was impossible not to admire his relentless drive to nail the music. For the German composers, he had a natural feel. The Russians he did well enough by enforcing the letter of the law, so to speak. But perfectionism only gets you so far. Playing French music under him was a little strange. You couldn't see the satin and lace, the candlelight reflected in silver serving dishes. The colorists, the impressionists, the elegance of Ravel—these were not available to him. Once when Szell conducted Ravel's shimmering *Daphnis et Chloë,* a reviewer wrote that the audience had been given a rousing *Daphnis und Chloë.*

Yes, the musical downside of this astute conductor's technique was that as we became perfect, we became overcautious. Newspapers labeled us "brilliant," but we felt as if we were playing scales. After a performance, while the audience was clapping and Szell was taking his bows, Joe Gingold would look at me and whisper, "So what?"

That year I had, for the first time, my own little orchestra. A group of doctors and other professionals and two members of our own orchestra had come to me wanting to form a chamber orchestra. My concertmaster was a chemist. Eric Von Bayer, who worked in the family pharmaceutical business, was my principal cellist.

We called ourselves the Cleveland Chamber Players, and a church offered its facilities. At our first rehearsal, the quality of the players took me by surprise. Afterwards, I got into my car in a euphoric state. I headed out the back entrance of the parking lot, where a large chain barred the way of traffic. My reverie became an expensive one as I smashed into the chain.

We played five concerts. Szell came to one, which was kind.

On occasion, Szell would toss pearls of conducting wisdom my way. "In order to be a conductor," he said one day, "you have to play the piano."

I said, "Toscanini played cello."

"An exception."

"Monteux played viola."

"Exception."

"Ormandy was a violinist."

Szell walked away.

That fall, wife and husband Vitya Vronsky and Victor Babin performed with us. They were pianists. The piece was one that Victor Babin had written, Concerto No. 2 for Two Pianos and Orchestra. It was a difficult work, but our conductor was Lord of the Details, so no sweat.

There was a challenging little spot in the closing bars of the first movement. The pianos played a cadenza and, at the end of it, instead of the orchestra entering all together, a few instruments led the way, one by one. Tuba, then clarinet, bassoon, horn, and finally the rest of us. Conductors normally would not conduct during a cadenza played only by soloists; in fact, such cadenzas were not even written out in the orchestra parts. Szell followed this practice, resuming his baton work as soon as the tuba was to enter. In many rehearsals, however, something went wrong.

At the final rehearsal before the performance, Szell made a new plan. In this case, the cadenza *was* written out in our parts, and Szell decided that he would conduct through it, so that the tuba player would be perfectly prepared for his entrance, as would the clarinet and all the rest.

It worked perfectly at that rehearsal. Szell was pleased. He even let it show.

"He'll never manage it," I said to Joe. It's always a risk, changing the plan at the last minute. If you sink into your automatic pilot setting for two seconds, you can get disoriented.

"This is Szell!" Joe said. "His little stick will guide us through every jot and tittle."

He was right, too. The Friday concert went without a hitch, every entrance on time.

"Told you," Joe said.

Saturday night we settled into our places, music on stands.

"Look out," I said.

He just shook his head.

The concerto started well. Szell conducted as before, and as we reached the cadenza he continued to conduct, and we followed along in our music. But in the middle of the cadenza, his hands began to wave in a frantic way that looked more like a person erasing a blackboard with two erasers than like a conductor. Joe and I, to maintain decorum, avoided looking at each other. Chet Roberts, our tuba player, decided that he knew where we were, so he started to play. Szell turned an incredulous face on Chet, who could only continue playing since once a tuba commits to a line it can hardly change direction without attracting attention. Other instruments made similarly independent decisions with regard to their entrances. I could see Joe shaking with suppressed laughter. My challenge was to avoid snorting. Also, the tears in my eyes blurred the music. Anyway, Joe decided to play and, as his assistant, I thought I'd follow suit. I got to the bottom of our shared page and turned it.

"I'm still on the left side!" Joe whispered.

And who knew where the rest of the violins were?

Slowly the orchestra came to a stop, as did Vronsky and Babin. The first movement had "ended."

The piano was, of course, Szell's own instrument, that which had brought him childhood fame. And he was scheduled to guest conduct the Chicago Symphony soon, in December 1956, and to perform a Mozart piano concerto on the same program.

"He'll never play." Joe stated this categorically. "He's scared to death of playing in public. He told me so. You watch."

Two weeks before he was to leave for Chicago, Szell walked into our rehearsal with his left arm in a sling. He'd had an accident, he told us all. A bad bruise.

He conducted our rehearsal that day with one arm. Except at one exciting climax in the music when the bruised arm snuck out and brandished about until its disability was remembered and it was tucked back into its sling.

As it turned out, the Mozart concerto he had played the previous year in Salzburg would be Szell's last public performance on his instrument. I never figured out how a man who, with a baton in hand, feared no one and nothing became intimidated by the straight, shining keys.

A second bitter Midwestern winter passed. My Mozart concerto was coming up, and I waited for Szell to call me in. He would certainly, Joe said, want to hear it privately first. The week of the concert arrived, and still he had not mentioned it. This silence increased Joe's anxiety more than mine.

But when I stepped on stage for the first rehearsal, I noticed that the whole orchestra sizzled with tension over what was going to happen. Szell started the Concerto No. 4 and gave me the nod at my entrance. I began to play. I kept playing, Szell conducted the others, and not a word was said. The orchestra began to relax and their playing became more musical. Joe was all smiles.

In the second movement I got worried. Szell was a top-notch conductor of Mozart. It was his great strength, working with Germanic music. He would not be expecting too much originality from his assistant concertmaster who was lucky to get a solo, and Szell did not always take surprises with grace. But there was a certain place near the end of the movement that I loved. It was the second time around for a particular melody. The first time I always played it simply, but then the second time I played it all on the D string and with a large helping of *rubato*, or freedom. I hadn't heard any other violinist play it that way, but it seemed to me supremely Mozartean. When the passage came, I followed my heart. I saw some surprised looks in the string section.

But Szell was with me as if he had known I was going to play it that way. We went right into the third movement, and at the end he nodded his pleasure to me.

It was during my time in Cleveland that Szell was able to consolidate his gains in the way that meant most to him: exhibiting his achievement with his own Cleveland Orchestra in the great cities of Europe, the very places that had known him as an up-and-coming *Wunderkind*. We were to go on a big tour. The peak for him would be two concerts in Vienna, where he was trained, and where the little György Szél was dubbed "the next Mozart."

When we heard who was to be our soloist the first night in Vienna, Joe and I were upset and went to Szell.

"I don't want to play with that man," Joe said. "He collaborated." With the Nazis, he meant.

"I don't either," I said.

"That's politics," Szell said. "I don't like it either, but it has nothing to do with music. You have to play that concert."

In May of 1957, we boarded two planes and flew to Brussels. We were a large company, of course, with all sorts of personnel besides the musicians. Our manager was George Smith, and we had along a brand-new associate manager, A. Beverly Barksdale.

We played all over. Antwerp, Brussels, Bremen, then London. Then Spain and Portugal: Barcelona, Madrid, Lisbon, Oporto. More cities in France, Germany, Switzerland. We had become what Szell wanted us to be, and for the most part the reviews were giving us our due.

We snaked around from city to city by train, which is no way to live. Each time we reached a hotel, every man ran for his room, his bathtub, his bed. Joe Gingold and I always shared a room. When we rode a train through the night, it was cozier: three berths to a compartment.

One night a lot of noise came out of a compartment near mine. Alfred Zetzer, bass clarinetist, was on the bottom. This was practical because he was rotund. He was one of the hairiest men I have ever seen and slept in only pajama bottoms. The berths were crowded, and as he rather filled his, he began to feel claustrophobic. So he moved his thin mattress and blanket and pillow to the floor.

So far so good. Back to sleep.

Later, the little guy in the top berth, hornist Ernie Angelucci, needed to get to the men's room. His berth, being the uppermost of three, was high up. He jumped down.

A long whoosh blew out from what he landed on—a large hairy mound.

"Aaagh!" he shrieked. An enormous animal had taken shelter in their compartment.

Now the musician in the middle berth, principal clarinetist Bob Marcellus, sat straight up out of a sound sleep and hit his head so hard on the berth above that he was knocked out.

Ernie bravely battled the enraged beast as it tried to rise up from the floor.

The story by daylight was that little Ernie had knocked the wind out of the hairy Alfred, and Alfred had been certain the train had crashed and its roof had fallen in on him.

Several things happened in Berlin. At the Kempinski Hotel, we were given, for once, single rooms. I felt awful, my stomach tumbling and my skin hot and sweating. The doctor who traveled with us had gone out for the evening. With self-cure as my only alternative, I got myself to a shop in the hotel that sold vodka. Back in the room, I ordered up a large pot of hot tea. I took aspirin and drank a vodka-tea mixture. Repeat. Eventually I fell asleep. In the morning the bed was soaked, but the fever was gone.

Go ahead and try my cure. No charge.

The trip was hard on all of us but hardest on Szell. In Berlin he went looking for places he remembered from his youth, when he had worked with Richard Strauss at the Berlin Opera. He found nothing he could recognize. Not just the buildings but the streets themselves were obliterated. Then he knew what World War II had done to Berlin.

Also in Berlin, act one of a large drama was played out. Secretary Charlotte Flatow forgot to arrange buses to the airport, resulting in a mere delay, not a disaster. We got to Stuttgart. Nevertheless Szell outdid himself the following day in flaying a victim, our manager George Smith. Perhaps Smith even bore some guilt in the matter of buses to the airport. At any rate, before the whole orchestra, Szell verbally tore flesh from bone.

Not the sort to brook such treatment, Smith took the report, and his resignation with one week's notice, to the president of the orchestra, Frank E. Taplin of the North American Coal Corporation of Cleveland.

Taplin supported Szell in the decision to fire Smith immediately, with no notice whatsoever. That was how A. Beverly Barksdale was raised to the position of manager while still in training just to assist that position.

From Stuttgart we went to Switzerland. These concerts played half a century ago run together in my memory, but floating above the daily grind of waiting and travel and packing and repacking is the music we made. One concert stands out. In Basel, Szell surpassed even his own high standards in conducting us in Beethoven's Sixth Symphony, the *Pastoral*. Soloist Rudolf Serkin enchanted the audience with Beethoven's Fourth Piano Concerto. The music programmed, the hall, the sound environment, the audience—all was flawless.

At another concert we played a not-very-accessible contemporary work. The audience whistled, a fierce insult in Europe. That was rare.

After Geneva and Paris, it was time for Vienna. Szell had been back many times as a visiting conductor. Now he brought his own orchestra, which he had himself raised to international prominence. It was a huge moment. No matter what else we felt, we all wanted to make him proud.

We accompanied the Nazi collaborator in the Brahms violin concerto, but Joe and I did not look at him or shake his hand afterwards as he left the stage. Yes, a breach of protocol. One that was repeated at various times in various cities in the wake of World

War II. The Nazi crimes were too fresh and personal to overlook completely.

On the night of our second concert in Vienna, it was Szell's sixtieth birthday. It happened that another Nazi collaborator, Berlin Philharmonic conductor Herbert von Karajan, knew Szell and sought him out backstage for a chat. Joe and I saw them hugging and exchanging news as we headed onto the stage, where the rest of the orchestra awaited us.

Joe tuned us.

The lights dimmed and the audience fell quiet. Everyone waited.

No conductor appeared.

There came a voice from the back of the orchestra: "Open the gate and let him out!"

The picture of him as a caged lion was too perfect. To a man, we were seized with uncontrollable laughter that we nevertheless each controlled, at whatever physical cost. Diaphragms were squeezed into knots. Faces were red with sweat. Tears flowed. We did give in to smiles and, when Szell finally appeared, that is what he saw.

He returned the favor, giving us a broad smile and throwing the audience a kiss. He was happy to be in his childhood city and saw that we shared his joy. In whatever way we might.

Szell's joy in the concert flowed on into the after-party to celebrate his birthday. We gave him a first edition of *Don Giovanni*, and saw tears in his eyes. That was a moment to remember. The party went late into the night, and it was one of our best times with our great conductor.

Vienna, in its reviews of the Cleveland Orchestra's performances, claimed his Viennese background as the source of his genius.

Now it was time to penetrate the Iron Curtain. Today it sounds like a mere metaphor, but for decades that curtain was political reality. They couldn't come out, and we couldn't go in, except under strict surveillance. Our violinist David Arben had remained in the

United States at the urging of the State Department. As a Polish refugee, he could be detained.

The train left Vienna and entered Czechoslovakia. Out the window, there always seemed to be another watchtower in sight, with Soviet guards pointing their guns at us. We were never supposed to get off. At stations, armed guards strode rapidly up and down the platform, outnumbering any passengers embarking or disembarking.

Our concert in Prague was canceled, rescheduled, and canceled again. So our train passed through Czechoslovakia toward Poland. Joe and I shared a compartment. It was a hot June, and trains were not air-conditioned in 1957. The engines were coal-powered, and blew out a continuous stream of coal dust. We had to ride with the windows open and brook the soot that came in for days on end. We held rough paper towels under a trickle of water in the tiny sink and wiped our faces and hands.

At one point, when we came to a station, we were stifling and some of us had to get some air, maybe even soda, guards be damned. The guards said something to us, probably "You will not leave the train!" But no one translated it, and we walked past the gun barrels and into the station. There was no soda, but at least we got to walk a bit.

We crossed into Poland hot and thirsty beyond imagining. Of dirt I will speak later. In Krakow the officials in charge of us—you didn't travel through Eastern Bloc countries without plenty of "hosts" watching over you—ushered us into a building that reminded me of a gymnasium except that tables were set for eating. This was a good sign. We asked if there might be anything cold to drink. What joy when cold bottles of beer were handed all round. We held them to our foreheads and rolled them down our faces first. Ah, the back of the neck.

The next day Joe and I went to Auschwitz. We both came from Russian Jewish families who had left many behind when they came to the United States, and we both grew up with the tacit assumption that a good portion of our extended families would not have survived the war. A taxi drove us to the outskirts of the area where the camp had been, and we walked all around, finding the very grasses, weeds, and shrubs strange because of their benign appearance. The Poles had placed a small monument there to honor their dead, and Joe knew Polish and read it to me. The Nazi camps were not attracting visitors in large numbers then, as they do now.

We performed in Katowice, Poznan, Lodz, and then Warsaw. But do not imagine that hotel rooms awaited us in all those cities. We lived in the train until we reached Warsaw. The showers we had enjoyed back in Vienna were a distant memory. So when we arrived in Warsaw and actually checked into a hotel, however second rate, our anticipation of running water and springy mattresses would be hard to exaggerate.

When I saw the gleaming, white bathtub, I wanted to get right in. But of course the first bath would be for Joe. He was concertmaster and my senior, besides the fact that I loved him as a brother. I knew he would be as quick as he could so that I could have my turn.

My skin seemed to crawl as I waited. A long time passed. I heard the water turned off, then on again, then off, then on.

Finally the door opened, and he came out wrapped in a towel.

"I'm sorry, Anshel." He looked anguished. "I'm really sorry."

"I'm sure it's fine—what do I care if the water's cold?"

I stepped in and confronted something I had never seen. A bathtub that looked like someone had rubbed shoe polish all over it and then tried to wipe it out again, without much success.

My own cleansing process did not improve the condition of the porcelain. But we were pretty clean! There was nothing for it but to stretch out on those actual beds in our underwear and enjoy the moment.

A knock came on the door, and a maid entered carrying towels. The presence of two nearly naked men didn't faze her and she headed into the bathroom. Words erupted from her in a quiet but shocked tone of voice the whole time she worked in there. Joe, understanding her of course, looked amused.

"She said she'd never seen anything like it in her life," he said when she left.

Haircuts were next. We sat in chairs next to each other in the barbershop. The barbers chatted away in Polish.

They quoted a price when they were done, and Joe said in Polish, "We'll pay what you usually get, and you don't deserve a tip."

He had been listening to the barbers as they fine-tuned their plan to triple the fee for their American clients.

Our concerts in Poland met with wild enthusiasm, with clapping and stomping and curtain calls. To Polish musicians, we gave away any strings and music supplies we could spare, since they couldn't get much. Louis Davidson gave away a trumpet. What the players we met from the Warsaw Philharmonic wanted most was freedom. They wanted to get out of Poland. Many were Jews, which didn't make things easier for them. We were pleased over the years to hear news of émigrés taking places in orchestras all over America.

Flying to Amsterdam, our hearts felt like they were soaring above the clouds with the plane. Who can forget what it was like to find a Dutch street café and order an Amstel beer? Two if you wanted.

Tagged onto the end of the season, after the exhausting trip, were concerts in Detroit and Ann Arbor. Joe was ill. He was also nearing retirement, and I knew that Szell would be watching closely to see how I handled replacing the concertmaster in these performances.

I was pleased to have *Till Eulenspiegel* on the program. Playing it under Szell's eye was not as dangerous as conducting it under his eye. What fun—the violin solo where Till climbs the steeple and pees, described by the high E-flat falling into a glissando all the way down to the lowest note on the instrument, the open G string.

That E-flat at the top is usually held for just a short moment, but I held it quite long. Szell looked at me and then I continued down with the glissando. I wasn't sure if he liked it, but I did.

I must have been feeling my oats because I somehow found the nerve to invite Szell to dinner after the Detroit concert.

"I'd love to!" he said. He did like good food.

It had to be someplace really nice, so I settled on the well-known Carl's Chop House. We changed out of full dress before we left the concert hall. His chauffeur drove us to the restaurant.

At dinner, he said nice things. More than I had any right to expect. "You're going to make a really fine concertmaster one day. So I suppose I'll lose you. But I hope it's not for a long time."

"I really don't see that happening anytime soon, Dr. Szell." The check arrived and I reached back for my billfold. My pocket was flat. Empty. I had left it in my full dress suit, now back at the hall in the trunk. I could feel the sweat coming out on my forehead.

"I have to apologize. My wallet—it's in my suit at the hall."

"You seriously thought I was going to let you pay? Listen, Anshel. How much time do you have left on your contract?"

"A year."

"Let's do a new one. You should have a three-year contract. I want to keep you here."

I was supposed to say thank you, yes. But there was some nagging discomfort. Three years was so long.

"You know, I'm sure, that I would never hold you back from something better," he said.

On the strength of that promise, I agreed. He had the contract prepared as soon as we got back to Cleveland, and I signed. Before long he had also scheduled another solo for me, Lalo's *Symphonie espagnole.*

He also assigned me to play the Tchaikovsky Violin Concerto once while he was traveling. Louis Lane would be conducting. I had come across the suggestion somewhere of cutting some of the orchestral part of this concerto, a very difficult part that the players don't particularly like. It did require changing one note in the basses to make a key change. Louis thought it was a good idea, and the orchestra was very happy with it. So I cut eighteen bars in the full score that Louis would be conducting from, and the players made the change in their own parts. It went well. I played the violin part in that section very fast, as I liked to, and the orchestra was able to pick it up at that tempo.

The next time the Cleveland Orchestra put that concerto in a program was when violinist Nathan Milstein was our soloist. Szell announced that we would be rehearsing it, and all the players glanced up in surprise. It wasn't the sort of thing we needed to rehearse without the soloist because we all knew it so well.

But Szell proceeded to open his score and "randomly" fell on the place where I had cut eighteen bars.

"What on earth— Who would do this? Such an idiotic thing! Some stupid person has cut part of the ending section of the concerto! And actually *changed* a bass note!" And so on.

Joe thought it was hilarious, but I was fighting mad. Louis had already told me that he had mentioned our change to Szell and that it had worked out very nicely. Szell was creating an opportunity—with the unnecessary rehearsal and the score falling open to that page—to roar his will at me.

I went right up to him at the next break. "Dr. Szell, I feel like punching you in the nose right now."

He put his arm around me. "I love it when you're mad at me."

The weird thing is, I think that was true.

While I was in Cleveland, I began to serve the Aspen Music Festival in Colorado as concertmaster of their summer orchestra and as coach for the chamber music ensemble. A huge tent housed the Sunday afternoon concerts. The predictable thunderstorms added considerable percussion to the performances and also camouflaged any wrong notes.

Aspen was a little town with unpaved streets at that time. If it hadn't been for the skiing business, it would have become a ghost town like so many others. Still, no one wanted to live there in the summer. The brilliant plan of holding summer festivals changed everything. To this hamlet came such musical stars as sopranos Jennie Tourel and Adele Addison; cellist Zara Nelsova; violinist Roman Totenberg; conductor Izler Solomon; Peter Schickele (later known as PDQ Bach), who worked backstage; and composer Darius Milhaud.

We always rented a house for our family quite cheaply for the summer, once right at the foot of Ajax Mountain, just across from the chair lift. Another year, we were next-door neighbors to Milhaud and his wife, which was, I'm sorry to say, a challenge for them. Our children David and Jennie usually played outside.

One day Mrs. Milhaud knocked on our door. "They're driving Darius crazy! How can he compose with all that noise?"

We told the children to stop being children.

Watching my son and daughter having fun inspired me. With a tempting field across the street from our house, I couldn't resist getting together some softball games. We challenged the students. Keith Brown set his trombone aside to pitch for the faculty team. I played shortstop.

After a morning rehearsal in Cleveland, on a dreary January day in 1958, I came home and began fixing lunch. The phone rang and I heard Marilyn, my wife, chatting with someone. She came to get me.

"It's Eugene Ormandy."

"It can't be."

"Anshel?" the voice said. It was his. I just didn't expect it to come through my own phone.

"How would you like to be concertmaster of the Philadelphia Orchestra?"

I closed my eyes and I was a little boy. I was in the dining room of our apartment, where Stan and I were in the Philadelphia Orchestra, concertmaster and assistant concertmaster.

"I'm ready," I told Ormandy in 1958. What I wouldn't have given to let the words stand unmodified. "But I signed a three-year contract. I've got two more years to serve in Cleveland." My current position with a world-class orchestra under the illustrious George Szell came out sounding like a prison sentence. Which is how it felt.

The silence of Ormandy's disappointment stretched on. I let my breath out and sucked in more.

"You'll have to ask out," he said.

As if one could simply *ask out* from the dominion of Szell. I thought of how, even behind those enormous glasses, his glacial blue eyes bulged out at us during rehearsals. Dr. Cyclops.

"Now that I think of it," I said to Ormandy, "Dr. Szell did say he would never keep me from something better."

I went early the next morning and knocked at Szell's office.

The door flew open and his large, deeply lined face jutted out above mine. The lenses of his glasses reflected the ceiling lights. "You're not going anywhere! You'll stay right here for the next two years!"

Then the door slammed shut. I seemed to be in Oz, the wizard's projected face still hanging in the air above me. He was all-knowing. Or else he had my phone bugged.

The dust of reality settled back over my life. Of course things that good didn't happen to me. I called Ormandy back with the gloomy news, knowing that he would now call the next violinist on his list, and that would be that.

"I've got a better idea," he said. "Krachmalnik is leaving. He's not even finishing the season." Jacob Krachmalnik was his concertmaster. "But my assistant concertmaster can function as the acting through next year. I'll hold the position for you, and you can just wiggle out of the last year of your contract."

I had never heard of any conductor of a major orchestra holding his concertmaster position in abeyance for a whole year. Such a move would require changes of programming to keep all the solo violin parts within reach of the assistant concertmaster. Ormandy confirmed the offer in a letter. I could not possibly refuse.

This time I arranged the meeting with Szell in advance.

The door opened slowly enough. A. Beverly Barksdale, Cleveland Orchestra manager, faced me. Lanky and weak-chinned, he was less intimidating than Szell. I felt quite at ease and strode in to find Szell seated in a chair next to his desk. Standing at my full 5'10" and with the confidence of Ormandy's insistence, I was ready for this.

Several chairs were ranged about the room as well as a chaise lounge. But Szell stood, ever the conductor, and motioned me to take his own chair. I did, although it placed me far below him.

"Do you realize, Anshel, how vital you are to this orchestra? And to Joe?" He was hitting a nerve. He knew Joe and I were close friends.

"That means a lot to me." My voice came out at the level of Szell's gray pants.

"You're also vital to *me*."

"Dr. Szell, I am honored."

"Good." All six-foot-one of him towered over me and waited for the apology he would graciously accept. The brown linoleum floor reflected the morning sun in glaring patches.

"I grew up hearing the Philadelphia Orchestra," I said.

Across the room, Mr. Barksdale's eyes widened in fear. A comparison of Szell's orchestra with another was not a welcome subject. The superlative status of Cleveland was taken for granted.

I continued. "Everyone considers Philadelphia one of the greatest in the world."

Szell looked stunned, and Mr. Barksdale stiffened and stared at his knotted hands.

"I want to leave at the end of my fourth year, in 1959." It seemed reasonable to me, each of us giving in partially.

"No chance!" Szell snapped. "You signed the contract. You *will* fulfill it—both years!"

Now I jumped to my feet and took a step toward him. "*Concertmaster!* It's an opportunity to be concertmaster!"

Szell hopped back and grabbed a wooden chair to hold in front of his chest.

"Gentlemen!" Mr. Barksdale begged from his safe haven across the room. "We should discuss it calmly."

"Do you think I'm going to punch you?" I asked Szell.

He set the chair down but scooted behind the chaise lounge.

His action worked on me, and I took another step toward him. "I never wanted to sign that contract."

"Well, your name is on it, and no one cares what you were feeling at the time."

"Please!" Mr. Barksdale said. "Let's all sit down!" He set the example by shrinking further into his own chair.

"You said you'd never keep me from a better position."

"That's a worse position!" Szell spit the words at the floor as if the members of the Philadelphia Orchestra lay there.

"Calmly, gentlemen!"

"Mr. Ormandy says he will hold the position for me for one year."

The words were like an electric current, startling both men. They could not fail to recognize it as a dramatic move on Ormandy's part.

Now I spoke to Beverly Barksdale. "I'll stay one more year. I want to be released from my last year here."

Mr. Barksdale looked at Szell, who still stood behind the chaise lounge.

After a tense pause, Szell nodded agreement.

I regret having been the cause of a permanent rupture in the friendship between those two great conductors, Szell and Ormandy. They never spoke again. If there was a way to be a lightning rod instead of an igniting spark, I didn't see it.

Ormandy asked me to keep my new position under my hat until he made it public himself. Not telling Joe Gingold was a kind of torture. And I constantly wondered what on earth was going on in Philadelphia.

The Cleveland Orchestra did its usual spring tour eastward. Playing at Carnegie Hall was always thrilling. But we had to get there, and boredom was our traveling companion.

With a nice flexible deck, we could banish it for hours. What had begun as backstage poker had expanded to include bridge and hearts and accommodated itself to hotel rooms—usually mine because it was large. The stakes were 10, 25, and 50 cents, with three raises the maximum. You could lose a good bundle if you weren't careful. Most of us smoked and by four a.m. you could hardly see the players on the other side of the bed, which served as a table. Occasionally a hotel we stayed at regularly might give us a playing room at no charge. Then I got to breathe clean air while I slept.

On train trips, the shuffling of cards began before the train pulled out of the station. On this particular tour, we entertained ourselves pretty well through New York State, stopping for concerts at places like Utica and Troy. One day I had a nice foursome of bridge going when Szell passed us on the train and looked into the compartment. We were just starting the bidding.

"One no-trump," a player said.

Szell gave in to a wistful smile. "I love bridge. Hardly ever have time for it now."

"Dr. Szell—" One of my companions was already on his feet. "Please take my place."

"Oh, yes, you must!" we all said. We collected the cards and began redealing almost before he had time to decide. So he sat down for a moment's relaxation as one of the guys.

A little shock went through us, such that we weren't about to make eye contact with one another. Still, we were glad to have him.

He seemed to have a decent hand and bid fairly aggressively till it was up to four hearts. He was the player and his partner the dummy for that hand. He made mistakes, and my partner and I set him by three tricks. It had been a makeable hand, just badly played.

"I've got such a headache," he said. "I think I'd better go rest."

We understood. You have to stay in shape for playing bridge.

One day on that same trip, I was in a hotel room near Cornell University dressing for a concert. The phone rang.

"Hello," I said.

I had not been sheltered from rough language, but what I heard through the telephone took this art to a new level. I had to wait until the caller stopped for breath.

"Who is this?"

"You took the job out from under me!" he growled. Then his vocabulary descended again into the nether realms.

I did recognize the voice. It was Jacob Krachmalnik, Ormandy's departing concertmaster.

"I had nothing to do with—" But I was not given space to comment. After a few more choice phrases, he hung up.

It didn't come together instantly in my head. I knew something about the concertmaster in Philadelphia. When I started at Curtis in 1939, Jake Krachmalnik was in his last year. He had been a friend of my brother's and had visited our home. My family did find him funny, though scratching one's armpits like a monkey at the dinner table wasn't our usual sort of humor.

Joe Gingold filled me in on his tenure in Cleveland, in my same position. Joe had not enjoyed having him as an assistant. He had been relieved to see Krachmalnik depart, although he was a marvelous violinist.

But, Joe said, he got on surprisingly well with Szell. Dr. Cyclops had warmed to Krachmalnik's coarse manner. They had a comfortable friendship.

Eventually, after talking with Joe and also with friends in Philadelphia, it all came clear. Krachmalnik had been chafing under Ormandy and behaving obnoxiously in rehearsals. He wanted solos, but usually visiting artists got them, especially the major violin concertos. Ormandy was sick of Krachmalnik, who was tenured and felt secure enough to let his discontent show.

My playing, also, was not unknown to Krachmalnik. Sometimes the visiting soloist with the Philadelphia Orchestra was me, and then protocol required him to shake my hand before I left the stage. I became a serious threat when Ormandy, uncharacteristically, let slip to a few orchestra members that he wanted to hire me.

The news reached Krachmalnik, and he called his former boss, Szell, to warn him of my likely departure—obviously I would accept Ormandy's offer.

But Szell had good news for Krachmalnik: "No, Anshel can't leave. He's signed a three-year contract."

Apparently, Krachmalnik imagined his position was entirely buttressed. His next move is known by many. He demanded that Eugene Ormandy give him a solo appearance. One of the major violin concertos, like Brahms or Tchaikovsky. And not just in Philadelphia—*in New York.*

It was Ormandy's opportunity, and he didn't waste it.

"Sorry, Jake, but I can't offer you a solo anywhere in the upcoming season." I know just how Ormandy would have said those words. A sincerity that was 99 percent convincing but undercut by a single percent of pleasure.

"Then I quit," Krachmalnik said.

"Put it in writing."

Puzzling it out, I can only assume he thought his resignation letter would not stand; Ormandy would not be able to do without him, once he discovered that I was tied down in Cleveland.

The piece no one had imagined was that Ormandy would let him go and hold the position open for me for a year. That outstanding move on Ormandy's part caught everyone by surprise. It pressured Szell to let me out of the third year of my contract.

So, yes, there was some truth in the accusations I listened to on a hotel phone in upstate New York. However unwittingly, I did play a role in Jake Krachmalnik's exit from Philadelphia.

Robert Shaw joined us as assistant conductor during my time in Cleveland. He was already an outstanding choral conductor with the famed Collegiate Chorale, and now his own Robert Shaw Chorale. He also had prepared choirs for Toscanini. But this humble man wanted to learn orchestral conducting, too, and who better to choose for a teacher than George Szell? Szell wanted something out of the deal for himself, so Bob Shaw agreed to lead the volunteer Cleveland Orchestra Chorus. He endeared himself to every one of us players.

No one comes to public performance without some problem, and Bob's was perspiration. Perhaps other musicians could ignore this, but those of us holding priceless violins at the foot of the podium had to take note of the perspiration flying off his face. This is very bad for the finish of an antique violin. After a concert, his music stand looked like it had been washed.

Never mind. We were always uplifted by the leadership of such a noble man. Szell helped him to get his own post as conductor of the Atlanta Symphony, and it was well deserved.

We all sweated more than normal in the Cleveland Orchestra. Jokes circulated about rehearsals being no less stressful than performances, but they weren't actually funny to us. It got to every player at some level and in some way.

Our outstanding oboist, Marc Lifschey, was a fun-loving person, and we all liked him. My salient memory of Marc was during a recording session. Leon Fleisher was playing piano with us. There was a long oboe solo. Marc played it and then he took his oboe apart.

"I can't stand this anymore," he said without actually looking at Szell.

"This is a recording session, Marc. I think your problem can wait till the session is over."

"I can't play anymore. Not with your stick in my face for every note." He was now cleaning the oboe.

"What are you doing?" Poor Szell. It just didn't compute for him.

Marc closed his instrument case and stood up. "I quit."

I know there's more to the story, but that's the part I observed. He did leave for a year to play for the Metropolitan Opera Orchestra. Then he returned to Cleveland for several years. I think Marc found a better home when he became principal oboe in the San Francisco Symphony.

I will admit something unpleasant. When I learned of the collusion between Krachmalnik and Szell to keep me away from Philadelphia, an unworthy inclination was hatched in me. I could finish out my contract with Szell in vengeance. I could deliver for him nothing more and nothing less than the notes on the page.

"And you think that would be hurting Szell?" Marilyn asked. "You owe it to your colleagues and your audience to give it your best. You owe it to yourself."

I owed it to her too. I continued to give my best to the Cleveland Orchestra. In December 1958, I played the Brahms violin concerto, my last solo there.

Let me say again that my debt to Szell is immeasurable. Playing under his direction was an education in conducting. And yet, every one of us in the Cleveland Orchestra got heartily sick of having every note scripted, especially in solos. That devours the soul of the artist. Perhaps it's that more than anything that goaded so many of the musicians to refer to him by various four-letter expletives. And then there was the moniker "Commander of the Luftwaffe."

As often as I heard this, I was uncomfortable with it. Of course Szell was a fellow Jew, even if he often flew under the radar. Also, we chose to play in Szell's orchestra and were paid for it. His exacting harshness, sometimes bordering on sadism, could not seriously be compared with the measures of the Third Reich. Like so many other musicians, Szell had come across the Atlantic expressly to escape Nazi power and influence in Europe. His meanness, however unfortunate, was born of a desire for artistic perfection. And he felt the same compassion for Nazi victims as most Americans did.

Once Szell asked me to recommend a soloist for a special concert that Bob Shaw would be conducting.

"Why don't you give it to David Arben?" I said.

Szell loved the idea and I knew it pleased him to advance a Nazi victim. David took on the Mendelssohn Violin Concerto.

The performance is one I remember well. David played beautifully, and maintained his quality even as a child began to make a lot of racket in the balcony. The child's mother quickly picked her little girl up and hustled her out, but the screaming was terribly loud.

It was also terribly familiar to me. It was Jennie, as Marilyn carried her out.

Someone took a good photo of David Arben playing the Mendelssohn. Joe Gingold and Robert Shaw were in the photo too. David autographed the photo and gave it to Joe Gingold. It was to resurface one day and come to me.

The musician has an intense relationship with the composer. I would never meet Johannes Brahms, for example, face to face. But while working out how to bring to fruition all the beauty in his violin concerto, how could I not imagine the composer's pleasure? Surely this was the primary response I would want, if I could have it.

Usually our season ended in May, but for 1959 my contract in Cleveland included the summer because the Cleveland Orchestra had signed on for some commitments in the early summer. Initially, I was pleased, as we all were.

In February, Ormandy called again. He invited me to join the Philadelphia Orchestra for a tour of several weeks in May and June.

"We're playing in Helsinki," he said. "Jan Sibelius will be there. I want you to play Sibelius's violin concerto for the man himself."

Opportunities of that caliber don't come twice.

I went to Szell with all the humility I could muster. He would know exactly what this meant to me, what an unforgettable experience it would be.

"Absolutely not," he said. "I want you in the orchestra."

The Philadelphia Orchestra set off on tour without me.

And I, with the Cleveland Orchestra, went to Philadelphia. Every summer Philadelphians enjoyed their orchestra weekly at the Robin Hood Dell. When the orchestra toured, the Dell scheduled substitutes. Cleveland was on that schedule. There is some honor in playing Robin Hood Dell as assistant concertmaster in the Cleveland Orchestra. But it was lost on me in 1959.

Szell was kind to me at the end of my tenure with him. He shook my hand and said he would miss me. Parting with so many friends was hard, but I did not have to say goodbye to David Arben. He was leaving Cleveland and joining the Philadelphia Orchestra along with me.

Leaving Joe was the worst. I loved him and would do anything for him.

Almost anything. The only time I refused to do something he asked of me was when I said, "No. *You're* his concertmaster. *You* tell Szell to zip up his fly."

At a time when our personal finances were headed toward the bass clef, Marilyn and I moved to Philadelphia with David and Jennie and into our first home—complete with a mortgage (my parents had furnished the downpayment). It was September of 1959, and we waited impatiently for the first paycheck while the orchestra negotiated for a new contract and went on a three-week strike.

But I had something to do. For years, Dr. Szanto had kindly lent me his Ruggieri violin. Now I felt I had to go up a level, though I could not imagine how this was going to work financially. I knew exactly where to go. In this country, violins of the quality I needed rested under the watchful eye of Rembert Wurlitzer in New York.

Everyone knows about Wurlitzer pianos and organs; the company has been around since 1856. But only people who needed to know about the best stringed instruments in the world knew about Rembert, grandson of the founder of Wurlitzer. He had a different mission and, in 1949, excused himself from the family business to start his own in New York. When superior eighteenth-century instruments from Cremona surfaced, they usually found their way to Rembert Wurlitzer both for authentication and for restoration. He sought out and hired the most skilled repairer of old stringed instruments and set him up, along with his assistant, in a workshop in New York.

I had met Mr. Wurlitzer when I was sixteen and soloed with the Philadelphia Orchestra for the first time. For that concert, he lent me a violin that was just right for me. He lent out violins just as the Steinway family did pianos. Now I hoped I would qualify for a longer-term loan.

Nagging at me as I drove was the memory of trying to play the Kochansky Stradivarius. When I made music, I liked to go at it with all I had. The last thing I wanted to do was overlay my playing with a blanket of instrument anxiety, a concern that I had to do things a certain way or the violin wouldn't give me what I wanted. Was that what Golden Era violins from the Italian town of Cremona, the Eden of violin making, demanded? I hoped I had not gotten this far only to find that I was playing all wrong.

Mr. Wurlitzer only showed me the best violins he had. I believe he had some Strads, but not the best. The moment that matters is when he placed in my hands a 1743 Guarnerius del Gesù. I knew that the Guarneri family were making violins in Cremona right along with the Stradivari. I put it to my chin and played a few phrases, no doubt something Russian. The sound pleased me.

So I took a good look at it. The wood of both the spruce front and the maple back was gorgeous. However, the purfling—the thin wood edging along the curves of the front and back—was plain. The finishing of the f holes was ordinary, as was the carving of the scroll.

"It was never about the look with the Guarneri," Mr. Wurlitzer said. "Just sound. Del Gesù was the one of the Guarneri bunch who got it exactly right." His life was a bit of a mess, and he died at age forty-six, in 1744, the year after this violin was made.

The Stradivarius sound is often described as feminine because its higher registers carry to the back of a large hall. The Golden Era ones have a touch of masculinity also. But my problem was with pressure. I press into the music, and on a Strad that can make the string give a scratchy noise like your throat when you've talked too much. The Guarneri del Gesù have a more masculine sound and are valued for their strength and power. No matter how hard I dug in with my bow, this 1743 example seemed to support my playing and answer me back.

The description on the Cozio.com website captures exactly what I found that day at Wurlitzer's:

> Tonally, his instruments retain much of the sweetness of a Stradivari, but have a seemingly unlimited depth and darkness of sound, irrespective of the pressure of the bow. . . . [I]t is the later instruments that have come to represent all that is characteristic of del Gesù—the unbridled creativity, the astonishing disregard for the details of workmanship, and the sheer daring of design and construction. . . . The rapid spread of del Gesù's fame in the mid-nineteenth century was largely due to the patronage of Paganini, who played the "Cannon" [del Gesù violin] of 1743 for most of his career.[2]

Mr. Wurlitzer was patient while I took the time I needed. As I experimented, my confidence grew—I wouldn't have to sacrifice my own expressiveness out of fear that the instrument would let me down. I left with it, on loan.

---

2. *www.cozio.com/Luthier.aspx?id=10*

Chapter 5

THIS IS THE PHILADELPHIA ORCHESTRA

FINALLY, THE DAY CAME. Most of the musicians were onstage, and I certainly didn't want to be last. But Ormandy stopped me.

"Don't go out. I'll introduce you."

I was nervous. I followed him out, and the players continued chatting and fiddling with their instruments until they finally noticed that I was with their conductor.

And that surprised me. Here the players did not instinctively freeze in place when the conductor came through the stage door, as they had with Szell.

Ormandy introduced me and I was surrounded by friendly greetings. I asked principal oboist John de Lancie for his "A" and tuned the woodwinds and listened until they sounded good, and gave them my nod. But as I went on to tune the brass, and then the strings to the same note, I was thinking about Bill Kincaid, principal flutist. He hadn't looked up once. While you tune a section as concertmaster, normally each player is looking at you because you are going to nod or else signal for raising or lowering. But Bill was not going to meet my eyes to get my approval.

I had offended him when, at sixteen, I won the conducting contest and conducted the Philadelphia Orchestra in the Polovtsian

Dances. I had asked Bill Kincaid to change his phrasing, to the delight of his rival, Marcel Tabuteau. Tabuteau had retired, but here was Bill Kincaid displaying ill will.

I wasn't sure how to rectify it, but I wanted to.

When Ormandy stepped onto the podium and asked the orchestra to please be quiet, I forgot about all that. He said *please!*

"We haven't got much time before the tour. Let's start with the Overture to *Die Meistersinger*."

The orchestra played the opening chord, C major. I lowered my violin and simply listened.

My assistant concertmaster Dave Madison said, "Are you okay?"

It was the sound. That sound like no other orchestra, the lush sound I had always known, now vibrated all around me. I was overwhelmed.

"Are you all right?" Ormandy asked.

"I'm fine."

There I was, concertmaster of one of the greatest orchestras in the world.

I started to play. I had the habit of keeping my eyes on the conductor at all times, so right away I noticed the enormous difference in style between Szell and Ormandy. You knew what Szell wanted you to do and, somehow, if he wanted the violinist next to you to do something slightly different, that was clear too. Ormandy had a way of communicating with us as a body so that we had a sense of communicating with each other too.

There was less precision, less micromanagement of the players. In beginning a piece, I was accustomed to watching for the conductor's initial downbeat and getting my bow going at the instant he reached the bottom. When I did that here, I got a distinctly dirty look from Ormandy.

I remembered: the delayed downbeat. It had been explained to me when I had tried out my teenaged conducting skills. Now I was on the other side of it. The whole orchestra cooperated in giving itself a split second's pause to get together—to wait until they *smelled* the music—and come in with that strong, rich sound.

I was expected to color within the lines, I knew. Ormandy had laid down some boundaries from the start.

"I want you to stay at least ten years," he said. "And I want you never to conduct in Philadelphia."

"Why would you ask that?"

"Because I don't want another Hilsberg."

Point taken. Besides Hilsberg's bid for Ormandy's position, I was aware of a second attempt to capture that coveted post. Pianist José Iturbi had tried and failed, even with the help of one-time board president Curtis Bok and a few other deep pockets.

Lining myself up as third pretender to the podium was never my plan. I said I would abide by Ormandy's requests. Summers didn't count, of course, when he vacationed. The orchestra played at Robin Hood Dell and had to be conducted by someone, and I never refused.

Like Szell, Ormandy was Hungarian. In spite of that, or because of it, he was suspicious of his countrymen. It was from him that I first heard the saying that if a Hungarian follows you into a revolving door he will nevertheless come out in front of you. It seemed to me that I, as a mere Russian, should present no threat at all.

There was one other thing he asked of me early on. Rehearsals had not begun on schedule in the fall of 1959 because the orchestra went on a three-week strike for a better contract.

"Attend all the union meetings," Ormandy told me, "and tell me what's going on."

The assignment did not appeal to me, and I went only to the final meeting where the orchestra voted to accept management's proposals.

Immediately, we were preparing for a tour through New England. We would play Richard Strauss's *Rosenkavalier Suite*, which the orchestra performed often, and some other pieces. Each concert would end with Strauss's *Sinfonia Domestica*. Ormandy asked the orchestra members if they wanted to rehearse *Rosenkavalier* and received a resounding "NO!"

I must have looked surprised, because my colleagues informed me summarily that "This is the Philadelphia Orchestra."

At Hunter College, the first stop on the tour, soprano Hilde Gueden joined us to sing Mozart's *Il re pastore*. I had not performed this piece before, even though it had a lovely obbligato for solo violin. It's not terribly difficult, but this was my first concert in New York with the orchestra.

"If it will make you feel better," Ormandy said, "go find her and play it with her."

Hilde had a magnificent voice. She also had a lot of other things going that a man might notice when she was in her dressing room wearing only lingerie, with the door open, which was necessary so that I could stand out in the tiny hallway and practice with her.

There was no room for a music stand, so I needed someone to hold my music. I collared Seymour Rosenfeld, our rotund second trumpet player, and pushed him into her doorway with the music. His glance fell on Hilde. The Sears catalogue, the main source of such vistas, had nothing comparable to offer.

"I'm sorry!" he squeaked at Hilde.

Concentration was not a problem for me, but reading the notes on the pages violently shaking in Seymour's hands was a challenge.

The obbligato went well enough, but my more salient memory of the concert is of the *Rosenkavalier Suite*, which our identity as the Philadelphia Orchestra had excused us from rehearsing. The suite is a conglomerate of themes from the opera *Der Rosenkavalier*, with additions by a number of conductors and arrangers. I had never played it before, and the violin part was so poorly marked that it was hard to distinguish what was to be played and what was not.

In the concert, I made it through to the middle section where I reached two lines that read both "play" and "tacet" (silent). I took a chance and followed the "tacet."

But my assistant concertmaster Dave Madison played, so I knew I'd guessed wrong.

Ormandy glowered at me as if to say *Why aren't you playing?*

On the next page came another "play/tacet." This time I did play. Wrong again. Ormandy shook his head.

Next we went to Burlington, Vermont. At dinner, our assistant conductor, Bill Smith, came rushing into the room, eyes wildly searching.

"Anshel! Mr. Ormandy needs you!"

I had ordered something delicious-sounding. My stomach rumbled, and the choice between food and Ormandy didn't seem particularly complicated. "I'll be there in a minute."

Bill saw through my delay tactic. "Right now. He's waiting."

I found him in his dressing room. One of our clarinetists had been hit by an automobile and, though not in serious condition, he could not play the concert. Without him, we could not perform *Sinfonia Domestica*. I joked that maybe I could play the clarinet part on the violin. Of course, all musicians know that violins don't transpose and that clarinets are in B-flat or A.

Ormandy wasn't up to humor. In fact, the whole orchestra was on edge. No one else could play the clarinet part. It's not as if we were in a major musical center and could locate a clarinetist who happened to be able to play the part.

"Can you play the Brahms Violin Concerto tonight?" Ormandy asked me.

No one asks this because no sane concertmaster will say yes.

"I don't go around practicing it."

Actually, I didn't go around practicing much at all. Usually I could get by on my sight reading skills—but the Brahms concerto?

"The librarian brought the parts for when Isaac Stern joins us," Ormandy went on. To add a little gloom, he said, "Otherwise we have to cancel the concert."

"Maybe," I said, and headed off to my dressing room to practice the concerto . . . or rather to find out if I could remember it from when I'd played it in Cleveland a year earlier. If I found any difficulty with my memory, I figured I could do a little practicing from the conductor's score with Bill Smith turning the pages. The pages would turn much more often, of course, in the full score, where each instrument gets one line per page.

Not five minutes later, Ormandy knocked on my door. "We also don't have a score," he said. "We both have to do it from memory."

He had gotten mixed up about when Isaac Stern would be playing the Brahms with us—it wasn't until after this tour. But our librarian had packed the parts for all the players. It was merely the soloist and the conductor who would have to wing it.

Various musicians looked in on me to offer sympathy. "He'll understand," they said. "Just say no." They were being sensible. Nobody does this, let alone a musician new to the orchestra and with no music at all. They were nervous for me, being put on the spot like this. Their support was indispensable.

I asked Ormandy for more time. I got thirty minutes. "And could you at least put the concerto at the end of the program?"

He agreed most pleasantly. The other players started looking at their own parts.

Brahms had such unique musical ideas in his writing that it required its own kind of memorizing. How the brain does these things is mysterious. I remembered the concerto.

I had developed management skills for the issue of nerves, too, as a musician must. There were times when I was soloing, and a rest came for me while the orchestra played. *What's my next note?* I sometimes thought. *When do I enter?* If I tried to think notes—*Is it F#? Is it A?*—my memory might shut down. But if I didn't go outside the music and think in words or note labels, if I just followed the musical conversation I was having with the orchestra, I could quite naturally pick up my lines. Often I could set my mind free and rely on what passed between my fingers and my ears.

I would love to claim that agreeing to play a major solo without rehearsal or even music on the stand is evidence of a grand courage at the core of my nature. However, the only person who knows me better than I know myself has concluded that it's the flip side of my social anxiety disorder. Marilyn thinks it's abnormal to handle social situations like parties by picking a symphony to conduct in your head and nodding to people as conversations seem to require it. It works pretty well, though. A musical conversation is easier to navigate and to remember than a social one.

That night in Burlington, while the Philadelphia Orchestra played the long introduction to the Brahms concerto, before the violin begins, the beauty of their playing astounded me. They hadn't had much time either. I was honored to be in the company of such musicians. I didn't see any option but to hit that concerto out of the park.

The performance of Brahms reinforced my conviction that practice does not always make perfect. I took my bow and walked off stage as the clapping continued.

A surprise awaited me backstage. There, right next to Ormandy, stood Bill Kincaid offering me a shot of bourbon.

"Don't take it!" Ormandy said.

It was delicious. Afterwards, I went to take my next bow.

After the concert, Bill invited me out for dinner and drinks. And then a nightcap.

"You were such a little shit in 1948!" he said. "I wanted to break your neck."

I was happy that we were friends at last, even if I couldn't quite keep up with him in the beverage department. Bill always said he never drank before a concert, and no one who heard him play his flute had any reason to suspect otherwise.

As for David Madison, my assistant concertmaster, it would have been impossible not to be friends. He had served as acting concertmaster for a year, and now was obliged to retreat to assistant. A lesser person might have found this difficult. Our shared dressing room was next to Ormandy's. My violin was locked in a cabinet where there was also room for Dave's. Before rehearsals, he laid out and opened my case. The music would be on our table and, if I had a solo, open to the page.

By this time, I had discovered the usefulness of buying the full score of whatever we were playing. Mr. Happich's wisdom had stayed with me, and the interest in hearing all the other instruments had expanded into a desire to see all the parts paralleled on the page. I liked knowing how the music I made fit into the larger picture. Then once I knew my own part, my orientation to the whole freed me to look at the conductor rather than my music.

The conductor's preparation begins with working through a score and marking it with his preferences. The orchestra librarian copies the markings onto the music for each instrument as applicable. Ormandy encouraged me to change the bowings for the violins any way I wished, but suggested that I consider the skill levels of the whole section as I did so. In addition, I could call out instructions for the violins as they occurred to me at rehearsals.

At an early rehearsal, I turned to the section and said, "Slur the next two bars, and start up bow."

"God damn it! What's wrong with the way it is?" came from somewhere toward the back.

Many of the players had been in the orchestra back when Stokowski was conductor. Along came I, all of thirty-one years old, telling them how to play.

We came to another section where Ormandy made a change that I thought required a bowing adjustment.

"At number 370, start up bow and change four bars later."

Again I heard the discordant voice.

When my third change provoked a grumble, I stood and asked Ormandy for a moment's break. Having placed the voice, I made my way to the back of the first violin section and leaned over Herman Weinberg's white hair to whisper to him. Then I straightened and said, "Okay, Herman?"

He smiled and nodded in agreement, and I returned to my chair and thanked Ormandy. The rehearsal continued.

Later the players all wanted to know what I had said to Herman, and I made no secret of it. "If I hear your voice again, I'll smash your violin over your head."

Herman and I became great friends. But that was later.

During one of my early performances with the Philadelphia Orchestra, Ormandy turned to the violin section abruptly, and something flew out of his mouth. It landed just under my chair and seemed to me to be a tooth or a dental crown. I certainly didn't want to step on—and possibly break—the maestro's tooth! With my foot I managed to move it into a position in reach of my arm. It was an unattractive brownish color, but then maybe it was a back tooth. Obviously it wasn't healthy, or it wouldn't have been so easily dislodged. I caught sight of Ormandy: he was shaking his head at me, no, no, no. I nodded yes. I would certainly keep this object out of harm's way.

We were in a busy passage of the music, and I had to wait until the violins had at least ten bars of rest—enough to allow me to free my arm to pick it up. The thing was very sticky.

It was not a tooth. It was some kind of lozenge. I dropped it instantly, but it left a sugary film on my fingers, which were now required to do Ormandy's bidding again on my Guarnerius del Gesù, which belonged to Rembert Wurlitzer. Touching the fingerboard was out of the question. I sucked on my fingers, but they still needed a good rubbing dry. I considered my trousers.

It seemed to me that for just such moments as this did orchestras hire assistant concertmasters. I leaned over and dried my fingers on Dave's back. It felt to him like a reassuring series of pats, and he smiled over his shoulder.

That's how I learned that just before each concert Ormandy placed a brown lozenge in his mouth to prevent dryness.

As I thought about it, something to suck on wasn't such a bad idea. My mouth got dry, too, and it wasn't possible to keep anything to drink on the stage. I got myself a bag of hard candies. Before rehearsal

I would pocket a bunch. As soon as a sufficient number of bars of rest coincided with a dry mouth, I would unwrap a candy and pop it in.

And here came my next entrance—time to put fiddle to the chin and bow to the strings. But I was holding a candy wrapper, which I had wadded up.

Oh, well. I tossed it over my shoulder along with my concertmaster's dignity.

Veda Reynolds sat behind me in the second stand and in the path of the missive. It usually hit her on the head or in the face. Or sometimes her violin took the hit. I might consume ten of these candies in a two-hour rehearsal. Wouldn't it have been nice of me to pick them up later?

I'm not that nice.

Veda wasn't the exclusive victim. Occasionally I chose someone else. I convinced myself that this habit actually *was* concertmasterly of me because it kept everyone loose and smiling.

My first experience of recording with the Philadelphia Orchestra was at Philadelphia's Town Hall. We were doing a piece that called for a significant solo from the concertmaster. I began it, but then I stopped. Almost without knowing why, I stood up. The other players watched sympathetically, thinking I was nervous.

"I have to stand," I said to Ormandy.

Immediately he shouted up to the production booth, "Howard, set up another microphone for Anshel. He wants to stand." He understood instinctively that I needed to have my head in the place I knew so well as a soloist and not in the concertmaster's chair. Howard Scott, our production manager, immediately complied, and after that I always had my own microphone in recording sessions. For certain pieces, like Strauss's *Ein Heldenleben* and *Also Sprach Zarathustra*, Rimsky-Korsakov's *Sheherezade*, and Bartók's first Portrait, I always had to do this.

The Soviet Union loomed forebodingly over everyone in those days, especially those of us with Russian roots. People like my parents longed to hear Russian musicians, but the U.S.S.R. kept its composers and musicians locked behind the Iron Curtain most of the time.

In 1959, Premier Nikita Khrushchev conceived a plan to improve relations with the West. Artistic exchanges were an efficient tool, especially when they were high-profile media events. He allowed three illustrious composers to travel to the United States. The visit would include Philadelphia, where we would perform their music with the composers present. It was a huge coup for Ormandy and the orchestra, and we were all excited.

We all knew the music of composer Dmitri Shostakovich, and Dmitry Kabalevsky we knew by name, and some knew his music. The third, Tikhon Khrennikov, was lesser known, but we understood him to be a musician of high standing. We would perform the great Shostakovich Symphony No. 1 and his new cello concerto, Kabalevsky's Overture to *Colas Breugnon*, and Khrennikov's Symphony No. 4.

The three arrived with quite an entourage, most of whom we could pretty well assume were KGB agents charged with preventing defections.

"The only one of the composers who's a card-carrying Communist is Khrennikov," Ormandy told me. "He's always watching the other two and eavesdropping on their conversations."

Conversations, under those conditions, were rather *pro forma*. Except that during a rehearsal break Kabalevsky came into my dressing room and leaned his tall frame against the mirror. In excellent English, he began to extol the virtues of performing, and even of *living*, in our country.

Nervous about who might be listening, I waved my hand toward the open door. He gave a careless shrug as if to say, "I don't care."

The visit electrified our music-loving city, and we played those concerts to full houses, my parents among them. Critics traveled to hear them and raved in their various news organs. But for me, the best was yet to come. With the composer present in the studio, the Philadelphia Orchestra was going to record two Shostakovich pieces, one of them his First Symphony, with all its lovely violin solos.

I loved those solos. I knew them backwards and forwards. The music was Romantic in nature, and I felt every note of it in my Russian soul. My first love was for the previous generation of Russian composers who had knit the melodies of the motherland so elegantly into their music—for Glazunov and Rimsky-Korsakoff and others, and above all Tchaikovsky. Now that older music seemed to saturate and embolden my playing of these contemporary composers who stood on the shoulders of the dead. I don't know how else to explain the satisfaction I felt.

Usually playing for an audience is more thrilling than playing into a cluster of recording gadgets, but this time was different. I was caught up in it and gave it all I had. At the end of the final movement, I felt I had captured its beauty and did not think I could ever play Shostakovich better. I returned to my poker game.

After a while, I went back to the booth, though I rarely wanted to hear our music before it was mixed. As I entered, I realized how much I wanted the composer's reaction. Szell had prevented me from playing Sibelius for Sibelius, and I felt that playing Shostakovich for Shostakovich was making up for it. The playback began, and I was standing right behind the composer. He sat at a table, his head inclined forward.

He didn't move. He didn't react at all to what I felt was some of my best playing ever.

Khrennikov stepped over to Shostakovich and bent down to whisper something to him in Russian. Shostakovich barely nodded.

I knew Ormandy had asked for retakes of some parts, but not of my solos, so I left to join the poker game.

But soon Ormandy came to get me. "Shostakovich has asked us to do the solo over again. He wants it faster." I saw worry on Ormandy's face.

"I like it the way I did it."

"He's the composer," Ormandy said, though with little conviction. "Also, he's Shostakovich."

"I'm still not going to play it any faster."

"Well, do it over again anyway," he said. "How you do it is just
how you do it. But I don't think they're going to like it."

I may have played it faster by a hair, but I doubt it. Anyway, it
passed.

Later, Ormandy and I talked about it, trying to guess what had
really happened. I had a creepy feeling about whatever Khrennikov
had whispered to Shostakovich. Ormandy was inclined to agree
that the demand for a retake had started there.

Today anyone can read about Tikhon Khrennikov. When I met
him, he had two titled positions. For almost two decades he had
been Director of the Red Army Central Theater. Stalin praised
his music for the stage. In 1948 Stalin cracked down on artists
producing "decadent" work influenced by the West. The reliable
Khrennikov was named First Secretary of the Soviet Composers'
Union. From this platform he called for a return to accessible and
optimistic Socialist Realism and personally chose whose work
would be performed and whose compositions were denounced.
He did plenty of the denouncing himself, shredding the careers
of Shostakovich, Prokofiev, Myaskovsky, and others whose music,
he felt, reeked of emotion or the merely personal. His own work
enjoyed broad attention and praise within the U.S.S.R.[1]

Needless to say, the Kremlin's policing of the musicians on the
Western tour of 1959 fell to Khrennikov. What I eventually realized
was that when I exposed the emotion Shostakovich had hidden in
his notes, I wasn't doing him any favors.

Ormandy's own deep musicality shines out in incidents like
that. Yes, my playing was bourgeois, but far be it from him to make
me cool it down. Soloists and orchestra members alike knew that
Ormandy's response to music was too strong, too visceral to bend

---

1. *www.classical.net/music/comp.lst/acc/khrennikov.php.*

with any prevailing winds. Under his baton, musicians could seek their personal best and know that it would be not only allowed but respected.

In my view, a conductor's skill shows most in his ability to accompany a soloist. Ormandy was able to grant enormous flexibility to soloists, giving them full freedom to go wherever the music led, and still he could bring the orchestra alongside at every moment. During my first year in Philadelphia I marveled at him again and again, whether following Gary Graffman playing Tchaikovsky piano concertos or Hilde Gueden singing. I had experienced it before as a soloist, but I gained a different appreciation of his excellence in accompaniment as I participated in the orchestra.

The bond between Ormandy and me was very strong. No one would call him a humble man, but the real beauty of music brought out a humility in him, a profound respect for both the composer and the performer. It was a joy to play for someone who so thoroughly loved the music right along with you. Where beauty is perceived and expressed, love is not too strong a word to describe the response, and those who respond to beauty together, also feel bound to each other.

The Tiffany clock he gave Marilyn and me for Christmas in 1959 still sits in our living room. Taped to the box was an envelope so tiny it fits in the palm of my hand, containing a note saying that he loved me as a father. And I did feel that he treated me as a son. Of course, he and Gretel had no children.

I felt comfortable with Ormandy from the start. "Would you like me to pick you and Mrs. Ormandy up?" I offered for one of our early out-of-town concerts.

"Sure! That would be great."

The Ormandys began to rely on my chauffeuring. We laughed a lot in the car. Whenever Mrs. Ormandy came along to New York, she would send a stagehand to the Carnegie Deli to get us corned beef sandwiches for the drive home.

"What did you get for sweets?" was always Ormandy's question.

At the end of my first concert with the orchestra at Carnegie Hall, Ormandy bowed and left the stage. As usual, continuing applause called him back for a second bow, and a third. When he left the stage the third time, it seemed to me that the audience had stopped applauding.

Here again, protocol dictates the concertmaster's moves. When the applause for the conductor stops, the concertmaster stands and exits, and then the members of the orchestra follow. Since the audience had quieted down, I started to make my way toward the side. But then the applause resurged. Offstage, Ormandy heard this and began to return, so that we encountered each other on stage.

"Where are you going?" he demanded.

"The applause stopped."

"No, it didn't," he said.

I continued off stage, and he continued on. Who knows what the audience made of that?

When it was time to leave, I brought my car around to the stage door for the Ormandys. He was already talking as he climbed into the front seat. "Why on earth did you walk off while they were still clapping for me?"

Mrs. Ormandy rescued me: "Gene, the applause did stop for a short time."

"I have too many friends in the audience to have the applause stop!" he informed us both.

Nineteen years after leaving the Philadelphia Orchestra, Leopold Stokowski finally received an invitation from Eugene Ormandy to guest conduct in February 1960. Stokowski had raised the orchestra from regional to international acclaim, and yet never been invited back. This is most unusual. What can have prevented the conventional honor normally shown to a previous conductor of long tenure?

The usual answer flies to the sticky subject of Stokowski's supposed sexual exploits. Now the board member whose wife's name was too intimately tied with Stokowski's was no longer associated with us. Surely it was merely that indelicate situation that had delayed the invitation.

Stokowski's return was a major event in Philadelphia. The newspapers reminded us of all he had done to polish the orchestra, which gave luster to the city. Those few members of the orchestra who dated back to the previous era were jittery, spreading their anticipation to the rest of us—"He's coming back! Three concerts!" Dave Madison had told me what concerts had been like back then, the godlike aura he managed to exude as he strode onto the stage, a magnificent specimen of humanity, six foot two with gleaming white hair that swooped over his head like meringue.

I remembered his visits to New Orleans and San Francisco. He had impressed me more than any conductor I had ever played for, even though I could not see myself opting for such a showy style. It was the vigor of his conducting that thrilled the players. His changes to scores attracted criticism, but I thought they were usually justified. When an orchestra is paying 110 players, the board is displeased to come to a concert and find only 80 of them on stage, even if the composer wrote parts only for 80. So in pieces written for smaller orchestras, Stokowski would add instruments and write the parts, not necessarily introducing new notes.

We sounded different under Stokowski. It was partly his added transcription to the scores. But also the force of his leadership. We sounded however he wanted us to sound. Of course the Philadelphians gave him curtain calls. When he returned the third time, he motioned for the audience to sit. First, he gave the smile. Such a knowing smile, boyish even on the old man. Knowing, specifically, that many of the women in the audience were suffering rapid heartbeats.

Then he spoke: "As I was saying—"

The audience erupted in laughter. They were still in love with him. He said generous things about the orchestra, its continued quality, about Ormandy's work with us, about the dedication of our board. He paved the way for annual return visits.

In February of 1962, Stokowski had *Scheherazade* on the program for us, Rimsky-Korsakov's symphonic suite full of violin solos. Afterwards he sent me a kind letter, which I still treasure. Here are words from him that thrilled this musician's heart:

> [*Scheherazade*] has nostalgic qualities which are different from any other music I know, and your playing showed that you completely understood this unique mood. For example, at the beginning of the 4th movement your first solo had that kind of dreamy tenderness it should have, and the next solo the powerful agitation and even brutality that is its character.[2]

That's what we all want to do. Really *get* what the composer meant.

During that visit, we played the piece Stokowski's way on Thursday, Friday, and Saturday. On Sunday—with no rehearsal—the orchestra recorded *Scheherazade* with Ormandy, effortlessly switching back to *his* way.

Writers about music often mention the long shadow of Stokowski. Anyone close to the five-foot-five Ormandy knew that, in his own mind, no height of musical achievement could add to his actual stature. He was a short man. The extra-high podium helped, but not enough. Obviously, height has nothing to do with conducting talent, and others have found it no hindrance. but for Ormandy it was a problem. Stokowski's physical height alone was enough to haunt Ormandy. Add in Stokowski's dancer-like grace, the head of hair, the magnetism he exercised over women, and his glamorous style of batonless conducting, and up rises a shadow perfectly designed to torment a profoundly talented but sensitive man like Ormandy. Who could compete with the elegant silhouette we all knew from Walt Disney's *Fantasia*?

---

2. Letter in the author's possession.

In April of my first year, I played the Tchaikovsky Violin Concerto with the orchestra, and afterwards Theo Pitcairn sought me out backstage.

"Do you really like that violin?"

"I love it."

"When do you have to take it back?"

"Monday." You could only borrow a Guarnerius del Gesù violin from Rembert Wurlitzer for so long.

Theo wanted to come along. That simplified my transportation plan. His driver pulled up in front of our house, and we rode up to New York in style.

I dressed neatly as I usually did, and Theo wore his baggy coat, floppy hat, and wrinkled suit. That was just Theo.

Mr. Wurlitzer greeted us both, and I handed over the case. As he opened it to inspect the instrument, I had a moment to wonder what he thought of my companion. The hat Theo held in his hand, now that we were indoors, might have been through several lifetimes. Perhaps during one of them it was in style.

But most of my wondering was about why Theo had wanted to come with me. It raised my hopes, and they were well founded.

Soon he addressed himself to Mr. Wurlitzer: "Would you take a check? I need a pen."

Mr. Wurlitzer found a pen.

After he wrote up the sale and tucked the check for $22,000 into his cash register, Mr. Wurlitzer said to me, "I want to do something for you."

As if I had done something for him?

He left us for a few minutes and then summoned us into a room where he had laid out all his best bows. It did not take me long to find a favorite.

"Good taste," he said. "That one was made by François Tourte."

I was pleased to know that. No maker of bows stands above him.

Some months later, Theo brought documents to Marilyn and me, drawn up by his lawyer. He had planned the transfer of the violin so that over a period of five years it would become half mine and half Marilyn's. Payments to him were to be made when possible, but no interest was charged and no penalty was stipulated. That we were unable to pay for this treasure was obvious from the start and not something that concerned that generous man. Just a year or two later, he converted the violin into a gift, half to me and half to Marilyn. "You've made it your own," he said. "I don't want to hear anybody else play it."

About the François Tourte bow, the funny thing was nine times out of ten I preferred my bow by John Dodd, an English contemporary of François Tourte. The Tourte bow gave a more rounded sound and perhaps served the violin better. But the Dodd bow made difficult playing easier, and so served me better.

Another thing occurred late in my first season, and it foretold trouble. Max Carol approached me. I knew his son Norman, concertmaster of the Minneapolis Symphony.

"You know I preside over the Philadelphia Little Symphony," Mr. Carol said. "Would you have any interest in conducting it?"

I made myself stand there calmly as glee leaped in my chest. I remembered that day when I had been caught conducting an imaginary orchestra in the office of the Philadelphia Musical Academy. Joseph Barone was visiting from L'Ecole Monteux, and he recruited me for Monteux. This Philadelphia Little Symphony was another of Mr. Barone's projects. He had founded it, along with one like it in New York, to provide opportunities for young soloists and conductors to develop their gifts. I wanted in.

But reasonable judgment had to prevail. "Mr. Carol, of course I would want to confer with Mr. Ormandy. I promised him I wouldn't conduct while I'm his concertmaster."

No excuse like "this situation fell outside our agreement" was available to me here. I simply took the risk and brought it up to Ormandy.

"But they're bankrupt!" he said. "They don't even exist."

"I didn't know that."

"If they want to start up again, go ahead. Conduct away." The wave of his hand said it all.

Armed with that permission, I told Mr. Carol I was available and hoped for the best.

Which was not to be. They had no funding.

At that time, we began rehearsing for my next solo with the Philadelphia Orchestra. It was to be another Brahms—his Double Concerto for Violin and Cello. Our principal cellist Lorne Munroe would join me. Five minutes into the first rehearsal, Ormandy stopped. So everyone else stopped.

"Why is it that everything you play sounds like Tchaikovsky?" he demanded of me.

The comment stung. Nothing is wrong with Tchaikovsky. But Ormandy was implying that my playing was not in the Brahms style, that I was incapable of rendering different styles of music each in its own way. Had I really so utterly failed Dr. Szanto, who urged me to access the music as it was born in the mind of the composer?

The barb was at odds with Ormandy's usual kind communications with me and with his daily reliance on me. It appeared to be an isolated outburst. Fortunately, it was followed by a return to normal.

Later I saw the connection between the verbal attack and the recent giving of his blessing to conduct, even if the orchestra in question was defunct. The giving was done with one hand as the other drew back to prepare a punch.

Later yet, I saw the pattern. His "blessings" were always this and that.

When the Dean of Temple University called to ask if I would conduct their orchestra, I knew Ormandy wouldn't care. It was a student orchestra—just kids. However, I found them full of surprises, unexpected proficiencies, that sweet desire to please. The school was willing to work around my schedule. It was a happy arrangement in every way.

Most of the time, Ormandy looked out for me. When I tore my pant leg on the way to a Monday night concert, he lent me a pair of his own pants. (I wore them as low as possible.) He wasn't even above sharing his personal secrets for avoiding embarrassing oversights onstage. He always checked his pants zipper before he walked on, and he told me to do the same.

"It's too late when you're onstage. Your full dress jacket won't cover it. I call it the glissando." He demonstrated, sliding his finger up and down the zipper as you would make a glissando on a string instrument by sliding your finger up and down the string.

How could I not be reminded of Szell's interpretation of the glissando in "Till Eulenspiegel" as the moment when Till turns and pees down from the steeple?

In a candid moment, Ormandy told me about an experience he had when he was conductor of the Minneapolis Symphony and still quite young. He arrived at the hall for rehearsal. The players didn't know he was there yet, and he overheard one saying to another, "That Ormandy is a son of a bitch."

Appalled, he closed himself in his office. This was intolerable! What should he do? He phoned Arthur Judson, his manager at Columbia Artists Management, Inc. (CAMI).

"You won't believe what I just heard. A member of my orchestra called me an S.O.B! Behind my back, but still—how can they dare?"

Judson burst out laughing. "Ormandy! Congratulations. You've just become a conductor."

This anecdote gave me pause. Maybe it should have given me a full stop. The nature of the position requires a conductor to make difficult decisions with regard to players and their futures. One must either arrive with a thick skin or grow one.

Being concertmaster, on the other hand, was not so onerous. I liked it best when I could lead with a light touch. When a piece of music divided the violins into several parts, it was traditionally the concertmaster's job to play the top line and assign players to each of the other lines. But our superb violinists needed little guidance. When it was necessary to decide on bowings for the section, I followed Ormandy's advice and accommodated the bowing directions to the weakest player.

On one occasion where the violins were divided into parts, Ormandy asked me, "Anshel, what *divisi* are we doing here?"

"I'll take care of it," I said. He turned his attention to the brass.

I stood up to address the first violins. "I'm playing the top line," I told them in a whisper, "and you're on your own."

They liked that.

Sometimes I would say to my section, "Play it like this." And I would play a down bow staccato, as I first learned from watching Heifetz and had now grown comfortable with. They laughed.

The laughter. We always needed that. Joe Gingold modeled it for me in Cleveland.

In late spring, Ormandy announced that next season we would play and also record Richard Strauss's *Ein Heldenleben* (A Hero's Life).

"Of course you know it," he said to me.

Of course.

I had never played it. Never even heard it. And wasn't about to get all hot and bothered about it. Surely my sight reading would get me through.

"Is it true?" some of the orchestra members asked me. "We're really going to record that?"

So I asked the librarian for the music. The violin part was disjointed. The soloist would need to know exactly what everyone else was playing just to come in at the right times. Technically also, it was extremely difficult. I bought the score, studied the orchestral parts as well, and actually practiced for several weeks.

I ended my first season full of joy. So did Veda Reyolds, who sat behind me, and she celebrated the end of our last rehearsal in the Academy of Music in her own way. As I was putting my music away, a tickling feeling came over my head and shoulders and little white balls fell all over me, bouncing off my curly hair, my shoulders, my violin, pooling in my lap, scattering all over the floor. The white things made hardly any noise, but maybe I just couldn't hear it over the raucous laughter of the rest of the orchestra. I examined one of the white things, pulled it flat. It was a candy wrapper.

All year, behind me and in view of everyone else, Veda had been quietly gathering the candy wrappers I tossed at her and plotting revenge.

We weren't quite done for the year. The orchestra always went to Ann Arbor for the May Festival at the University of Michigan. We played our nightly concerts in Hill Auditorium, but Keith Brown and I kept our priorities straight, just as we always did in Aspen.

Softball was the thing. We pulled together the Philadelphia Orchestra Team. An enemy helps a group unite, and ours was formidable: Sigma Chi, known as the fraternity of athletes. Not only were they younger than we, and more devoted to the gross motor skills than the fine—they didn't even need to stay sober. They polished off several kegs while handily trouncing us. I doubt they came to our concerts.

At least Keith and I could rebuild our self-esteem a few weeks later in Aspen, where our faculty team stood a chance against the students.

Marilyn and I were glad to have that extra summer income. Most orchestra musicians had to cobble together their living in those days of shorter seasons. Just paying for the fancy clothes was a challenge, and as concertmaster I didn't dare cut corners with frayed cuffs or worn-looking pants. You could get away with more in the back, where our fourth hornist Herbie Pierson always smeared black shoe polish on his leg under the big tear in his pants.

In September, Ormandy announced that everyone should be ready to start working on *Ein Heldenleben* soon "because Anshel doesn't practice."

Little did he know, this was an exception. Of course I had set it aside for the summer, but now I was on task. When we went to Baltimore for a concert, I even kept my violin with me on the train so I could take it home. Everyone else put theirs on the truck that transported our instruments back to the Academy of Music.

On the train, I placed the violin most carefully on the rack above my chair and went to play poker. And I had a great run of cards! Maybe the proximity of the violin was good luck.

The next afternoon, I arrived at the hall and as usual Dave Madison had my music set out and the violin case open, everything ready for the day's work.

"Did you sleep well?" he asked.

"Fine. Thank you for asking." It wasn't Dave's normal question, so I gave him a quizzical look.

"Did you have a chance to practice?"

Now I looked at the violin, lying in its case. Then I remembered setting it on the rack on the train. And I remembered getting off the train, carrying only my suitcase, not the violin. I actually felt nauseated and faint.

"How is it possible?"

"I saw you out the window when you got off at your stop," he said. "I went and got it and took it home with me."

Neither of us told anyone what could have happened but hadn't, thanks to Dave.

As the time to rehearse *Ein Heldenleben* with the orchestra approached, I asked Ormandy, "Would you like to hear me play it?"

"Look, I hired you. It's your interpretation I want. Whatever you do with it, I'll follow you."

The composer Richard Strauss was a retiring man. In these tone poems, he found a way to express himself. The long violin solo in *Ein Heldenleben* represents his wife, a notorious control freak. She was also a marvelous soprano. I finished working it up, gave it my final personal touches and, only then, listened to some recordings by other violinists. My interpretation was quite individualistic, but my changes were violinistic and seemed to me suited to Strauss's representation of his wife, both tender and capricious.

Something got into me at the first rehearsal. I asked Ormandy to start without me. My solo part was about five minutes into the piece. I walked off stage and stood behind the door, watching. Dave kept looking back. As assistant concertmaster, he would have to play that solo if I didn't return in time. He was sweating it—looking at the music, glancing at the door. All the other violinists shared his anxiety. At the last possible moment I came in, playing the solo as I walked.

Even Dave laughed. That was the kind of atmosphere the musicians in the Philadelphia Orchestra generated and Ormandy mostly tolerated.

I was also enjoying the artistic freedom he encouraged. One passage in *Ein Heldenleben* I played sul G, meaning entirely on the G string, though Strauss didn't notate it that way.

"You're not going to do that in performance, are you?" Ormandy asked.

"Why not?"

"You won't hit it every time."

Of course he allowed me to play it sul G, and I never missed it. Playing that passage on the G string allowed me to express more fully the tongue-lashing Strauss's wife seemed to be giving her husband. It contrasted nicely with the following less angry passage, and then the third part, which suggests—without quite delivering—an apology.

Again, the contrast with Szell was striking. In Cleveland, personal style was at your own risk, if not *verboten*.

We all felt comfortable finding our own best musical pathways in the Philadelphia Orchestra. At the same time, playing together requires a complicated network of inter-musician signaling. A quartet does this by watching one another. In an orchestra, the conductor can communicate with everyone. Under Ormandy, I also felt comfortable establishing my own signal pathways for particular pieces of music. For example, in Brahms's Symphony No. 1, the second movement contains solos for violin, oboe, and French horn that are somewhat intertwined with one another. At one point the French horn and solo violin are in conversation. It was extremely helpful during that movement for the oboe and horn to be able to watch my bow. I always moved my chair a little and sat at an angle that kept my bow visible to them, and they positioned themselves so they could see me. Ormandy understood what we were doing and appreciated our commitment to the music.

Playing an instrument does involve the whole body, but it was only in the Philadelphia Orchestra that my left leg came in for attention. Most violinists sit with their feet placed apart, symmetrically, or crossed at the ankle. But I used my right foot for support, and my left did whatever it felt like doing in response to the music, unbeknownst to me. The more I was taken up with my playing, the farther I tended to stick it out. I never could manage to think about it and rein it in while playing the violin.

Theo Pitcairn came to almost every Friday concert with other family members, and they always came backstage at the end. Dick Yardumian and his wife Ruth E. (pronounced "Ruthie") came with him. Before Ormandy's time, Ruth E. had organized the youth concerts of the orchestra under Stokowski. As long-time supporters, they were treated like family by Ormandy and many members of the orchestra.

I suppose Theo preferred the daytime concerts because he could get back to Bryn Athyn nice and early. I certainly don't think he came for the social experience. Those Friday concerts were a different animal. Informally referred to as the Ladies' Concerts, they were especially favored by the high society of Philadelphia, called "the Main Line" after the Pennsylvania Railroad that ran through the affluent suburbs extending northwest from the city. The ladies in attendance were known for being restless during the performance. Stokowski once even turned around and rebuked them for being too noisy. I can only imagine how it thrilled them to arouse his anger.

To me, various ladies said, "I loved your leg!" Who knows what my left leg was up to while I was deep into Beethoven?

Ormandy, of course, had no choice but to continue the Friday afternoon concerts, and he conducted them as if the Main Line ladies were as passionate about the music as he was. This, in spite of their applause habits. Clapping seemed a burden to them, and in any case they weren't about to remove their gloves just so we could hear their hands collide. I suppose they had to keep their gloves on, too, because each seemed to have some urgent need to get out as fast as possible. They began leaving almost the minute Ormandy's baton gave the final flick for our last note to end. He then stepped off his podium to shake my hand, muttering, "They can't wait to get out of here!" He was barely able to get off the stage before the silence engulfed him.

However, those faithful women bought their tickets every week and generously supported the orchestra. I admired Ormandy's conducting at full tilt for them, just as he once did in a snowstorm when only 300 people could get to the Academy of Music.

That fall, we were able to give a special pleasure to Theo. He was always zealous for Dick Yardumian's success. And Ormandy and I were on the same page as we offered the world premiere of the revised Yardumian Violin Concerto in November 1960. I could see Dick's growth as a composer as I played the new version. A year later we would perform Yardumian's Symphony No. 1. Ormandy and I worked together most collegially on editing it for our orchestra.

My fellow musicians could not have realized that Ormandy was courting Theo Pitcairn by performing Yardumian compositions. Theo was very fond of Dick and his family and rewarded all who advanced his career.

Occasionally I saw how that worked from close up. Once I was at Dick's house in Bryn Athyn, and Theo was with us, when the phone rang.

Dick answered it, and then covered the receiver and whispered to us, "It's Ormandy." A minute later he said into the phone, "Sure, I'll ask him and call you back."

"He wants to record *The Messiah* with the Mormon Tabernacle Choir," he told us. "Columbia is willing but they won't pay for the soloists. He needs $20,000."

Theo thought about this, but not for very long. "Okay," he said. "I'll give him some Pittsburgh Plate Glass stock to cover it." Georg Frederic Handel's *Messiah* was deeply meaningful to Theo.

After that, the orchestra began performing it every year to a sold-out house. After one or two of these, Ormandy shifted the responsibility for conducting this moneymaker to his assistant conductor, Bill Smith.

While we were in Salt Lake City, we recorded another work, a little song Ormandy had never heard of. It was called "The Battle Hymn of the Republic." He didn't split the royalties on such a minor piece, but just let the choir have them all.

None of us dreamed it would be a gold record. In the present sad days of financial troubles, I wish the Philadelphia Orchestra had some of that money.

Like all the orchestra members, I addressed our conductor as "Mr. Ormandy." But one day when I was driving him to an out-of-town concert he suggested a change.

"Anshel, when we're alone you can call me Gene."

I tried to imagine it: *Hi Gene. Looks like we're in for some traffic.*

"Well," I said, "could I just call you *Boss*?"

He liked that.

One day I picked up the Boss and his wife Gretel (for some reason her name was easier to say than his) for a concert. I always tried not to push his buttons on the way to concerts, but sometimes he pushed them himself. On this particular day, he fiddled around with my car radio till he found classical music. Respighi's *Pines of Rome* was playing on one station.

After listening for a few moments he said, "That's the worst performance I've ever heard of *The Pines.*"

"Who is it?" I asked.

Gretel, I noticed, giggled.

"I have no idea," he said. "It's just terrible."

"Be careful, Gene," Gretel said.

"What!" he snapped. "You think that's me?" Then he turned to me. "Stop the car. I'm going to call and find out who it is."

"We're on the New Jersey Turnpike," I reminded him.

Gretel was laughing out loud. "Gene, we don't know what station it is."

We waited for the end of the recording. I thought it all sounded quite good. Finally the announcer said, "You have heard the *Pines of Rome* by Ottorino Respighi as performed by the Minneapolis Symphony conducted by Eugene Ormandy." And he identified the station.

"The man is wrong. He's crazy. That's not the way I did it in Minneapolis." A Howard Johnson's came into view. "Take that exit. The station owes me an apology. On the air!"

I drove up to the restaurant and waited for him to get out.

But he was looking at me. "Go on," he said. "The operator will get their phone number for you now that we have the station."

"Boss, the operator won't be able to get the number. Not just from the station's letters." It wasn't a phone call I wanted to make.

"Forget it," he said. "I'll call from home."

Later Gretel told me he'd found that it was his own recording. "But then the reception on your Cadillac radio . . ." she said with a sly smile. "That probably distorted the sound."

Once, most generously, Ormandy invited me to share a program with him, where I would conduct one of the works the orchestra performed. He asked me to give him a list of symphonies I'd like to conduct and we would choose from that.

I listed the biggies—Tchaikovsky's Fourth or Fifth, Dvořák's "New World," Beethoven's Fifth or Seventh, Brahms's First or Second.

He said, "No, that one I'm working on for next year . . . we did this one the season before last, New York is doing that one now," etc., etc. "Anshel, why don't you do Dvořák's Symphony No. 4?"

It's a lesser known work. He had done it with the Minneapolis Symphony and went to the storage room to get the recording of it. "Take this home and think about it. You'd do a beautiful job on this."

A few days later I handed it back. "I really want to do Brahms Fourth, Boss."

"Why would you want to do that?"

"I can do it."

"It's really difficult."

"I'm absolutely sure." And I was, in my great big head, sure. It had to be a major symphony, something everybody knew. The trouble was, "everybody" included the Philadelphia Orchestra, who had played it under Ormandy more than once in their magnificent Philadelphia style. They didn't need me.

As a matter of fact, I needed them. I wasn't all that experienced, and its difficulty was above my reach. I had some ideas of how I wanted them to do things, but it was like pulling an elephant. They didn't budge. Of course, it was their kindness toward me, their desire to help me "succeed" that moved them to just play it as they had always played it under their great conductor, regardless of what I thought I was doing. And I did think I was doing something, pushing and pulling and trying to bring certain instruments out. All to no effect. I stumbled, and they masked it.

An orchestra that good can be relied on to mask a lot of stumbling. Van Cliburn's extraordinary talent doesn't need my defense, and I'm betting it can sustain the following anecdote without damage. I think he was playing the Brahms Second Piano Concerto. Beautifully, of course. Until in the middle of a movement, he had a memory lapse. Soloists will often skip ahead when this happens, and the conductor must catch on and move the orchestra ahead to wherever the soloist finds his footing. It happens.

But Van didn't do it that way. He went back to the beginning of the movement, but not exactly the beginning. He would later describe it as "floundering around for what seemed like minutes" until he found his place. Ormandy turned to look at Van in astonishment, as if to say, What am I supposed to do with the orchestra?

The audience, naturally, gave Van a standing ovation.

In my second season in Philadelphia, KYW, then the local NBC affiliate, approached me. They were putting together eight TV programs on well-known soloists, including violinist Jascha Heifetz and pianist Arthur Rubinstein. They filmed me giving introductions to each one and then saying goodnight to the viewers at the end. It was easy work.

After those programs, the station gave me my own series, introducing and interviewing the guest artists who performed with the Philadelphia Orchestra. *Portraits in Music*, as it was called, aired on Saturday evenings. Mendelssohn's "Italian" Symphony provided the perfect theme music.

Of course, Ormandy was one of the first celebrities I interviewed.

"You have to write out all the questions for me in advance," he said. "I don't want any tricks."

I tried to imagine what a concertmaster could gain from playing public tricks on his conductor. I never came up with any advantage to tricking him though, so I simply asked Ormandy the questions I'd given him in advance. Once we got going, he didn't mind my asking a few more questions that grew naturally out of the conversation.

Once on *Portraits in Music*, I was faced with an awkward boy pianist whose mother brought him into the studio. He was nervous, and I wanted to help him relax so, when the studio lights came on, I started with a throw-away question: "Are you married?"

"Noooooo," he said. Still nervous.

A little later when I heard him play, it became clear that no one needed to worry one bit about the young André Watts. He would do just fine.

Arthur Fiedler came that year also, to guest conduct, and of course we wanted him on the TV show.

He came over to me backstage. "Nobody ever wants me to do serious music anymore," he complained. "Nothing but the light stuff. You know I'm really a classical guy."

"But that's how you made your wonderful reputation. And the Pops saved the BSO."

"True. It really was the only way I could see forward for Boston."

"Will you have time for an interview?"

"Yes, let's find a way to make that happen. They're not even letting me off for dinner till 8:00."

So we met again at 9:30 in the evening and settled ourselves in the warm glow of the stage lights.

"When did you start conducting the Boston Pops?" I began.

The cameras were rolling, and I was expecting a quick answer, but none came. I looked at Arthur—his eyes were closed! The big dinner had caught up with him. I gave him a little kick. "The Boston Pops—when did you start it?"

He startled awake. "Oh! That was, uh, in 1830."

"Really? You look wonderful, for your age!"

We started over, and managed to record a smooth conversation.

By this time, our paths had crossed quite a few times, and I liked Arthur Fiedler a lot. Because of that, and because he was so kind, I brought up a painful memory after the interview. I couldn't help unburdening myself. "Do you remember that terrible sound that happened when you were conducting the San Francisco Symphony?"

"You mean in the Cow Palace."

"Exactly," I said.

"Who could forget someone deliberately trying to sabotage a concert?"

"It was me. I was trying to get my bow off the string and. . . . it somehow went wrong."

"Oh, no, Anshel, you're thinking of something else. That wasn't a sound you're capable of making."

"But I did."

And so we went, round and round, the dear man never willing to believe me.

Once on *Portraits in Music*, I had to go it alone. If you have a TV show, eventually it will happen to you—the last minute phone call that your interviewee is ill. When it happened, there just wasn't time to arrange anyone else, so I fell back on an old favorite, the Chaconne. Everyone loves Bach, so I just talked about all the things he manages to say in one short piece of music and then played it.

In 1961, the Philadelphia Orchestra embarked on a transcontinental tour that would go to California and end in New York. It began in Ann Arbor with our traditional May festival.

A few days later, we packed ourselves into a train and headed south to Indiana. I was less squeezed than others, since Ormandy arranged a large private compartment for me. This was necessary to accommodate the card games we players always had going, though perhaps that was not in the boss's mind.

In Fort Wayne, we performed in an old movie theater. Of course the dressing room space was inadequate. Ormandy kindly invited me to share his room.

In the performance, we came to the final piece of the concert, Stravinsky's *Petrouchka*. We had played it in Philadelphia just a month earlier and Ormandy had conducted it most impressively from memory.

We began, and quickly I noticed that his movements were rote. In fact, it was like watching my grandmother wash clothes on a washboard. His arms moved up and down without even completing the standard fourfold movement of conducting— the sequence of down, left, right, up. He gave no direction to the strings or woodwinds, and did not even pull the brass in at their entry. His music stand was empty. But he really did know *Petrouchka* inside out.

Just not at that moment.

I looked around and saw the musicians beginning to be disconcerted. Stravinsky is difficult music. Sweating, I shifted toward the orchestra to make eye contact with various section leaders and raised my violin a bit so the bow was more visible, to help them until our conductor got his bearing.

Ormandy still raised and lowered his arms mechanically. On his face was a look of frozen fear. His beats were not even in the right places, as if not a single note of Stravinsky's piece was available to his mind. He was wandering in a territory all his own.

We knew this work. I was sure we could play it decently, if we could just all keep together. I felt completely unprepared for what I had to do, but there was simply no choice. The players had to follow something, and in this case it wasn't going to be Ormandy. Fortunately, the bowing action adds to the visibility of a violin, but it was not enough. I knew that. With my head, my feet, my elbows too, I tried to lead the orchestra. A lesser group of musicians could never have gotten through such a difficult piece in this way, but somehow the others saw what they needed and played where they were supposed to. What a great sigh of relief ran through us all when we reached the end.

The audience, I think, was none the wiser. They even required an encore.

I knew Ormandy would not want to see anyone, and I wished my things were out with everyone else's. But I had to go into his dressing room because we were sharing. I would just retrieve my stuff and get out of there fast.

He stood staring into a large mirrored wall. Which meant that he was facing me in the mirror.

I started packing my violin quickly.

"What did I do? What did I do?" he said.

"Boss, *Petrouchka*'s a difficult work."

"I know. But what did I do?"

"Well," I said, "you made it more difficult." I would really like to revisit that moment and think of something more helpful to say. I just haven't thought of it yet.

Two days later Ormandy conducted *Petrouchka* perfectly from memory. What happened to him can happen to any of us.

Because our music was beautiful and moved our audiences, we were always supposed to be poker-faced. Who can do that? Especially on those grueling tours. We developed radar, constantly looking for something to amuse us.

We always had a couple of encore pieces at the ready, usually a Bach air or an arioso. Something guaranteed to please. Ormandy had to decide when an encore was required and then work the transition. Often the last piece on the program was something weighty, and he would say to the audience, in his winsome way, "What can we offer you after Tchaikovsky?"

Our cellist Sam Belenko had a sonorous basso voice. Once when Ormandy asked his question of the audience, he got a reply from the orchestra in that deep voice: "NOTHING." Sam's head was down, but everyone knew who said it.

Never had Ormandy gotten so honest an answer. He had to know his whole orchestra could barely contain itself. But he pulled out one of the Bachs with a straight face, and we recovered our composure.

We rolled through the country on the train—Chicago, St. Louis, eventually California. Toward the end it seemed like we were playing the *Rosenkavalier Suite* almost every night. John de Lancie and I found a way to stave off boredom. At the place where a short violin solo interacts with an oboe obbligato, we developed a kind of guessing game. The solo is really just part of a waltz and not written with the intention that the violinist will do anything special with it. But the trip was so long! I would add a little finesse, a little extra seasoning of a different flavor every time. John could see by my bow what I was up to, and he was quick to follow, playing simultaneously with me and matching the flavor. Just plain fun, whatever took our fancy on a given night.

Maybe it was our utter independence of the conductor in these few little bars of music. After the performance one night, Ormandy said to me, "Why don't you play it straight for a change instead of fooling around?"

The next night I played it very straight. So straight it could have passed for an étude played competently by a young student.

We got back on the train to ride through the night. I couldn't get to my compartment without passing the Ormandys.

"Anshel," Gretel called to me. "Gene would like to see you."

He was looking out the window into the black night and motioned for me to sit down. Then he turned and looked at me for almost as long as he had looked out the window. Finally he said, "I liked it better the other way."

"Me too."

The western part of the tour ended in Las Vegas, and most of us were exhausted and ready for some recreation. I was happy because the countless performances of Strauss's *Ein heldenleben* and *Also sprach Zarathustra* were behind me, as well as a recording. After our concert, I returned to the Sands Hotel.

"Let's meet in the bar," I said to David Arben, my friend since Cleveland days.

It was smoky and noisy, with the slot machines dinging. We weren't surprised to find a bunch of our colleagues there too. The surprise was when twelve beautiful women in high heels and fishnet stockings and a few other small items of Vegas attire pranced onto the stage all holding violins. After a man in evening dress introduced them, some idiot from among my friends shouted, "The concertmaster of the Philadelphia Orchestra is sitting at the bar!"

"Well, well, well!" the man said. "I happen to have a Stradivarius upstairs. Would the concertmaster favor us with a tune?"

"No," I said, along with many more words like *Let the ladies play*, and *I'm off duty*, and *Get me out of here*, none of which were audible over the din of my colleagues' hilarity. They wanted to see me up there among the girls, and so I was pushed along.

When the Stradivarius case was opened, I saw that it truly was a beautiful instrument, at least to look at, and when I put it under my chin and tried a few scales, I found a sound to match and sort of floated into the Tchaikovsky violin concerto, relieved to leave Strauss behind. The waiters stopped serving and the lights were turned down.

David Arben was at the blackjack table facing the other way. He had missed the entrance of the women and my being pressed into service. When it suddenly got dark and the dealer sat still, he thought he was having a Nazi camp nightmare. Finally the notes came through to him, and he was okay.

Nobody minded when free drinks were served after my performance. The manager also gave me an unlimited credit card to use anytime I was in the hotel.

But I went on with my normal life after that, so never used the card.

The everlasting transcontinental tour was almost over when Ormandy announced that we would add six concerts in Florida. This meant more money, so most players were pleased. But I wanted to see Marilyn and David and Jennie.

"You don't need me for those concerts, Boss," I said to Ormandy. "No solos are even scheduled."

"Take the week," he said. "You've earned it."

He made sure I was paid for that week. Often, he was kind as a father and innocuous as Dr. Jekyll.

Max Carol had not managed to resurrect the Little Symphony. But Ormandy *had* given me permission to conduct it, and I felt that applied to whatever Max put together. By 1962 Max and I had assembled something else: a chamber orchestra. He recruited local business leaders for a board. We wanted thirty-four players, and I figured we could get them all from the ranks of the big orchestra.

It was easy. Everyone wanted to join the Philadelphia Chamber Orchestra—Dave Madison as concertmaster, John de Lancie as principal oboe. Also cellist Lorne Munroe and bassoonist Bernard Garfield. Our soloists that first season included cellist Leonard Rose, pianist Leon Fleisher, soprano Adele Addison, and flutist William Kincaid (by now my good friend). Feodor U. Pitcairn, Theo's son, was president, I conducted, and we bestowed the title of honorary musical director on Ormandy with, more or less, his permission. I reserved the Academy of Music for our five concerts, on Sunday evenings.

"Go get a new full dress suit," Ormandy told me.

"Why?"

"It looks terrible from the back."

I never looked at my back. But I studied up and figured out that when you wave your arms around in a jacket it usually pulls the back every which way and raises the shoulders and separates the pleat at the bottom. He said I should go to his tailor, but I bought one off the rack that stayed in place well enough. It's all about the way the sleeves are set in. The armholes have to be close and fairly tight fitting so that, when your arms move, the rest stays put.

Trying to lead the whole orchestra in Brahms No. 4 had dented my confidence. But conducting those thirty-four players in chamber music pieces they had not performed with the big orchestra repaired the damage. They followed wherever I led, and my own interpretation found full expression. It filled me with joy to conduct them for the several years that I did so.

I felt natural and graceful in my movements. So I really have no idea how it happened with Leonard Rose, when he was our soloist.

Although, to be fair, Leonard carried on a lot of business before he was ready to go. He would switch his cello bow to his left hand and shuffle his chair around so he was facing just the right way, and then settle his body repeatedly into the chair, all the while holding his bow up in the air with his *left* hand. Which is very close to the conductor. And I had to raise my arms with a certain forcefulness at the opening of a concerto.

Still, I never intended to knock my right arm into Leonard Rose's bow and send it flying.

There was a little pause as he stared at me, agape, and Dave Madison retrieved the bow. The audience had a nice chuckle. It's a lot funnier if you don't know the bow is worth thousands of dollars.

At the end there was plenty of cheering and clapping, and then an encore. Wonderful reviews in the newspapers.

My success with the chamber orchestra did not fill Ormandy with joy. But since we performed only on five Sunday evenings each year, there could only be five Monday mornings that followed.

"You're in for it today, Anshel," somebody would always say when I arrived at rehearsal after a Philadelphia Chamber Orchestra performance.

Still, I calmly took my seat, hoping Ormandy would be proud of me. That we would have a father-son day.

"What's wrong with your section?" he would demand, a few minutes into the first piece. "Why are they playing like that? Can't you fix it?"

I should never have promised him not to conduct. I couldn't fulfill that promise. And I could easily survive five post-performance rehearsals a year with him storming around.

Orchestra members often had difficulty making ends meet with the thirty-six-week contract that was common at that time. Before my time, in 1930, the members themselves had organized public summer concerts at low cost in Fairmount Park. After a wonderful beginning, the Depression squeezed the life out of the project, and it continued to slide toward bankruptcy during the War years.

Frederic R. Mann was its savior, bringing organization and funding. He created the Robin Hood Dell Orchestra, which was really most of the Philadelphia Orchestra renamed for the summer. We got six weeks' pay for giving free concerts, not to mention a break from Ormandy, so it pleased us all.

During one part of every summer, only one seat in the orchestra was in the sun—mine. Did I deserve that? According to my fellow musicians, I did. "Because you're the concertmaster," they said. Go figure.

Freddie Mann always invited Ormandy to conduct in the Dell, but some animosity between the two men kept them apart like two positive magnets. Ormandy vacationed in the summers and did some guest conducting in Europe.

So Freddie invited others to conduct the concerts, including me. For the summer of 1962—and particularly to irritate Ormandy—Freddie asked me to conduct two concerts at the Dell in the same week, and I agreed.

Then our publicist Allen Sommers piled on. "Why don't you interview the soloists during the summer? You could talk to them at the rehearsal, put it on your TV show. That's sure to bring the crowds."

After that, Freddie would call me every so often to tell me which soloists he was lining up. "We've got Roberta Peters!" he said. "Isaac Stern!" He gave me the honor of conducting some of the world's finest soloists.

I said to Richard Tucker, "I've hardly conducted any opera!"

"Don't worry," he said. "I'll follow you."

Another week we had Richard's brother-in-law Jan Peerce, also a tenor. Jan did not like to wear his Coke-bottle glasses in performance. "When we get on the stage," he said to me, "could you clutch the back of my jacket if I get too close to the edge?"

Also we had Ormandy's nemesis, José Iturbi, who had made a grab for the Philadelphia podium. That didn't matter, since Ormandy wasn't around. But what a difficult interview! His answers consisted of yes, no, and maybe. He seemed irritated. So I had to blab away and fill the minutes.

Once when I was conducting at the Dell, Leonard Rose was to play Tchaikovsky's *Rococo Variations*. It was a beautiful night, the tops of the tall trees revolving in the summer breeze. Lenny was fussing around rearranging himself in his chair as usual. I was ready to start the orchestra since his entrance wasn't right away. I thrust my arms upward to provide the initial downbeat—and bashed into Lenny's bow. He had been holding it raised in his left hand again, as he settled himself. The bow clattered to the floor.

The look he gave me—*No! Really? Again, Anshel?* It was a special look from one musical Russian Jew to another.

The audience loved it. Fortunately the bow didn't break that time either.

Of course the Robin Hood Dell Orchestra had a softball team, and I played shortstop. Our usual opponents were the Dell cleanup crew. Usually they won. The journalists had fun quoting the Cleanups captain saying that his men "clean up the Dell bowl after each concert, which would make it about right for them to clean up the orchestra too."[3]

We lost for two years and then started winning the championship regularly.

My son David was getting the feel of the bat, so I coached his Little League team, the Mudhens. The way I managed it was by getting dressed for the evening's concert at Robin Hood Dell, then driving to the field with David and coaching four innings in my tuxedo. My assistant would have to coach the rest of the game so I could show up, reluctantly, for my concert.

For all the ecstasy of the Philadelphia sound, for the privilege of contributing to it, for all the richness of working under as great a maestro as Ormandy, I still resigned in my mind in each of the seven years I was under contract. Usually it was a Monday night when I wrote the letter—after a performance of my chamber orchestra. I didn't mail them. In 1962, though, I just walked out.

That year the Philadelphia Junior Chamber of Commerce invited me to a luncheon because I had been named among the finalists for their Outstanding Young Man of the Year award. Musicians rarely made their short list, and I was thrilled. But the luncheon was on a day when we had two orchestra rehearsals. I asked Ormandy's

---

3. George R. Stabb, "Dell Men Score Twin Win Over Cleanups, Prokofieff," *Philadelphia Evening Bulletin*, July 10, 1962, 3.

permission to leave the first rehearsal early. He gave it, but stipulated that I must not be late for the second rehearsal.

A taxi drove me from the Academy of Music to the nearby hotel ballroom. I soon found myself seated on a dais with the other finalists, Pete Retzlaff of the Philadelphia Eagles; civil rights leader Leon Sullivan; and Olympic medalist Jack Kelly, brother of Princess Grace.

When the video began I was startled to see myself as a boy playing the violin. A professional voiceover detailed my early admission to Curtis, study with Monteux, and other experiences. And soon the whole room was listening to my playing too—Vivaldi. It dawned on me that I was the winner. The luncheon itself was followed by a reception and congratulations from all the dignitaries. I was watching the time, and it was zooming by.

Treading a fine line between rudeness and gratitude, I excused myself when I could and rushed back to rehearsal—twenty minutes late. I slipped into my seat and quickly joined in.

After a few minutes, Ormandy called for an intermission. He stormed into his dressing room, a clear signal that I had better follow and explain. At least I had physical evidence. Plaque in hand, I knocked on his door and told him about the wonderful thing that had happened to me and that, truly, honored the whole orchestra. With an expression I took for interest, he examined my large plaque with the inscribed brass plate, laurel leaves scrolling up the sides.

Then he said, "Hang it in your toilet."

My chest contracted at the icy tone. I walked next door into my own dressing room. Emotion ruled, clear thought was out of reach. My violin lay on the table, and I packed it up, making myself be as careful as always. I didn't want to see the others. I went down to the street door and left the Academy of Music. I preferred to be unemployed and to be in the company of my wife. Marilyn, I had figured out, must have known all about the award in advance and helped with assembling the video.

"What are you doing home at 3:00?" were her welcoming words.

When our phone rang, she was quick to answer it and to accept, enthusiastically, Gretel Ormandy's invitation to have dinner at their house that evening. It took her much longer to persuade me to cooperate.

"Welcome!" Gretel said when we arrived. "Anshel, why don't you go and see Gene in his study." She was the cordial half of the pair.

"What's the matter with you?" he said in lieu of a greeting. "Don't you have a sense of humor?"

Unsure how rude statements delivered in a tone of rage could be seen as comic, I nodded vaguely. Then, strange as it was, he invited me to follow him into his bathroom.

"See?" A framed honorary doctorate hung on the wall above a towel rack. "This is where I put it."

To me, the display had the look of a temporary relocation.

Some time later, Ormandy told me he had recommended me for that award. He knew exactly why I was late for rehearsal.

I wanted to quit that day, but I also didn't want to quit. My violin and my John Dodd bow, or occasionally the François Tourte one, were giving back to me everything I put into them. Sometimes it was a problem, not being able to hold back. It's usual for musicians to conserve their energy, and also their musical passion, for performances. We use rehearsals to get the details down pat so that when we've got an audience we can go for broke. Sometimes, though, the music seduced me in rehearsal. Our assistant principal cellist Elsa Hilger had this problem as often as I did. I remember rehearsing the Ormandy transcription of Bach's *Toccata and Fugue*, both of us playing like the world was ending, utterly intoxicated with Bach, and the other string players raising their eyebrows as if to say, "What—you think we're in Carnegie Hall?"

Psoriasis ran in my family, and I got it bad on my fingers. I sometimes played notes on alternate strings to spare the most compromised fingertip. Dave Madison used to say, "Take it easy!" and hand me a tissue to wipe the blood off my fingerboard. When the music took over, I forgot all about the psoriasis.

Ormandy generously continued to give me solo opportunities, and I usually gave him what he wanted, which was creativity within limits. The occasional transgression against expectations did occur, and at least one of them I can blame on Nathan Milstein.

Whenever Nathan came to solo with us, he could be found before the performance flitting around backstage, never letting go of his violin for a second, and constantly noodling around on it.

One time he asked me what I would be playing next time I soloed. "Brahms." I said.

"What cadenza do you play?" he asked

This refers to the section in the concerto that allows the soloist to show off technical prowess as if inspired by a muse. There was room for creativity, but Brahms's close collaborator Joseph Joachim had written the cadenza especially for him, and it was used by every violinist I'd heard. So I said, "The usual."

"Why don't you spice it up? You know, do your own thing."

"You mean write my own?"

"Sure. Or at least put something fun in the middle. Make it yours!"

This was a delicious idea.

"But don't let anyone hear it," Nathan said. "At the rehearsal, just wave Ormandy forward—he won't expect you to make the orchestra wait through your cadenza. You can give them the last couple of notes so they know when to come back in."

When the concert came, and the cadenza arrived, Ormandy hushed the orchestra, and I started with Joachim's cadenza. But soon I set off into my own musical thoughts. I had planned it well, weaving in themes from the first part of the concerto, and adding what fireworks seemed good to me. I enlarged the cadenza by about a minute and a half.

Ormandy, as he heard the unfamiliar notes, gave me a look of astonishment. The orchestra, too, sat up and listened. But Ormandy shrugged and took it in stride, and of course I returned for the last notes to Joachim's cadenza so Ormandy would know how to bring the orchestra back in.

"What the hell were you doing in there?" he asked me afterwards. "Why didn't you play Joachim?"

"Nathan Milstein said I should write my own cadenza."

He twitched as if he had a gnat in his ear. "I should have known it was him."

On November 22, 1963, we were getting ready for one of the Friday ladies' concerts. Leonard Rose was our soloist, a pleasure to me both because of his exquisite playing and our friendship. I checked with him to make sure he was ready to start and then looked for Ormandy. He was busy with a group of the Main Line ladies, which was usual for a Friday. The orchestra had taken their seats on stage.

Just as I was about to go out to tune the orchestra, a stage hand came up to me. "Please, Mr. Brusilow, could you wait just a minute."

I waited five or six minutes. Ormandy was ready. I could see through the curtain that the orchestra was getting antsy, so I went out and tuned and took my seat. Another five minutes passed.

There was some quiet talking in the audience, but then this was a Friday concert and therefore more social. Finally I went backstage again. Immediately a member of the Women's Committee came to me and took my hand. She was upset about something.

"The President has been shot. The news is saying he's dead."

I went out again and told the players and asked them to stay seated until an announcement was made. We could see that word was spreading through the audience. No one that I saw heard of President Kennedy's death with dry eyes.

I don't remember who announced it to the hall. Of course, we canceled the concert. I went to find Ormandy, and Lenny Rose was in his office too. We sat together and gathered what news we could. Lenny had played at the White House just a week earlier. I took him home with me. He called his wife Minnie—everyone had to speak to their loved ones on that day. Marilyn made dinner, and we watched the sad news on TV together.

Number one on Ormandy's list of anxieties was having someone wrest the Philadelphia Orchestra away from him. It was *his*, damn it! And the fear was not ungrounded. The orchestra was not Alexander Hilsberg's. Not José Iturbi's.

Once I was driving him from Ohio to Michigan. We were approaching the Detroit Hilton.

"They all know me here," he said. "It's always like coming home. That bellman?" he indicated a guy by the front door. "I've known him for decades!" He stepped out of the car with a big smile.

Sure enough, the bellman rushed over. "Mr. Iturbi! It's so good to see you again."

"Are you crazy?" Ormandy looked at me for some kind of confirmation of the man's lunacy, but—oh, this was bad timing—I started to laugh.

"I'm Ormandy!" He stalked into the hotel while I dealt with the bags and parking. I joined him at the desk, though I was not fully in control of myself.

His mood was in freefall. "What an idiot! How can he think that?"

We went to our rooms. I stopped by his at the appointed time to go to lunch.

"Come in, Anshel!" He was cheerful again. "You'll never guess!" he said, as though I'd asked some question. "But I can tell you now. General Motors is giving me a Pontiac! Oh—" he retreated to the phone by his bed. "I'd better call downstairs so they know where to find me."

He called the front desk. "This is Mr. Ormandy and I—"

Some premonition led me to go look out the window, turning my back to him.

"ORMANDY!" He stopped again and then, most amazingly, spelled his name. He actually said, "O-R-M-A-N-D-Y."

Over at the window, I focused on the cars stuck in traffic way below, anything to keep from laughing out loud.

"I'll never stay at this hotel again! Ever!"

The Pontiac did arrive, and I drove it to Ann Arbor, where the University of Michigan's May Festival would conclude our season, as usual.

On the outskirts of town he saw a restaurant he knew.

"I like that place," he said. "No, it'll be crowded. People will know me, and I'm too tired for all that autographing."

"You sure you don't want to stop, Boss?"

"Oh . . . all right. I'll just put up with it."

I pulled in and parked the car.

The hostess looked very busy, but Ormandy approached her and said, "We don't have a reservation but I'm—"

"Right this way, sir."

She led us on a weaving path through table after table crowded with patrons who didn't spare a glance for the great conductor. Our food came in reasonable time, and I found it excellent.

"This used to be a great restaurant," he said on the way out, "but it seems to have gone downhill."

One time the great cellist Mstislav Rostropovich was scheduled to do a pension fund concert with the Washington Symphony Orchestra (now the National Symphony Orchestra). Everyone knew him to be persnickety, and in this case he refused to play under WSO's conductor, Howard Mitchell. Ormandy was invited to guest conduct. He didn't want to put up with Rostropovich, so he said he was busy. He recommended me to conduct, and I was supremely available. In fact, I was excited beyond belief! Rostropovich had already chosen two Russian pieces, Tchaikovsky's *Rococo Variations* and the Shostakovich Cello Concerto No. 1. So I programmed *Francesca da Rimini* and the overture to *Colas Breugnon*, too, for an all-Russian concert.

While we were getting dressed, I said to Marilyn, "I'm going to do something I've never done before."

She set her hairbrush down and stared at me.

"I know what I'm doing. It'll be fine."

"Anshel, don't."

"What? You don't even know what I'm thinking!"

"I don't need to."

A limousine took us to the impressive Constitution Hall with its fair-to-lousy acoustics. Rostropovich was in the dressing room next to mine, but he was practicing and I didn't knock on the door.

After the opening piece, when I left the stage, I told the stagehand to go out and remove my desk. Rostropovich was next, with *Rococo Variations*.

Yes, I wanted my desk removed because I planned to conduct it from memory. Not only did I know the score backwards and forwards, I had a recording of Rostropovich playing it and I had listened to it *ad nauseam*, from Marilyn's perspective anyway. By now I knew every ritard, every accelerando, every nuance, and really did not need the score.

At last, Rostropovich came out of his dressing room and passed me backstage without a glance. This was not surprising, given his reputation for being unsociable. I followed, according to protocol. While the orchestra was tuning, he looked over and noticed that I had no desk.

"Where is the score?" he said.

"It'll be just fine," I said.

"NO! NO!" he said.

I knew I was right. "Don't worry!" I said. I gave the downbeat, and away we went.

His playing was perfection, the accompaniment was everything I had hoped, and the audience gave us wild applause. Rostropovich seemed pleased.

The next orchestral piece also went very well, and then came the Shostakovich Cello Concerto, again with Rostropovich. In the third movement, the tympanist has an important part. But he missed his first entrance. Rostropovich looked at me and kept playing, as I kept conducting, while frantically trying to cue the tympanist back in. At the next missed tympani entrance, Rostropovich and I both said, "BOOM." The audience loved this, and we kept booming vocally as the tympanist kept missing his cues.

Afterwards, the members of the orchestra gave plaques and kind letters to Rostropovich and me. Then he disappeared, and Marilyn and I went back to the Hay-Adams Hotel.

It was not quite over. In the elevator, the door opened and who should enter but Slava Rostropovich, speaking rapid Russian with a friend. An elevator is a small space, and when he did not say hello, I knew it was a choice, not an oversight. I gathered that I had offended him.

Back in Philadelphia, Ormandy asked me how it had gone.

"The concert was terrific," I said. Then I told him how unfriendly Rostropovich had been.

He asked more specifically about my accompaniment of Rostropovich, and I mentioned that I'd done the *Rococo Variations* from memory.

"You did what?"

I repeated it.

"Anshel, Anshel, sit down." He was at his most fatherly. "It's not about how well *you* know the work. The score is there for the soloist. Rostropovich could have a memory lapse and just having the music there offers him security. You took that away."

Sometimes I really needed his parenting.

Conducting is hot work, and for years Ormandy complained about the poor air-conditioning in the Academy of Music. Finally he got his way. A special unit was installed under the floor, and his podium was vented so the cold air would blow right up at him. He loved it.

When there was a soloist, often the podium had to be moved. Then Eddie, our backstage regular, turned off the AC unit and covered the hole in the floor.

Once our soloist was Eugene Istomin. His piano had been moved onto the stage, and Ormandy's podium was moved to one side as needed. The orchestra entered, and I followed and tuned them and sat down in my seat, next to the piano. Then Istomin entered, with Ormandy following.

I realized that I was hearing an air noise. It was the AC coming out of the hole in the floor, which now happened to be under the pedals of the piano. Istomin sat down at the piano and started fooling around with his chair. All of a sudden his face registered something.

"It's freezing in here!" he said.

Ormandy was just about to start the orchestra, and Istomin's right pant leg was flapping in the arctic breeze. I caught Ormandy's eye and pointed at the hole in the floor.

He mistook my downward pointing for something else and quickly turned aside to check his fly. Finding no problem there, he looked back at me with irritation.

"It's the AC," I whispered.

He motioned me to go fix it, and I exited the stage just as the audience expected us to begin (I always enjoyed opportunities to mystify the audience). Backstage, Eddie quickly fixed the AC, and things then proceeded as normal.

Leon and Dora Brusilow before leaving Russia, c. 1920. *Author's collection.*

Leon and Dora Brusilow, c. 1930. My mother wears a fur neckpiece sewed by my father.
Author's collection.

Edwin A. Fleisher, William Happich, and an unidentified musician. *Courtesy of Free Library of Philadelphia, Fleisher Orchestral Music Collection.*

In the Russian outfit my mother sewed for my first performance and which, thanks to a shove from the pianist, the audience got to see. *Author's collection.*

Gregor Piatigorsky, my early rescuer; Alexander Hilsberg, my conductor in New Orleans, 1954–55; and Efrem Zimbalist, Sr., my teacher at Curtis. *Courtesy of Curtis Institute of Music Archives.*

Just playing, not long after I gave up football. *Author's collection.*

Jani Szanto, my beloved teacher at the Philadelphia Musical Academy. *Courtesy of University of the Arts Libraries & Archives.*

With my brother Nathan Brusilow. Behind us, our parents' fur store is shaded by the awning. *Photographer Leon Brusilow. Author's collection.*

Pierre and Doris Monteux at *L'École Monteux*, now called the Pierre Monteux School, Hancock, Maine, 1940s. *Author's collection.*

Relaxing outside, at the Monteux School, c. 1944. *Author's collection.*

Playing violin in class at the Monteux School, Sylvio Lacharité conducting, in the room we used both for classes and performances. *Author's collection.*

The two cabins at the Monteux School. Mine is on the left. *Author's collection.*

With Pierre Monteux at the school. *Author's collection.*

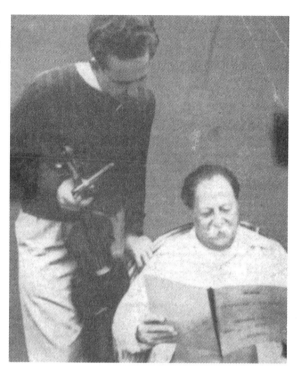

Musicians at the Monteux School, c. 1949. Seated in front: Richard Yardmian, second from left; Alvin Mills, left of the young woman. Standing: Joseph Barone, center in white shirt and dark tie; Harold Glick, third from right; me, far right. *Author's collection.*

With Marilyn, just married, December 23, 1951, San Francisco. *Author's collection.*

Bas relief above main door of Severance Hall, Cleveland.

With George Szell and the Cleveland Orchestra, Concertmaster Josef Gingold next to me, in Severance Hall, 1957–58. *Photograph by Geoffrey Landesmann, Courtesy of The Cleveland Orchestra Archives.*

Theodore Pitcairn, my generous benefactor. *Photographer George Salverian.*

With George Szell as he throws a kiss to the audience at the Philharmonic Hall in Warsaw, Poland, June 1957. Josef Gingold is partly visible on the left. *Photographer Dan Weiner. Courtesy of The Cleveland Orchestra Archives.*

Eugene Ormandy rehearsing the Philadelphia Orchestra at Town Hall in Philadelphia. David Madison sharing my stand, Morris Shulik and Veda Reynolds (wearing glasses) behind us in the second stand. David Arben, fifth stand inside, in a light-colored shirt. *Photographer Adrian Siegel. Courtesy of the Philadelphia Orchestra.*

In a recording studio, fall 1959. Left to right: assistant principal cello Elsa Hilger, principal clarinet Tony Gigliotti, producer Howard Scott, Eugene Ormandy (behind Scott's hand), myself, composer Dmitri Shostakovich, composer Tikhon Khrennikov. *Photographer Adrian Siegel. Courtesy of the Philadelphia Orchestra.*

With Gretel and Eugene Ormandy, 1962. Photographer Louis Luv. *Courtesy of Eugene Ormandy Archive, University of Pennsylvania Libraries.*

With Leopold Stokowski in 1960, backstage at the Academy of Music. Nice image of my Guarnerius del Gesù. *Photographer Adrian Siegel. Courtesy of the Philadelphia Orchestra.*

Card from Ormandy with his gift to us, Christmas 1960. *Author's collection.*

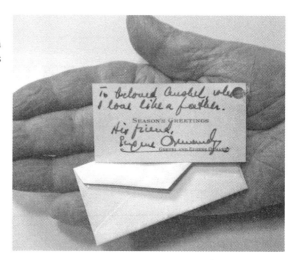

Real musicians can doze even during a rehearsal with Igor Stravinsky, no matter how many pairs of glasses he wears. Sharing my stand, Dave Madison; behind us, second stand, Morris Shulik and Veda Reynolds. Academy of Music, January 1964. *Photographer Adrian Siegel. Courtesy of Philadelphia Orchestra.*

In my dressing room with David Oistrakh as he plays my violin, Academy of Music, 1962–63. *Photographer Adrian Siegel. Courtesy of Philadelphia Orchestra.*

With Rudolf Serkin at Academy of Music, 1963–1965. *Photographer Adrian Siegel. Courtesy of Philadelphia Orchestra.*

Goofing around at a rehearsal of Debussy's *Prelude to the Afternoon of a Faun* (hence the two harps in the foreground) at the Academy of Music, April 1960. Behind me, Morris Shulik; center Eugene Ormandy. *Photographer Adrian Siegel. Courtesy of Philadelphia Orchestra.*

Philadelphia Orchestra rehearsing at the Academy of Music, 1963–66. Dave Madison sharing first stand with me; second stand, Morris Shulik and Veda Reynolds; third stand, William de Pasquale outside; David Arben visible on fifth stand inside. *Photographer Adrian Siegel. Courtesy of Philadelphia Orchestra.*

Rehearsing the Chamber Symphony of Philadelphia.

Rehearsing Chamber Symphony of Philadelphia with Renatta Scotto at the Academy of Music, 1966. *Photographer George Salverian. Author's collection.*

With SONY producer Howard Scott, toasting our recording agreement for the Chamber Symphony of Philadelphia. *Author's collection.*

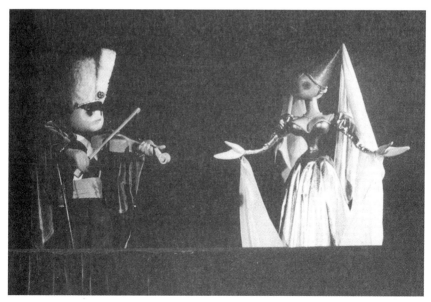

Two of the puppets Bil Baird created for the Chamber Symphony of Philadelphia's performance of Stravinsky's *L'histoire du soldat* in 1967. Left, the soldier with his violin; right, his girlfriend, from Act one, Scene one. *Photographer George Salverian. Author's collection.*

Chamber Symphony of Philadelphia, Hill Auditorium in Ann Arbor, Michigan, September 1966. *Photographer George Salverian. Author's collection.* First Violins from outside: first stand, Concertmaster Stuart Canin and William Steck; second stand, Robert Witte and Alcestis Perry; third stand, Helen Janov and Kent Rose; fourth stand, Thomas Michalak. Second Violins: first stand, Principal Rick Posner and Monica Witte; second stand, Marion Hersh and Lee Snyder; third stand, Olga Myerovich and Alicja Buczynska. Front row from left: Flutes, George Ervin Monroe and Israel Borouchoff; Oboes, James Caldwell and David Seeley. Middle row: Clarinets, Ronald Reuben and Principal Nathan Brusilow; Bassoons, Ryohei Nakagawa and Christopher Weait. Back row: Horns, two extras for tour, then Ward Fearn and Principal James London; Trumpets, Principal Louis Opalesky and Joseph K. Koplin. Timpani, Jack Moore. Violas from outside: first stand, Principal Carlton Cooley and Ralph Hersh; second stand, Murray Labman and Arthur Lewis. Cellos: first stand, Principal Willem Stokking and Catharina Meints; second stand, Samuel Belenko and Robert Perry. Basses, Principal Sam Hollingsworth and Henry G. Scott.

Facing the press with Ralph Rogers of the Dallas Symphony Association after not playing at the State Fair in Dallas, October 1970. *Photographer Gary Barnett/The Dallas Morning News.*

Rehearsing with the Dallas Symphony Orchestra in McFarlin Hall. *Courtesy of the Dallas Symphony Orchestra.*

With Mel Torme, perusing the score of *Irmelin* by Delius in preparation for performing with Dallas Symphony Orchestra. *Photographer Joe Gordon. Author's collection.*

Dallas Symphony Orchestra performing on its South American tour, spring 1973. Behind me: Concertmaster Philip Ruder; behind him, William Hybel; behind him, Peggy Miller. Continuing toward the right: at baton tip, Gloria Stroud; Principal Second Violin, Samuel Schwartz (glasses); timpanist Kalman Cherry (standing); flutist Harvey Boatright; violist Dorothea Kelley (blonde); Principal violist Ralph Hersh (glasses); harpist Julia Louise Herrmann. *Author's collection.*

With Colombian dignitaries left of me, and on my right my wife Marilyn and Hope Somoza, in Medellin, Colombia, 1973. *Author's collection.*

From Efrem Zimbalist, Sr., after my visit with him in Reno. "To my dear friend Anshel Brusilow with affection and admiration, Efrem Zimbalist, 1973." *Author's collection.*

Rehearsing University of North Texas Orchestra, cellist Mitch Maxwell, violinist Gary Walker in foreground. *Photographer George Salverian. Author's collection.*

New poster of my 1743 violin, now named the Brusilow Guarneri "del Gesu." *Reproduced with permission of The Strad: www.thestrad.com*

Chapter 6

THE BOW AND THE BATON

WHEN ORMANDY ENTERTAINED VIPS in his dressing room, he often invited me to join them. Sometimes reporters were around and pictures were snapped. When we were photographed standing next to each other, I used to lean down so our faces were close together and the height difference was minimized. Sometimes he whispered, "Thanks." I was only five inches taller, but to him every inch seemed to be a foot.

A number of times in these situations, he introduced me as his successor. Eventually, someone told someone who told a reporter. Specifically, someone told *The Evening Bulletin*'s columnist Frank Brookhouser. In his "Man on the Town" column, Brookhouser stated that rumors were abroad that I would succeed Ormandy when he retires.

Clueless, I arrived at rehearsal the next morning.

"He wants to see you," my colleagues said.

I went to his office.

"Shut the door."

I did.

He was pacing. "When did you talk to Frank Brookhouser?"

"Never. I don't even know him."

"Why did you tell him you were my successor? What an idea!"

"I've never said that," I said.

"As if he would have heard it somewhere else!"

"Well, he could have heard it from you. Or a concert guest you talked to," I suggested. It was another of those moments when a helping of tact would have served me well.

"I've *never* said that!" he said.

I shrugged my shoulders and went on my cheerless way.

On one occasion we were rehearsing Schumann's Piano Concerto with Rudolf Serkin at the piano. In the third movement, Ormandy summoned me. I laid my violin on the chair and hurried up to the podium.

"I want to go listen," he said. "You conduct. The score is open to where we are." He walked off.

I had studied the score and we had performed the concerto in Cleveland, so I knew it well enough to know that we were approaching a passage that is extremely difficult both to play and to conduct. I looked down at the score: it was open to a random place, nowhere near where we were. The musicians were now beginning the difficult passage. Obviously Ormandy was hoping we would have to stop.

From the piano, Rudi Serkin smiled at me and winked. I did what I had seen Szell do—ceased actual conducting and simply motioned for the orchestra to play softly. It worked perfectly. Ormandy came quickly back to the stage and thanked me. Rudi was all smiles.

Interestingly, when we came around to that passage the second time that morning, Ormandy did the same thing, just let the orchestra play its way through on its own.

Such challenging setups for failure punctuated our normally warm relationship.

And yet, I could never be sure if this or that instance was intentional.

No, the kind Dr. Jekyll watched out for my interests and those of my family by giving me special recording opportunities. The orchestra had recording sessions on Sunday afternoons. After the symphony or whatever major piece we were recording was finished, Ormandy would dismiss some members. With just those necessary for Vivaldi, we would record one of his violin concertos in the Four Seasons. Eventually I had done them all. It was usual for the conductor to get royalties of 4 percent, and for a visiting soloist to get 2 percent or 4 percent, but concertmasters didn't expect royalties because they were just doing their jobs. Nevertheless Ormandy did arrange for royalties to come to me for the Vivaldi concertos. Those checks helped our family considerably over the years. The royalties still come, though the pathways have meandered, today passing through Amazon.com, iTunes, and Napster.

An organization like the Philadelphia Orchestra must make itself accessible to everyone, not just the lucky folks who can come to the Academy of Music or Carnegie Hall. Sometimes we played in places like a high school in Englewood, New Jersey.

I pulled up in front of the Bellevue-Stratford where the Ormandys lived. Ormandy was waiting for me at the curb. He tossed his navy cashmere overcoat and the brown Homburg hat that didn't match into the back seat of the car, and we were off.

Gretel was not with us. She rarely attended any of the "run outs," as we called the concerts in easy driving distance, unless they were at Carnegie Hall.

I stopped for gasoline.

"Why do you always stop for gas after I'm in the car?" he asked.

"I'm always hoping you'll offer to pay for it."

"But they give you travel allowance to pay for the trip, don't they?"

"Don't I get something for driving?"

He just shook his head. Then he said, "You do know the way?"

"Sure." I had a general idea. Anyway it was only 5:30 and the concert was at 8:00.

At 7:00, he ordered me to ask for directions at a gas station.

"Just twenty miles farther up the road," they said. The highway we were on became deserted. Not another car in sight.

"Speed up," Ormandy said.

I spotted lights ahead. "There it is."

"Thank goodness!"

We found ourselves in a store parking lot.

"What's this?"

"It's Bloomberg's Furniture Store."

"I never wanted to play in Englewood in the first place," he said. "No one even knows where it is! Turn around." He was getting antsy, as was I.

Next we saw a police car going about ninety with lights flashing.

Ormandy shouted "Catch them! They can guide us!"

"I think I would need an airplane."

"Follow them—they'll take us to the concert!"

They disappeared into the blue yonder. It was 7:30, and I noticed that we were on a small road leading into a wide opening. It was the entrance to the George Washington Bridge into New York City.

"I am NOT going into New York," Ormandy stated. "Not one of my friends is there, nor my family. Even my brother Martin has gone to Japan with the Philharmonic. Get out and tell the man in the booth that you have Eugene Ormandy in the car and that we MUST be allowed to turn around."

I actually did this, and the man was kind enough to allow the U-turn. "It's no more than six or seven miles up the road," he promised.

But Ormandy was dejected. "I don't care anymore. I don't even want to get there. Bill Smith can conduct."

When it was nearly 8:00, we really were near the high school and were now caught up in the concert traffic.

We arrived. But an officer waved us away.

"Get out of the car and tell him who I am!"

I did this. The officer told me to follow the police car, and they would help us park. The squad car began flashing its lights, and I followed it, of course *away* from the high school.

"My God! Where is he taking us?"

We parked in a neighborhood some distance away and the policeman drove us to the back entrance of the auditorium, which we reached at 8:00.

It was locked.

Ormandy swung wildly between depression and rage, and I was afraid he would explode. As usual, this struck me as funny.

"Wait here," I said. On my way around to the front, I passed an open window. It was frosted so I thought it was the men's room. I could hear some players' voices.

"Hey! Open the back door for us! I'm with Ormandy and we're locked out."

Henry Schmidt, the personnel manager, let us in.

"I'll be ready in fifteen minutes," Ormandy said.

"Oh, never mind the hurry," Henry said. "We can't start. The other bus of players is lost somewhere in New Jersey."

One morning the phone rang at home, and it was the president of the orchestra board, C. Wanton Balis. He asked me to come to his office.

Mr. Balis was a slim man of about six feet, with just a fringe of hair. His dress was formal, as befitted a respected member of the Main Line society set. No doubt he was trained in manners, but this occasion seemed not to call for them. He did not offer me his hand. Nor did he invite me to sit in one of the chairs in his handsome office. I stood.

"There's a problem, Mr. Brusilow," he said, leaning back in his chair and looking at me across his large desk. "And you probably know what it is." Of course, he referred to the Philadelphia Chamber Orchestra.

"I don't actually see it as a problem," I said.

"You're overstepping your bounds. Your chamber orchestra performs repertoire that belongs to the Philadelphia Orchestra."

"We program early Mozart—just strings, two oboes, and two horns. Our early Beethoven and early Schubert are the same. The big orchestra never does any of that."

"You just did the Boccherini Symphony."

"I'm not aware of the big orchestra ever playing that. Anyway it's a chamber symphony."

"Symphony is symphony. That's all the public takes in."

I thought the public deserved more credit, not to mention more variety of music.

"Also," he said, "you make them play on Sunday—the day of rest."

I knew better than to foreground Jewish and Christian differences. "I don't *make* anyone play. It's up to each player."

"You took them out of the city and used the name of the Philadelphia Orchestra."

We had just returned from New York, it was true. "I say only that they are *members of* the big orchestra."

Now I brought out my guns. "Every successful concert we give"—and this was the real problem, the success—"enhances the image of the big orchestra. Especially by playing repertoire the Philadelphia Orchestra wouldn't be playing."

"But you are not the one who trained them to be what they are."

There were things I could have said to him, about the players needing extra income since the season ran only thirty-six weeks, about letting young conductors have a chance, but I didn't, for once. The conversation fizzled perfectly, since C. Wanton Balis did not have a way of forcing my hand. It wasn't as if there were some rule I was breaking.

The players always needed to make ends meet. In the summer, the Robin Hood Dell Orchestra brought them a little extra income, but not enough. The orchestra board did want to extend the season, and plans were underway to open a new venue for the orchestra to play part of the summer in Saratoga Springs, New York.

One thing Ormandy hated above all else was losing his best play-ers to another orchestra. In 1963, our principal cellist Lorne Munroe turned in his resignation so he could join the New York Philharmonic.

"Why on earth would he want to go play up there with that group when he can be in the Philadelphia Orchestra?"

"Can't imagine, Boss."

"Find me someone, Anshel."

"Listen to Bill Stokking in the cellos."

"Who?"

Well, there were a lot of us in his orchestra; I suppose he forgot some of us. "William Stokking—that guy in the back. Wavy brown hair."

The next day Bill Stokking played for Ormandy and me. Ormandy turned to me, stunned. "He reminds me of Emanuel Feuermann!" He referred to the cellist who had died twenty years earlier and ascended to reign over cello heaven.

I told Bill he'd done well.

A few days later Ormandy was beaming. "You'll never guess who I got!"

I couldn't.

"Sammy Mayes! Sucked him right out of Boston."

One thing Ormandy loved above all else was fleecing another orchestra of its best players. Sammy Mayes was a marvelous cellist. In my head I still revisit playing the gorgeous second movement of Tchaikovsky's Piano Concerto No. 2 with Sammy Mayes and with Gary Graffman at the piano. It's nicknamed the "triple concerto" because Tchaikovsky does virtually transform it into a concerto for piano, cello, and violin in the second movement. Ten minutes of musical unity and pleasure can last the rest of one's life.

Bill Stokking lost out there. However, he was to have his day yet.

For a benefit concert, Harpo Marx came to Philadelphia to give a harp solo—he was truly gifted—and to conduct another piece. At rehearsal he came out in costume and got us all laughing with his bicycle horn shtick.

On the night of the concert, I glanced into his dressing room and saw a strange, little man sitting at the mirror and wondered where Harpo could have gone. Only when he turned around did I recognize him without his wig and outfit.

"Can I do anything for you?" I asked him.

"I'm scared to death!" he blurted out. "I'm not a conductor!"

At this point I remembered my experience when Ormandy handed off the Schumann piano concerto to me at the hard part, with Rudi Serkin chuckling at the piano.

"Harpo, just do one thing. Give us a downbeat, and then step back and have a good time. We'll be with you."

With a good orchestra, it works out okay.

Danny Kaye made occasional visits too. He was beloved by all of us for his ability to mimic Ormandy's walk. Ormandy was generous about inviting lots of us into his dressing room to enjoy someone like that. I remember a moment when Ormandy excused himself to go to the restroom. When he came back to the room, the front of his trousers was all wet.

Danny seized the moment. "Oh my God—look! The conductor of the Philadelphia Orchestra just pissed all over himself!"

"No, no, no, it was the spigot—it was too fast and splashed out!"

The room exploded in laughter.

Danny conducted us beautifully all by ear. He didn't read music and had learned it by listening.

Jack Benny came too. He was in a different category, in Ormandy's mind. Jack was extraordinarily generous in offering his draw to support many orchestras. When his name came up for a benefit we were planning, Ormandy drew a line.

"I don't conduct for comedians."

I would be quicker to criticize this if I could forget the day I refused to play lunch music for the likes of Efrem Zimbalist and Madame Lea Luboshutz at Curtis.

The plan would have met its kibosh if Isaac Stern hadn't convinced Ormandy to go ahead. Isaac was slated to play with Jack and he had no problem with it at all. Ormandy reluctantly agreed.

Jack Benny also came for a summer concert in 1962 at the Robin Hood Dell. He and I were playing the Bach Concerto for Two Violins together. I loved being his straight man. Hollywood composer and conductor Johnny Green led the concert, and we had a capacity crowd.

Backstage, Jack and I were running our fingers up and down our fingerboards while Johnny conducted the opening.

"I could walk out there right now and do an hour monologue and not even think about it," Jack said. "But when I walk out with the violin in my hand, I'm shaking."

I tried to imagine the torture of doing an hour of standup comedy. He was a brave man.

Not all of our guest musicians were famous. Young composers were invited to hear us play their work. Ormandy often allowed the composer to sit near the podium and even to request changes.

"Just reach over and tug my pant leg if you want us to change something," he would say.

One young man tugged Ormandy's pants just six bars in. "That A was flat back in the horns," he said.

Ormandy had us take the phrase again.

About twelve bars later came another tug. "The trombones are too loud." Next the woodwinds were too soft. We watched Ormandy's temper begin to fray. It wouldn't be long now . . . here it came.

The words seemed to come through clenched teeth: "The best composer is a dead one!"

The young man sat as if his arms were encased in concrete. He had no more changes to request.

Tickets for our concerts in Baltimore every season were scarce. Families actually willed them down. The Christmas concert topped them all, even though Ormandy refused to perform any Christmas carols. We played Viennese waltzes and other light fare.

At the end, he spoke to the audience and wished them a happy holiday season.

Once, from the back, came a voice terse with sarcasm: "Why don't you play 'Jingle Bells?'"

Players and audience alike were stunned. For many seconds, Ormandy appeared frozen. Then he said stiffly, "Thank you, and goodnight."

"Can you believe such arrogance?" he said to me backstage. "Who does he think he is? He will *never* hear us play again."

"How are you going to find out who said it?"

He shot me a very small smile. "I'll find him."

That would be impossible, it seemed to me.

Little did I know. Ormandy found out who it was and had the management confiscate his season tickets. They were not restored until the man drove to Philadelphia and personally apologized to Ormandy.

The world of classical music has more than its share of Jews, and naturally we often felt a camaraderie with each other. With a Russian Jew, especially one trapped behind the Iron Curtain, I had a double camaraderie. Violinist David Oistrakh was one of these. The first time he came to solo with us in Philadelphia, he came into my dressing room.

"I see violin?"

I handed him the Guarnerius del Gesù. He immediately started playing something on it and continued for several minutes. Then he lowered it and looked at me.

"Vont to sell?"

I confess I was horrified.

"If ven vont, I buy!"

The thought of my violin vanishing into the Soviet Union I couldn't bear. I liked David very much, however; we were to become as close as friends can be, across that political barrier.

Another time, David Oistrakh soloed with us at Carnegie Hall, and I offered him a ride back to Philadelphia. I was driving Ormandy, too. I brought my car around to the stage door, and Ormandy got in front, as always, and David got in back.

"Oh, Cad-ee-lak," he said. "Consairt-master nice job? Mmm." He knew very little English.

I grinned at him. "Yes."

Ormandy started to talk to David in German.

I suppose I didn't like being left out. During a lull in their conversation I said something to David in Yiddish.

"What did you say!" Ormandy barked. "He's not going to be able to understand that bastard German."

I asked David in Yiddish if he understood me.

"*Yah, vou den. Ich farshtay yayder vort,*" he answered. Meaning, "Of course. I understand every word."

It was rather quiet for the rest of the ride.

I can't speak to why Ormandy kept his Jewishness in low profile. I heard that he explained it this way: his French grandmother had translated her surname Goldberg, meaning "gold mountain," to the French *or mont,* which morphed to Ormandy. He substituted that for his original surname, Blau. Others say that his arrival in the United States as a young man on the S.S. *Normandie* influenced his choice, Ormandy rhyming with the ship's name. [1]

In the spring of 1964, I was looking ahead to summer, when I would conduct at the Robin Hood Dell. During the regular season, I was conducting the Philadelphia Chamber Orchestra, but that was only thirty-some players. Thinking about working with most of the Philadelphia Orchestra in the Dell, an ambition took hold of me.

---

1. With Gary Graffman's permission, I will share the ditty that he and Leonard Bernstein sang just before they performed the Dies Irae variation of Rachmaninoff's *Rhapsody on a Theme of Paganini.* When they were about to walk on stage, Lenny sang to Gary, following the Dies Irae: "Gary Graffman is a Jew." Gary sang back, "Leonard Bernstein is one, too." Together they finished, "Ormandy won't allow his real name is Blau!"

I called Freddie Mann. "I want to do *The Rite of Spring* this summer."

"Stravinsky? Are you crazy? It takes an enormous orchestra!"

"I can get them ready in one rehearsal. We just played it in March with Georg Solti, and the players know it. You'd have to hire the extra musicians, but I promise no rehearsal overtime."

"I don't know. You'd need something really easy to pair with it."

"Good idea! We'll start with Beethoven's Fifth. Most of the players can do it in their sleep."

"Yes," he said. "That would work. And I'll scrape up some money for the extra players."

Imagine my excitement when it was arranged that at our usual May Festival in Ann Arbor, Igor Stravinsky would be there. He was to conduct a piece of his own music with us. We had a two-hour rehearsal with him, with a break in the middle.

That's when I saw my chance.

"Maître," I said to him, "would you sign my score of *The Rite of Spring?*"

"Yes, of course, but where do we sit?"

I dragged two orchestra chairs to a quiet backstage area near the open delivery doors. It was a beautiful spring day with a breeze. No one was around.

"Print your name so I know how to write it."

I did, and he autographed my score.

"Why do you carry this?" he asked.

"I'll be conducting it in July with the orchestra."

He searched my face. "Don't do it the way the others do. They rewrite it to make it easier to conduct. The rhythms are important, and I don't like them changed. If the Philadelphia Orchestra can't play it the way I wrote it, they shouldn't do it at all." Then he said, "All conductors, they are guilty of fraud."

"What do you mean?"

"I write my music the way it is. I have a bar with four beats, with three beats, with eight beats. But conductors ignore this."

"Maître," I said, "I promise not to change a single thing. I'm using this score, just as you wrote it. You know, I studied many years with Monteux."

"Monteux! There was the man. He could do my music!"

I couldn't resist: "Even at the opening, with all the brouhaha?"

"Monteux looked at me." Stravinsky said, looking to the side as if it were 1913 and Monteux stood just there. "I just motioned him don't stop. But Nijinsky? He's crazy! All the noise came from the audience and he changed everything, the dancing, the choreography—he just did whatever he wanted! The music was okay, though."

He looked around at where we were sitting, reorienting himself in the present. That calmed him. "Do it like Monteux," he said, and patted me on the cheek like a little boy.

Then he began to talk about his life in Russia, long ago.

Suddenly Mrs. Stravinsky appeared. She leaned over to whisper in his ear.

He turned back to me. "See? When you get old, they have to tell you when to go to the toilet."

After that I devoted myself to the Stravinsky. I knew exactly what he meant about rewriting the score of *The Rite of Spring*. Bill Smith had rewritten it for Ormandy in such a way that it sounded almost exactly like what Stravinsky wrote, but was much easier to conduct. But I used the original. Every waking minute I studied the score, but it wasn't enough. When I went to bed at night I conducted it in my head, seeing how far I could get before I fell asleep. Then I listened to a recording with the Suisse Romande Orchestre conducted by Ernest Ansermet. He did it very well. I listened a few times and then put it away. As the July concert date approached, I got farther into the score before falling asleep.

One night I conducted the work from beginning to end.

The next night I began in the middle of the score. And the next, toward the end. Anywhere except the beginning. I was consumed with it, had to know it from every angle.

On the day of the concert, we rehearsed Beethoven's Fifth for fifteen minutes, just parts that might cause problems, and the Stravinsky for two hours. The orchestra was with me.

My parents were coming, so I asked the parking manager to let them park in the back area usually reserved for musicians. No problem, he said.

At the Dell that night, our librarian Jesse Taynton came into my dressing room and asked for my score to the Beethoven. It was his job to take it onto the stage and set it out on the conductor's music stand.

"I'm not using it."

He nodded. We'd all done the Fifth so many times.

The orchestra played wonderfully, covering the spacious Dell with our famous sound.

At intermission, Jesse came in for my Stravinsky score.

"Never mind, Jesse. I'm doing it from memory."

"No, let me find it for you."

I had to keep reassuring him until he gave up. Was I showing off? I don't know. All conductors do it. There is something more to it, something like reassuring yourself that you do have a handle on the piece. It's not the same as playing music on an instrument from memory. When you're leading a large group of musicians, you don't want to feel that you have to keep checking an instruction manual.

On stage, I lifted my baton toward principal bassoonist Bernard Garfield, and *The Rite of Spring* was underway with the beautiful weaving notes that only Stravinsky could have conjured out of silence. We moved through the first part and then the second, every player fully engaged. The middle arrived and we swam through it in perfect coordination, just the way I had studied it. Then the finale with its dreadfully difficult rhythms.

Stravinsky was present in my mind, and I did my best to conduct it like Monteux. Of course, the times had changed, and no fights broke out. The audience stayed all the way to the end. In fact, they erupted in applause and—amazingly—so did the orchestra. Marilyn and I went home for some peace and quiet.

I did think I wanted peace and quiet, but when I got home something different was waiting for me. For several years I had been conducting the Temple University orchestra (which Ormandy tolerated well because they weren't professional). A large group of my students had amassed on my lawn to shout their bravos. I loved it. Bring on the noise.

We Philadelphia musicians knew when and where the reviews would show up, and we knew all the local reviewers. The next day a review appeared in the *Philadelphia Inquirer.* That was normal. Oddly, I'd never heard of the reviewer. No one else knew her either. She found the concert to be nothing special. Did she not notice the audience's response?

Stranger yet, the *Evening Bulletin* had no review at all. Both newspapers always reviewed the orchestra performances.

About a week later James Felton, the *Evening Bulletin's* regular music critic, told me what happened.

"Anshel, I'm so sorry! We were all out of town. Our bosses said it was mandatory that we cover the announcement in Saratoga Springs." He was speaking for all the regular music critics of the Philadelphia newspapers, and I appreciated his candor. What he explained was that every music critic had had to attend a press conference 270 miles away. "The board" of the Philadelphia Orchestra was announcing the orchestra's new plans for a summer festival. It had to be announced at the future location of the festival, *not* in Philadelphia. And although it was two years in the future, the announcement could not be given at any other time except the evening when I was conducting *The Rite of Spring.*

"I don't know who the young woman was who reviewed your concert," James Felton said. "But I do know that she was told just how to write it up."

Of course every musician knew that Ormandy was behind the board's press conference. He had the newspapers in his back pocket. The lesson I was supposed to be learning was that it was dangerous to conduct in his city.

The players had some fun at Ormandy's expense in later rehearsals. They'd say within his hearing, "Didn't Anshel do great with Stravinsky? He even used the original score!" They loved to irritate him because it was so easy to do.

Later my mother told me their experience at my Stravinsky performance. My father pulled the car up to the backstage parking area at Robin Hood Dell, as I had told them to.

The attendant had put up a hand to stop their car. "Only friends of the orchestra."

My father, always the joker, said, "What am I, an enemy?"

Apparently he was related to the enemy.

Sometimes Ormandy wanted to get rid of a player. For years he weeded out those who had played under Stokowski. Luckily for me, my dear assistant concertmaster, Dave Madison, had an engaging personality that kept him off Ormandy's shit list. Few others from the Stokowski era were exempt.

"I want to move So-and-so farther back," Ormandy would occasionally say. "He's not pulling his weight."

Knowing how random personality traits could annoy him, I almost always objected to these demotions, and most of the time he deferred to my judgment. I never told the players.

Once he fixed in his crosshairs a player in the back of the second violins. It started with dark looks on a Monday. A frustrated sideways whipping of the baton to stop us all while he glared at this man followed, and we had to back up a few bars.

The next day rehearsal hadn't gone more than three minutes before he started in. "You've been playing this music for twenty years. Do you think you could make the effort to learn it now?"

The man nodded, as if now he was going to play however it was that Ormandy wanted him to. Many players needed occasional correction, but I do not remember this player being noticeably worse than anyone else.

Wednesday Ormandy was angrier. We all chafed under the harassment of our colleague.

Thursday he stopped us with a jab of his baton and said to the player, "How can you sit there and make that noise? It's not even music. You don't belong in this orchestra!"

Each of us felt the sting. A desire was surging among us to somehow rein Ormandy in.

At the rehearsal break, seven players came into my dressing room.

"No one wants to stand for him tomorrow."

They were asking me to abandon the protocol that governs the beginning of every performance: The orchestra members enter the stage and sit in their places. The concertmaster enters, bows to the audience, tunes the orchestra, and sits down. Next the conductor enters and the concertmaster stands—and the players follow suit—as a sign of respect for their conductor.

"Don't stand when he comes on stage," they said. "If you do, no one else will join you."

No insult to Ormandy could be more public than this. It would hit the newspapers as the lead sentence of any review.

The weight of the issue made me almost sick. That evening, I called several players whose judgment I respected. Each felt repulsed by Ormandy's behavior. And yet none wanted to force my hand. They were glad the decision wasn't theirs. I lay awake most of the night.

In the morning, I went to Ormandy's office. I could tell by her expression that his secretary knew what was afoot. She shook her head no, advising me not to talk to him. But I went ahead.

In his office, I said, "Boss, the players have asked me not to stand when you come on stage."

I can hardly remember seeing a face more unhappy than his. Of course it had looked that way all week. "Do what you want," he said.

Then he got up and went into his bathroom, leaving me to stare at the four walls.

The morning rehearsal was gloomy, but Ormandy refrained from flaying his victim any further. I went to lunch with some of my buddies and returned still undecided.

We dressed, and at the appointed time, the players filed onto the stage and took their places. When the cellos had their end-pins secured, the oboes were satisfied with their reeds, and everyone looked ready, if miserable, I entered. I took my bow and then turned to the orchestra. At this time, first oboist John de Lancie was supposed play his A so that each group of instruments could be tuned to it, but I signaled John to wait.

"I've decided that we will all stand," I said *sotto voce*. "All of us. The cello section—" I looked at them. "And the woodwinds, everyone. John, let's have the note."

John gave his A, and I tuned the strings, the woodwinds, the brass. I sat down.

Ormandy entered and I stood. Some of the others stood immediately, and some rose reluctantly, but we did all stand.

The Philadelphia Orchestra had some dirty laundry, but I didn't want to share it with the public. The convention of standing for the conductor is worldwide. It is not applause and is not an evaluation of the particular conductor, but rather an honoring of the position.

The fall of 1964 was a wonderful time and a terrible time. Marilyn was pregnant. On Oct. 5, she got the children off to school and asked me to drop her off at the hospital. Just drop her at the door and drive off. That was what she suggested.

"No, I won't."

I called the orchestra secretary, and Ormandy was perfectly nice about my missing rehearsal. When I called in the afternoon with the news, he stopped the rehearsal to announce Melinda's safe arrival. Again, as he had done for David and Jennie, he gave us a sterling cup for the baby with his engraved signature.

We got a third chance to raise a musical child. David had done well at playing piano and violin, but didn't sign up for orchestra in junior high. He was summoned over the intercom system to see the music teacher.

"I wanted you to be our concertmaster!" the teacher said.

His answer was direct: "No." To us, he offered a bit more detail. "They think I'm going to play like you. It's not going to happen."

Okay. We appreciated his firm decision. Maybe Jennie with her sweet singing voice and discipline at the piano? She held out longer by several years.

As it turned out, the people our children have become are so much better than anything we could have designed.

Now along came Melinda to survive our parenting and become her own person. She loved being tested on such trivia as "What is Stravinsky's first name?" With each of our children, I got to be a kid all over again. It was all Monteux's fault. He had housed me at the Sakoviches', where I could measure what I *had* to have in life against what I merely wanted.

In addition to baby Mindy, I got something else that fall: a new contract—one with a barb.

First the good news. The orchestra season was at last to be fifty-two weeks, paid. The players were jubilant. This trend was spreading. Conductors, however, now had the burden of trying to schedule, program, and prepare for many more concerts.

The Orchestra Association also outlawed "moonlighting," and defined that term as performing outside the big orchestra with any group larger than six players taken from the big orchestra.

There was nothing subtle about this tactic. As soon as the moonlighting clause was made public, a reporter from the *Philadelphia Inquirer* called my house.

"What is your reaction to the new clause, Mr. Brusilow?"

"I'm mad as hell."

Hard on the heels of that was the call from the *Evening Bulletin*. There didn't seem to be any question in anyone's mind about the purpose of the fateful clause. The arrow pointed at me.

Ormandy was also questioned by reporters. However, he had no opinion because, he claimed, it was just a restriction the board had added. His hands appeared to be immaculate.

My chamber orchestra was not the only group affected. Philadelphians had also been enjoying the Amerita String Orchestra and a group of twenty-five called the Philadelphia Concerto Players. Players from the big orchestra staffed all three of these groups and chose to do so for artistic as well as financial reasons. Many people wondered why the players had agreed to these restrictive new terms. An article in the *Spectacle* said this: "Members of the orchestra, almost to a man, explain that they allowed the clause to get into the contract because they were told it would not be used to dissolve Brusilow's group or the Amerita."[2]

The moonlighting clause would take effect in the fall of 1965. Thus the last performance of the Philadelphia Chamber Orchestra, staffed by members of the big orchestra, was in April 1965.

I still wonder if the orchestra board had chosen to take over the Philadelphia Chamber Orchestra as it was, and use it to help fill the longer season, might that not have been propitious for both organizations?

These ugly affairs were cleansed in the public eye by fielding an altered version of the chamber orchestra the following year. It bore the same name, but the players were largely borrowed from a chamber orchestra that had recently been formed in Princeton. Ormandy was "Honorary Music Director," and a close friend of his conducted it.

---

2. Marie van Patten, "Chamber Music's Catch 22," *Spectacle*, [n.d., but 1965-66], 162.

Conducting was not something I was prepared to give up. If push came to shove, I would give up the violin bow before I would give up the baton. I typed up my resignation again and this time really sent it to the board president, C. Wanton Balis. As it happened, I forgot to sign it. It was accepted nonetheless.

Ormandy's feelings were mixed. He had to get this competing conductor out of his orchestra—out of his city! But he wanted the concertmaster. He asked me to stay while he searched for my replacement.

Once during that last year with the Philadelphia Orchestra, we were all standing around at 30th Street Station waiting for a train to Baltimore for a concert. Ormandy motioned me aside.

"Why would you give this up, Anshel? It's the best job in the world."

"I have to."

"Do you want more money? I could get that."

"Boss, I really want to conduct."

"You'd be miserable. It's a headache!"

Boris Sokoloff, the orchestra manager, joined us. "How do you know what orchestra you'll get?" he asked. "It certainly won't be on the level of Philadelphia."

"That's ridiculous!" Ormandy snapped. "A musician like Anshel will succeed wherever he goes!"

I could hardly give a better example of relating to Ormandy. His head was so full of contradictory opinions that he himself didn't know which one was coming out of his mouth next.

His brilliant conducting continued to amaze and educate me, even as our relationship became ever more unpredictable. I watched closely how he managed to accompany soloists so that they felt completely comfortable with the orchestra. Of course he knew the solo part as well as the soloist.

In one particularly challenging instance, Sviatoslav Richter joined us to play the Grieg Piano Concerto. Ormandy had conducted it times beyond counting with as many soloists. But

Richter's interpretation was so different that the concerto became a new piece of music. At the rehearsal, Ormandy sweated as I'd never seen him do, especially over a concerto, not even a symphony. I watched him master the situation, work out exactly what Richter needed from the orchestra and guide us in giving it. Because of his hard work, the performance was extraordinary.

We always held a benefit concert and ball for our stately concert hall, the Academy of Music. In my last season, Leonard Bernstein guest-conducted it. On the way to the Bellevue-Stratford Hotel for the ball, Marilyn and I found ourselves in the elevator with Lenny. I'd known him since Curtis days, and he was a close friend of my brother Nat's.

"Corigliano is retiring," he told me. John Corigliano was concertmaster of the New York Philharmonic. Lenny was leaving the Philharmonic too, and wanted the orchestra to be in fine form as Zubin Mehta took over. "The concertmaster position is yours if you'll come."

It wasn't even tempting. My face was set in a new direction, one without a chin rest. Several board members of my now-defunct chamber orchestra had taken the initiative to start planning a new, professional-level chamber symphony. Not one that performed five times a year or only in the summer, but a permanent one. They went to Theo Pitcairn with the idea and proposed me as conductor. Theo enthusiastically promised significant support.

This was my dream. I never did see myself as a great violinist, a virtuoso. Musicians like Heifetz and Milstein were possessed of a drive that was alien to me. I loved too many other things. And too many people. I can hear the difference even as I listen to myself on recordings. I did bring to the concertmaster job the constellation of skills that make life easier for the conductor. That is not the same as being cut out for a concertizing career.

My tenure with the Philadelphia Orchestra would end with a six-week tour of South America. Naturally, Ormandy programmed works by South American composers like the illustrious Argentine,

Alberto Ginastera. I came into the dressing room I shared with Dave Madison on the day we were to begin rehearsing Ginastera's Concerto for Strings.

Dave had my violin case open and the music on the stand, as usual. Unusual, though, was his expression. His eyebrows were drawn together and he avoided looking at me.

"Are you okay?" I asked.

"I'm fine. I just hope you're going to be."

I glanced at the music. "Solo Violin" was how it began. Next came notes written as quartertones, which meant they should be played out of tune. Easy enough.

Then I looked across to the opposite page. Mountains of black notes tumbled over each other, heap after heap.

"He's got to be kidding!"

Dave shook his head.

I was a good sight reader, but this was impossible. I would have had to work on it for weeks.

I hadn't though. I was starting right now. What was an honest violinist to do?

I wasn't one on that day, so I don't know. The composer deserved my respect, so I allotted to him the summit note and valley-bottom note of each mountain. I would only hijack the dozens that fell between.

Immediately, it seemed to me, we were all in our places, Ormandy giving the downbeat with his baton, and looking at me. I played through the easy part and then the mountain range faced me. So I gave Alberto Ginastera his valley note, zoomed my own way up a snaking trail, gave him his summit note, and skied back down at breakneck speed to his note at the bottom. Countless times, never the same twice, until I had fulfilled all the measures written in that way. The look on your face can fool a lot of people, and mine suggested conviction and bravado.

When my solo was over and a rest came, I picked at something on my knee. I had no idea if the others—including Ormandy—were staring at me, thinking things like *Why on earth did he put that A in there? And There's no E-flat in that measure!* My speed, though, gave me a cloak of secrecy. I didn't think anyone could pick out a single note and tie it to the written music.

It was a relief that Ormandy didn't say anything. Neither did anyone else, and we moved on to the rest of the piece where the whole orchestra played.

When we got to the end of the concerto, Ormandy said, "Good job," and patted me on the back! Others also congratulated me. I didn't like to say "thank you" when it was so undeserved.

The next day I came to rehearsal feeling pretty relieved about that piece. It was only when we opened our music, Dave and I of course sharing a stand, that the danger of my position became clear. Since I didn't know what exactly I had played yesterday, how could I play the same thing? If I improvised it differently, I would be outted.

I focused my mind and dove into those wild, black notes, hoping they would resemble what I'd played the first time.

No one said anything—so far so good! And so it went for the days of rehearsal. It got easier each time.

We performed the concerto in Philadelphia before we left for the tour of South America. This was my last performance at the Academy of Music, and there I was, committing fraud. Ormandy actually gave me a bow and the orchestra applauded.

Before we left, Ormandy told the orchestra that Ginastera wouldn't be able to attend our concert in his city, Buenos Aires. I tried to put on a downcast look.

Four of us took our golf clubs along on tour. We knew we'd have time to play. Ormandy would not schedule rehearsals in every city because "This is the Philadelphia Orchestra."

We performed on the beautiful islands of Trinidad and Tobago and then flew to the mainland. In Caracas, Venezuela, we gave an outdoor concert in extreme humidity and among such clouds of large and small insects that the crowd of people seemed curtained away, their hearty applause mixing with buzzing and droning.

The citizens of Rio de Janeiro welcomed us next. The American Embassy hosted us for dinner. An American attaché and his wife took me on the cable car ride to see the Christ of the Andes statue on the mountaintop. They also took me to Hans Stern, the jeweler, where I bought tourmaline earrings for Marilyn.

In each country, we played the national anthem, and Ormandy conducted them all from memory. The larger the country, it seemed, the shorter and easier its anthem. Uruguay's anthem is a tricky overture. Ormandy asked me to nod at him each time the meter changed from four to three, and back to four.

The people in the audience that night were gorgeously dressed. The women were studded with diamonds. Looking at the audience and then back at the music, I forgot about Ormandy.

He was staring at me with the question practically written on his face, *When do I change the meter?*

I nodded, and of course it was in the wrong place. I nodded again. Somehow we waffled through. Whether anyone in the audience recognized it as their anthem is anyone's guess.

The next morning in Uruguay violinist Bobby DePasquale and I wanted to play some golf. We asked a taxi driver to take us to a country club. He dropped us off, took his pay, and zoomed off.

Now we looked around at the lush grass rolling away and the manicured circles around the holes, but not one soul was in view. Finally an employee showed up.

"You want to play?" he asked in Spanish. "Really?"

We were sure. Two reluctant caddies were rounded up for us.

At the first tee, I watched Bobby in his red windbreaker hit a nice one out onto the fairway. It bounced a couple of times.

It was my turn.

Bobby appeared to have changed into a black windbreaker. That was strange. Closer to him, the black became a solid blanket of

black flies covering his red windbreaker. I looked down at myself—
the same. It was quite horrifying. We clamped our mouths shut so
as not to eat them, but they flew up our noses. We tried to play one
hole, but in just a few minutes we took up our clubs and ran.

On the tour, the Philadelphia Orchestra bounced around
from country to country, pleasing our audiences and having a
good time. Often Ginastera's "Concerto for Strings" was on the
program, and I became entirely comfortable with it. One day I
admitted to Sammy Mayes and Dave Madison that I had improvised most of it.

"I don't believe you," was Sammy's response.

"That's something I never would have figured out," Dave said.

We went to Argentina and played the Buenos Aires concert.
Getting that behind me was a big relief, even though I knew
Ginastera would not be present.

The day after that concert, we were leaving for Chile, but not
till evening. Time for some golf! Four of us promised a taxi driver
he wouldn't regret driving us all the way out to the club named for
golfer Roberto De Vicenzo, one of the most beautiful courses in all
South America. Sending those balls flying down the fairways felt
like a well-earned pleasure.

At the sixth tee, a golf cart came over a rise of ground and right
over to us, the driver waving.

"Teléfono! Teléfono for Brusilow!"

I told the others I'd catch up with them and got into the cart
with the driver.

Waiting for me all that time on the phone was our assistant
manager. "Ormandy wants to fly out as soon as you four get back,"
he said. "There's a huge storm brewing in the Andes."

"We're a long ways out of the city," I said, "but we'll start back."

He felt a need to press the point home. "You know how he
is about flying." Everyone who traveled with the orchestra knew
Ormandy hated a bumpy ride.

As the golf cart toodled me back to find the others, I had time to appreciate the mountains in the distance glinting white in the sun. The fairways showed the parallel lines of fresh mowing.

My friends leaned on their clubs as I approached. Just by their position, I could tell they dreaded some bad news that would ruin our day.

"Ormandy wants to leave as soon as we get back," I said. "Let's play the rest of the course." Our priorities were aligned with one another, and it was a pleasant game.

We had a problem getting a taxi, and by the time we pulled up to the hotel it was five o'clock. A staircase led up to the lobby. Ormandy posed at the top.

"Where have you been?" The look on his face said, *Kill, kill, kill.*

"We were so far away. It was impossible to find a taxi!" You can only look so innocent with a golf bag at your side.

"Let's go."

"I'll go pack. Five minutes."

"I had someone pack your stuff."

In less than an hour we were on the plane to Chile. The wind blew the clouds aside and a yellow moon sailed into view and lit the snowy peaks all during that calm, smooth flight.

In Santiago, Salvador Allende attended the concert. He was late, so we started late. This made Ormandy so mad I think he would rather have skipped the Chilean national anthem.

Exhaustion was settling in by this stage of the tour. I vaguely remember a concert in Guatemala.

Mexico City was the final stop. A field house had been converted into a concert hall by constructing a stage at one end and setting out two thousand chairs. There was no backstage and no dressing or preparation area for the players. Ormandy had the use of a big tent to greet dignitaries and guests.

I came down to breakfast in the hotel on the morning of the concert. Ormandy sat in front of a plate piled with food.

"Anshel!" He was beaming. "You'll never believe who's coming tonight."

I considered the president of Mexico, or a Mexican composer.

"Ginastera!" Ormandy breathed ecstatically. "Isn't that wonderful?"

"Yes," I said. "That's wonderful."

At least we weren't playing his piece.

Ormandy chewed on a piece of bacon. "I'm changing the program, of course," he said.

I have claimed that I wasn't nervous before performances. This would be the exception. I considered getting "sick." As a matter of fact, I had begun to feel sick. But Dave couldn't play it in my place. I considered closeting myself for the hours that remained and trying to learn the actual notes Ginastera had written for his Concerto for Strings. There wasn't nearly enough time.

A terrible thought occurred to me: what if Ginastera had already heard me on the radio, hijacking his music? He could be coming to set the record straight?

Ormandy decided we should rehearse. Afterwards, I wandered around behind that huge wooden stage looking for a hiding place, since there were no dressing rooms at all.

Back in a corner, a few old chairs stood near some dark, dusty curtains. I was able to pull the curtains over the chairs to create a small room. It was so dirty I had to be careful not to touch anything. I had a view of the stage entrance. Dave was looking around for me, so I came out.

"Where were you?"

"Oh, I wanted to warm up."

Now we were on stage. Ormandy came out. The Ginastera was the first piece on the program. I had no options. I played it the same way I had been doing throughout the tour. At the end, Ormandy acknowledged me with a bow and did the same to Ginastera.

Intermission came, and I went back into hiding.

When I saw the other string players heading back toward the stage, I came out again and joined them. Then Ormandy entered the stage and leaned down to ask me, "Where have you been?"

I just smiled and we went ahead and played the rest of the concert and an encore. Then I scurried back to my corner and closed up my violin. I knew the shortest route to the exit. I would have to take my violin with me since the trunk where the instruments were stored and transported was not on my path. I just had to get by Ormandy's tent and then there was an exit to the street. It was dark and many people were milling around the tent, so my chances were good. I clutched my violin against my side, ducked my head, and practically jogged.

"Anshel! Anshel!" Our manager Boris Sokoloff was someone I didn't feel I could ignore, even during my last week ever with the orchestra. He beckoned, and I stepped into the tent.

Not far from me stood the tall and robust Alberto Ginastera. I thought, *If he hits me, he'll kill me.* And immediately he did start toward me with energetic strides. I felt petrified. But his arms came up from his sides not with fists but with open hands, and he embraced me and kissed me on both cheeks.

"I never dreamed it could sound like that! *Magnífico!*"

Suddenly everyone in the tent began to applaud. Ormandy was beaming—which could mean anything—and I was sweating bullets.

"I was so honored to play your concerto in your presence," I managed to say to Ginastera.

Had I finally done it? I had missed out on playing Sibelius for Sibelius because Szell wouldn't release me. I had played Shostakovich for Shostakovich in such a way as to get him in trouble for writing bourgeois music. Now had I played Ginastera for Ginastera and managed to please him . . . with my Brusilowized Ginastera?

The next night, again in Mexico City, was our last concert on the tour, and also my very last concert with the Philadelphia Orchestra. My fellow musicians honored me by standing together as I entered the stage to tune them for the last time. Funny how a tribute from your peers gets to you. We did appreciate our audiences' approval, but it seemed easier to come by. Your colleagues have the scoop on you.

Memory has a sovereignty all its own, and mine gives me no access to Ormandy's farewell that evening, though it was probably kind. I do have a photograph of the final handshake on stage.

What I remember is a conversation I had with him shortly after returning to Philadelphia from the tour.

I wanted to be up front about the new Chamber Symphony of Philadelphia I was putting together. Of course he knew about it, but I went to his office to tell him how auditions were going.

"I'm happy for you. I really do wish you success," Dr. Jekyll said.

Not smart enough to quit while I was ahead, I said, "But it's really too bad the Chamber Orchestra couldn't continue. The players loved it and so did I."

Mr. Hyde emerged. "You took my best players—musicians *I* had selected and trained. With one or two lousy rehearsals, you played to large audiences and took all the accolades. I couldn't let that continue."

Here was the admission that Ormandy himself was behind the moonlighting clause. I didn't have any response.

"You promised you wouldn't conduct. You promised to stay at least ten years. You lied on all counts."

Since I can't defend myself against that charge, I'll change the subject to one where I can claim some innocence. Some months later, when I was no longer in the Philadelphia Orchestra, my phone rang. The person on the other end of the line tried to speak, but his words were lost in laughter. Over and over he said, "Anshel!" and tried to start talking. I recognized the voice, Sammy Mayes.

"He's programmed it again this fall," he finally managed to squeak. "The Ginastera. And Norman played that solo."

Norman Carol, Max's son, was the concertmaster Ormandy had hired to replace me. He was a fine violinist with no conducting aspirations.

"Oh, no!" I said.

"Oh, yes! He starts the solo, and Ormandy flicks the stick at him. 'No!' says Ormandy. 'What on earth are you playing?'"

If I had imagined that Ormandy would program Ginastera again, honest to God, I would have called Norman.

But what would I have said?

Sammy went on: "So Norman says, 'I studied it. These are the right notes!' and Ormandy says, 'It's all wrong.' And then he looks at *me*!"

I felt a twinge of remorse, thinking of Sammy on the hot seat.

"And Ormandy says, 'Sammy! That's not what Anshel played, is it?' So I have to answer, and I say, 'It doesn't sound like it, Mr. Ormandy.' And all the while Dave is sitting with his hands over his face. He doesn't want anybody asking *him* anything about it.

"So Ormandy says to Norman, 'You need to learn this music. This is the Philadelphia Orchestra!'"

Some months later, I ran into Norman Carol. Before I could get the apology out of my mouth, he said, "If I had a gun, I'd shoot you!"

I suppose it's just accidental that I had completely morphed into a conductor by the time I was fixed in someone's crosshairs.

Chapter 7

THIS ISN'T THE PHILADELPHIA ORCHESTRA

I STILL REMEMBER THE HUSH WHEN the lights went down. The Philadelphia Union League was packed with its members and friends, coming out to a private concert, to see something new. It was September 30, 1966, and my Chamber Symphony of Philadelphia was on its home turf, after two initial concerts out of town. As if to make room for us, the big orchestra had gone on strike. I was feeling my elbow room.

The concertmaster had tuned the players, taken his bow, and been welcomed by the audience. I walked on and enjoyed their enthusiastic applause too. Soloist Gary Graffman began Beethoven's Third Piano Concerto. I kept the orchestra with him wherever he chose to take us. The slow movement began.

Then a strange sound, a deep resonant D, came from somewhere and intruded upon Beethoven. A startled look crossed Gary's face, but he regathered his focus and kept going. The sound merged passably with his notes and, in any case, was dying out.

Before it was gone, the D came again, this time clashing with Gary's notes. Now I placed it. Just up the street was the PNB Building with its massive Founder's Bell. It was eight o'clock, and we had six more gongs to go.

Comprehension swept over the audience in the form of rustling, coughs, whispers. Gary was cool—in fact, I suspected him of being amused. Gary and Naomi Graffman think I voiced the word "Ormandy," which was hilarious to those who heard it. I don't remember that. But everyone knew the animosity the man felt toward me and my chamber symphony. If anyone did suggest Eugene Ormandy's somehow being able to ring the Founder's Bell during our concert, I can believe it would have struck a chord.

In the *Philadelphia Evening Bulletin,* James Felton had described our forming as "the birth of a second permanent professional orchestra in Philadelphia."[1] In the long run, that was the material point. One powerful man felt there shouldn't be two orchestras in the City of Brotherly Love.

It was caviar in a silver dish to me when the group of supporters had offered me my own chamber symphony. My previous Philadelphia Chamber Orchestra had performed five times per year, each of which annoyed Ormandy like a bee sting. My new chamber symphony would have a full season of thirty-four weeks, just as most big orchestras had then. This would be a whole nest of hornets in Ormandy's back yard.

Chamber symphonies at that time were part-time, calling members out to rehearse for a certain number of performances annually, but not attempting to schedule a full season of concerts or employ anyone full-time. Our plan was different.

During our preparatory year, I procrastinated about things like getting new concert clothes, but I had three priorities. First, I went to Theo Pitcairn myself to see if he was as excited as my backers said he was. I knew he was angry at the Philadelphia Orchestra board on my behalf and had himself tussled with C. Wanton Balis over the moonlighting issue. The Pitcairn support of the big orchestra came to a halt with my resignation.

---

1. "City's New Chamber Symphony Unveils First Season Plans," February 20, 1966, 7.

Theo loved the new idea. The sale of his El Greco painting *Saint John the Baptist* brought in $67,620 for the chamber symphony. The next year he would sell one of Monet's earliest Impressionist paintings, *La Terrasse à Sainte Adresse*, for $1.4 million, setting a new record for an Impressionist painting.[2] A good bit of that also came to us.

Theo spoke publicly about our vision and called it "a million-dollar project." A board of savvy and committed men and women came together easily, with Feodor Pitcairn as president.

My second priority was recording. From my new office on Broad Street, I telephoned Roger Hall in New York, head of RCA Red Seal Victor Records. We'd become friends when he was manager of the Philadelphia Orchestra.

"Come up here and tell me what you're doing," he said.

I drove to his office in New York.

"Ormandy will squash it," was Roger's first comment.

"You know me," I said. "Am I going to pick mediocre players? We've got the Academy of Music booked for twenty-one concerts, and we'll tour all over."

He did an about face. "I suppose with just thirty-six of you, you can play in smaller cities that can't hire the big orchestras." Not much had to be explained to Roger. He knew music inside and out. "You'll be able to do some music that hasn't seen the light of day in living memory, all those great pieces that just don't sound good with a hundred players. Okay then. We'll make some records."

His second comment was to my liking, and that first one, about Ormandy, I decided to disregard.

A week later, I drove to New York again to sign a recording contract for the Chamber Symphony of Philadelphia—before we had a single player under contract.

Thirdly, I got busy auditioning. Musicians from all over the world answered the call. The choice of a principal clarinetist was

---

2. *Life Magazine*, Dec. 15, 1967, 33; "Sold in London," *The Philadelphia Inquirer*, June 29, 1968.

easy. I suppose only readers who remember hearing my brother play will believe my judgment was unprejudiced. You wouldn't be likely to forget the rich tone Nat achieved on his clarinet with double lip embouchure, which means lips covering both the upper and lower teeth. I also needed a personnel manager, and I knew Nat's business skills would be useful there, so I suckered him into both positions.

Nat had been principal clarinet in the Kansas City Philharmonic under conductor Efrem Kurtz, who appreciated the natural musicality Nat brought to his playing. Nat's career tracked with that of his conductor and also principal flutist Elaine Shaffer. All three moved from Kansas City to the Houston Symphony.

While love was on the increase between Kurtz and Shaffer, en route to marriage eventually, no love was lost between my brother and Elaine Shaffer. He played with great originality, and she was not the only colleague who found this irksome.

"I can't play with Nat," she used to say. Or sometimes she would just give Nat a dirty look during a rehearsal. Then Kurtz would notice her and find some reason to lash out at Nat.

"The clarinets are playing too loud!" he barked at one rehearsal.

Nat said, "The clarinets don't have anything here, Mr. Kurtz. We're *tacet*."

"Oh . . . well"—he quickly checked his score and found that Nat was right—"I meant the second violins."

It seemed like Maestro Kurtz was a weapon that Elaine Shaffer could aim. Eventually Nat couldn't stand it. He returned to Philadelphia and sold refrigeration.

Luckily for both of us, he still practiced clarinet.

Together, Nat and I auditioned 1,042 musicians for our 36 positions. Some sent tapes, but many hundreds came to play in person. We needed players who could handle difficult music and who could get a good sound out of their instrument. Sight reading ability was important, as was experience and ready repertoire. Then, too, we wanted stage presence and a way of making music that was distinctive. And personalities that didn't poison the atmosphere. Some things we felt we could take for granted, like living within the limits of legality.

You shouldn't take anything for granted when hiring musicians.

Auditioning is work. You listen and listen until you think nothing can please you. But all of a sudden your ear thrills and you look up to see if it's a bald old man or a pretty young girl, and you don't care which as long as you can hear that sound some more.

We had whole days of just bass players. Rumble rumble rumble. Sam Hollingsworth from Nashville came to audition. Our boredom must have been obvious.

He settled his big, dark brown instrument on its endpin and said, "I will be playing Sonata No. 4 in D Major by George Frideric Handel."

I had performed this piece myself—because it was a *violin* sonata, which Sam intended to play on a bass! It became impressive as he played the whole sonata perfectly in tune, give or take a couple of octaves. We hired him as principal bassist and also tour manager.

One day a familiar woman auditioned for violin. I saw her name on the list: Florence Rosensweig. She'd been the concertmaster in Mr. Fleisher's Symphony Club when I was a kid.

"I remember you," she said, and she mimicked me: "I don't want to play the bottom line! I want to play the top line." She played beautifully and still had dimples, and I hired her.

For the top line, I went in pursuit of Stuart Canin. He'd won the Paganini Competition in Italy, and now had a tenured position teaching at Oberlin College. I wanted Stuart's gorgeous music in my concertmaster's chair. However, with two young sons, he wouldn't take the risk.

I listened to my other top candidate. A fine player, but not quite a soloist. Stuart was persuaded when I promised him solos both in Philadelphia and on the road. He also made many recordings with us, so I made it worth his while.

William Steck came to audition for a violin spot. He had quit the big orchestra a year before I did. When we were kids, Billy Steck's dad had brought him over to our apartment to play for my parents, and Dad recommended studying with Dr. Szanto. Billy auditioned beautifully for me, but he had a crummy violin. I lent him my Guarnerius del Gesù and placed him next to Stuart as assistant concertmaster.

When cellist William Stokking from the Philadelphia Orchestra wanted to join us, I said come along then, and didn't bother with an audition. It gave me a particular pleasure to hire him as principal cello because of the audition I had once set up for him with Ormandy. He had done well, but that was when Ormandy had the thrill of swiping Sammy Mayes from the Boston Symphony Orchestra.

As for stealing, it's true, I didn't feel so very bad myself about stealing Stokking. Or when Ormandy's second horn Ward Fearn came to join us either. I hired Carlton Cooley as principal violist and Sam Belenko in the cellos, but the thrill was less because they had left the Philadelphia Orchestra earlier.

It was time to gird myself up for the big hurdle—management. It was easy enough for our twenty-one Philadelphia concerts at the Academy of Music. Playing around the country, though, was another matter. In order for us to be a permanent chamber symphony, we had to fill a thirty-four-week season with engagements, and a manager could book those for us.

As a solo violinist, management contracts had always slipped away from me. In Paris, tears gathered in Jacques Thibaud's eyes when he told me that I would share first place in the Long-Thibaud violin competition and—the worst part—the other winner would get the management deal. Thibaud knew that was what mattered, not the prize money. When I defied Doris Monteux by marrying, access to management as a concert violinist vanished with the Monteuxs, ending that hope, for the time being anyway.

But this time I was a conductor. With a first class orchestra, a new kind of thing, "America's first permanent chamber symphony."[3]

Columbia Artists Management, Inc., or CAMI, is the giant in the arena of classical music management. Young musicians desire CAMI as a fairy godmother. When old, some come to see it as a wicked witch. It's actually more like a unilateral superpower, equipped with stimulus packages as well as WMDs. Arthur Judson was one of its two founders in 1930. In his eighties, Judson was fired by CAMI.

But he wasn't done. He pulled some experienced managers together and formed Judson, O'Neal, Beall & Steinway. Since I had known Arthur Judson from earlier days, I went to see him. Judson directed me to one of his partners, Harry Beall. I liked Harry very much and he was eager to represent my chamber symphony.

Before making a decision, I also visited with Sol Hurok. For decades, his agency, S. Hurok Presents, was the biggest competition CAMI had. Hurok encouraged me in my plan and expected it to succeed. "I can't represent you, though," he said. "I've got plenty of first-rate soloists, and they'd love to perform with your chamber symphony. But then Ormandy wouldn't ever use them again. And they can't afford to forgo the Philadelphia Orchestra."

"That can't be true!"

"Take it from me, Anshel. What I'm saying is true." To be more accurate, he said, *"Vas ich zoog, es emis,"* falling into Yiddish for solidarity—*what I'm saying is true.*

I also tried Herb Barrett, another manager. "I'm one of the most honest of the dishonest managers," Herb said. "I'd like to, but I *can't* take you." That Ormandy stood in the way was understood.

Harry Beall was our manager, and he was marvelous. Before I was finished hiring musicians, we had more than one hundred concerts scheduled. Fritz Steinway handled our publicity.

---

3. "An Orchestra Is Born," *The Philadelphia Evening Bulletin,* Sep. 30, 1966, 28; Jackie White, "Father of Chamber Symphony Visits Here," *The Nashville Tennessean,* January 29, 1967, 8C.

Finding soloists was still my job, and the obvious question is how I got two such fantastic soloists as Gary Graffman and Renata Scotto for our opening. Gary is not easily intimidated. He said yes to me, not the least bit concerned that he was also scheduled to play a benefit concert for the Philadelphia Orchestra the following February. It was frowned on for a soloist to play benefit concerts for two orchestras in a single year, but February was a different calendar year.

Normally, all communication to soloists came through their managers, but in this case Gary was contacted not by his manager but by C. Wanton Balis, president of the Philadelphia Orchestra. I had thought I was done with that man. Balis wrote Gary a note canceling his engagement with the big orchestra because he "shouldn't be playing with that chamber symphony."

Of course Gary played for us and no doubt had plenty of other engagements the following February.

A friend brought the other bit of luck. Ray Fabiani kept his fingers in a variety of local pies, such as professional wrestling and the Philadelphia Opera. "Hey, Anshel," he said. "You know that new soprano who's coming to the Met, Renata Scotto?"

"No. Yes." Unsure, I found myself sounding like my old teacher Dr. Szanto.

"I could get her for your opening thing. Would you like that?"

Scotto hadn't yet sung in the U.S, so her American debut was with us.

Three days after that Union League concert, with its unique accompaniment by the Founder's Bell, we had our gala opening at the Academy of Music to a packed house. With our full complement of twenty-three strings, twelve wind, and one percussionist, we opened with Mendelssohn's "Italian" Symphony.

These choices are personal, when it really comes down to it. I had to feel aesthetically alive to the music, sensitive to each strand that contributes to a total perfection. I had to win the allegiance of all thirty-six players facing me. That Mendelssohn symphony had been my theme music for the TV show *Portraits in Music*, and it brought me pleasant memories. It's that simple.

Gary Graffman and Renata Scotto were flawless. That night the Chamber Symphony of Philadelphia brought even the critics to their feet cheering.

When I signed the recording contract with RCA, I had asked Roger Hall, "What are the chances of getting Heifetz to record with us?"

"If you can get him, you'll have the world," Roger said. Jascha Heifetz existed on a musical plane all by himself.

I asked for his address.

"He's impossible to get in touch with. But you could try through Piatigorsky."

Of course I had met the cellist Gregor Piatigorsky, though perhaps I hadn't made the right kind of impression—as an adolescent boy sobbing on a twilit path at the Curtis summer workshop.

"Okay," I said to Roger. "I know him."

The following week, Piatigorsky met me at the door of his California house. He remembered all about my "homesickness" in Maine, and even asked about my parents.

The phone rang and he spoke Russian with someone for a minute, but at least it wasn't my dad this time.

Over coffee, we talked about his concerts and his wife's chess competitions. He never played with her because he couldn't win.

We found unexpected agreement on something personal to every musician—the greatest concerto ever composed. For me, it is Dvořák's Cello Concerto. Piatigorsky agreed! I had never played it with him, but I would have loved to.

I had played it with Leonard Rose several times with the Philadelphia Orchestra, and I couldn't hear that concerto mentioned without giving in to silent reverie. In the coda, Dvořák holds nothing back. He does not fear passion; he drives straight for the heart, for love. The interplay of melody parallels on a spiritual level the consummation of a marriage, the violin and cello as soprano and tenor voices. Lenny Rose and I anticipated the passage, and kept our eyes on each other through every note. He knew exactly what I was going to do, and I knew what he would do, even though each time we performed it we developed the musical conversation a little differently. The concerto has a beautiful drawn-out ending, shifting among sections of the orchestra until all come together in a moving celebration.

But I recalled myself to where I was, and what for. I maneuvered the conversation with Piatigorsky around to Heifetz.

"You want to know about Jascha?" The phone was ringing again. "That'll be him."

After another phone conversation in Russian, he returned. "He wants to know if he should invest in a particular stock. Do I look like I'd know about stocks? I told him, yeah, invest."

Then, since I'd broached the subject, he rewarded me with anecdotes about Jascha Heifetz. The afternoon passed, punctuated by phone conversations. "Him again," Piatigorsky would say afterwards. "He wants to play quartets next week. I said yes. But you know what he does? We all meet at his house, and he asks what we want to play. Suggestions are tossed around, and it ends up always it's what Jascha suggested. So we play, supposedly all sight reading. But Jascha, he's got the fingering down. He practices the piece ahead of time, and then he pretends to sight read. We're always at a disadvantage."

For dinner we walked to a restaurant near Piatigorsky's home and settled into a corner table. There he told me another story:

The University of Arizona asked him to arrange a violin-piano-cello performance with Heifetz, Arthur Rubinstein, and himself. Piatigorsky said all he could do was try.

He called Rubinstein first, the easier mark.

"Great! What shall we play?"

"Hold it, Arthur. We haven't talked to Jascha yet."

Next he called Heifetz.

"No. Arthur always wants his name first."

Piatigorsky called the university president and gave a gloomy report on the low collegiality factor.

"Supposing we give all three of you honorary doctorates?" the president said.

Piatigorsky made the rounds again: Rubinstein said, "Of course." Heifetz said, "Let me think about it."

Amused, Piatigorsky said, to me, "I don't remember anybody asking Piatigorsky."

Finally Heifetz agreed, and they went to the University of Arizona. After the doctoral ceremony, the trio was warming up backstage. Heifetz turned to Rubinstein.

"I will walk on stage first."

"Pianists go on first," Rubinstein said. "Then violin and then cello."

In the end, Heifetz and Rubinstein walked on stage elbow to elbow, as if they were glued together. Piatigorsky brought up the rear.

I never asked Piatigorsky how I should approach Heifetz to get him to record with the Chamber Symphony. The difficult thing was that he sweetly assumed that I had come all the way to California just to visit with him, not to use him for my own ends. I just asked if I could write Heifetz a letter and got the address and wrote the letter when I got home.

On Roger Hall's suggestion, I wrote that we hoped to record some particular music Heifetz had never recorded. He had recorded almost everything, so this was a tease in hopes of getting a response, and I had a good idea for what to record with him.

Eventually I got around to clothes. My former dress suit went to Herbie Pierson in the Philadelphia Orchestra so he could stop using black shoe polish on his leg. This time I went to Ormandy's tailor, the only one in Philadelphia who knew how to tailor the jacket for a conductor, with close-fitting armholes so the back stays in place as you wave the baton.

As I stood half-dressed during my fitting, a knock came on the dressing room door. "Telephone call for Mr. Brusilow. The caller says his name is Heifetz."

He must have called our house and gotten the tailor's phone number from Marilyn. I never jumped into a pair of pants faster.

"Mr. Brusilow, Jascha Heifetz here. What is the thing you said I haven't recorded?"

"I would love to record Vivaldi's *Four Seasons* with you."

Dead silence. Then he said, "When I decide to record *The Four Seasons* I'll let you know."

I asked a few other musicians if they thought that was a poor choice to offer Heifetz. They said, "Heifetz called you back???"

The season began. In Philadelphia and in far-flung towns starved for high-quality performance, we played music from early Baroque to post-Webern. Haydn and Mozart and Bach were the backbone of our repertory. Playing Mozart with thirty-six players was a joy, especially with piano and strings. And Bach—big orchestras weren't doing his Brandenburg Concertos, and we did all six in the first year.

Soloists had an experience with us they couldn't get anywhere else. When Henryk Szeryng played the Bach violin concerto before intermission and the Beethoven after, he was so excited he couldn't stop talking about the balance between the orchestra and the solo violin. No conductor can prevent 80–100 musicians from occasionally competing with a soloist. With a chamber symphony, one could get the equilibrium nearly perfect.

The reviewers spoiled us. I should have been storing up their encouraging words.

Philadelphia is a supremely musical town, but New York is still New York. I had scheduled our series of seven concerts there in the new Philharmonic Hall, although I was more familiar with Carnegie Hall. On November 9, 1966, we were given one hour on the stage at Philharmonic to prepare for our debut.

What does a conductor do in an hour? I didn't move large structures around to experiment with the sound, obviously. I didn't scramble my players into unfamiliar seating patterns. I couldn't actually hear them very well. They, too, had disoriented expressions on their faces as if they were listening hard, trying to catch the pitch of instruments in the distance.

We just used the regular platform, warmed up, and rehearsed a bit. Then we played our program.

The reviews were devastating. At least my players were spared. *The New York Times* laid all of the blame for a performance without "grace or style" at my feet. So thickly that I needed new shoes.

I did plan the program badly, putting together too many bits and pieces and choosing things too well known. As for the sound, I guess I hoped the audience heard it differently than we did on the stage. Were my musicians even playing? Were their instruments stuffed with cotton? To me, it seemed that we were getting about 10 percent of our capacity. No doubt I was not at my best.

Of course the sound problems of that venue (now called Avery Fisher Hall) have become legendary and continue to this day, in spite of creative efforts to redress them. But in 1966 many of us in the musical world were still puzzled by what was going on in the brand-new music venue at Lincoln Center. We were playing on a wooden surface with solid concrete underneath it. *Solid concrete.*

For the second concert in New York's Philharmonic Hall, we moved forward onto an extra front portion of the platform, which is hollow. When the cello pegs went into that floor, the difference was enormous. Now we were able to get 75 percent of our sound capacity.

The work was hard, the hours long. In the mornings, after a short night's sleep, Marilyn would put a cup of her superb coffee just far enough from the bed that I couldn't reach it. Would she bring it to me, please? No, she would not.

So I got up and faced another day. Besides the rehearsals and the business, I worked over the scores. Always, my priority was to be faithful to the composer. At thirty-eight years old, I could understand only part of what a composer was trying to say, and I could convey to my talented players only what I understood. We were good. And yet, I was still learning.

In some ways, conducting is not a young man's art, or at least not supremely so. After years and years I learned that there are many ways to be faithful to the composer. First you must become secure in your personal technique. Then you can begin to find your own way to hear what was in the composer's head, and to convey your way of hearing it to the players. That is why conducting continues to be satisfying for a whole lifetime. It is never the same.

Some parts of a conductor's job are pesky. For instance, you have to keep the string players at their best. I know too well how tempting it is to overdo the vibrato because it compensates for the difficulty of really playing together and staying perfectly in tune. You can mush around with vibrato. And then there's the soft and loud problem, which is enough to make you seasick. It's easy to press the bow firmly into the strings when your hand is right over the strings. But when your hand is way out, and the far end of the bow is on the strings, it's hard to apply the same pressure. In a smaller orchestra, I needed every player to keep the same amount of pressure on the bow, no matter which end was on the strings.

The small orchestra was just right for playing eighteenth-century music as the composers themselves had heard it. With a large orchestra, the conductor has to double or even triple parts written for a single instrument. This is necessary because all the musicians are being paid, and dismissing half of them to play poker backstage just because you're doing Mozart looks to boards of directors like "wasting salaries." The advantage the large orchestra gains is that if you have four flutes and one messes up, the other three can generally cover it.

I wanted perfect ensemble playing without hurting the musical line. What that means is that no one can make a mistake. My musicians didn't have any cover. With fewer instruments and top-notch players, I knew we could achieve a fresh clarity and transparency of tone.

I planned to explore the small orchestra repertory more ambitiously than had been possible in the five annual performances of the doomed Philadelphia Chamber Orchestra. That was the center of my programming goal for my new symphony, and something that gave me great pleasure.

The challenges of my plan surfaced quickly: audiences in cities that rarely heard live symphony wanted the chance to hear, finally, pieces they had loved for years through the media of their day. So I did "infringe" on the territory of big orchestras, too. It wasn't always possible to please Philadelphia audiences one week and an audience in Miles City, Montana, the next.

On the other hand, there was room for creativity. Thinking about Stravinsky's delightful theatrical piece *A Soldier's Tale* (*L'Histoire du Soldat*), I wanted to surprise audiences in some way. Stravinsky wrote a narrator's part, telling of a soldier who sells his violin to the devil and winds up losing more than he gains.

The previous year, *The Sound of Music* had come out, and everyone was talking about the marionettes used in "The Lonely Goatherd" sequence. Bil and Cora Baird had made the puppets, so I called them to ask if they could make us some for *A Soldier's Tale* by January 1967.

"We'd love to!" Bil said. "But you know the translation of Stravinsky's script is pretty outdated. Let's have Sheldon Harnick fix it up."

Harnick was busy writing the libretto for *Fiddler on the Roof*, but he made time to develop a masterful adaptation of Stravinsky's fiddler-soldier tale too.

In January 1967, we performed the Stravinsky piece with puppets three times in Philadelphia and once at Carnegie Hall in New York.

Shakespearean actor Morris Carnovsky narrated. Other orchestras performed it with Baird puppets afterwards, but we were the first.

It was the best of times, it seemed to me. Audiences were large, reviewers raved, Westinghouse wanted a TV special. In the midst of the excitement, I was also planning our second season. We needed soloists, and Rudolf Firkusny came to mind. A great pianist and a friend of mine, surely he'd want to play with us.

And maybe he would have. I never found out.

Our manager Sam Flor sent a request to Firkusny's manager at CAMI. No reply. When I prodded Sam to get an answer, he called the CAMI manager again.

"Firkusny's not available to us," Sam reported.

"Why not?"

"Because we can't use any of that manager's artists."

This locked out only a dozen or so soloists, but for some reason it made me mad.

When I'm mad I should go stick my head in the sand. Instead, I picked up the phone and called the guy at CAMI. I knew him somewhat and had found him personable.

"Any soloist who performs with the Chamber Symphony of Philadelphia," he said, "is unlikely to be engaged by Ormandy again."

Sol Hurok had said the same thing to me, but it pained Hurok. This CAMI guy was just a mid-level manager in a huge operation, and I didn't see what gave him the right to be so stubborn. Even in a personable tone.

Marilyn would have told me to go mow the lawn or take a nap and think about it later. But she was at home, and I was in my office.

I wrote a hot-headed letter to the president of CAMI, Kurt Weinhold. Unfortunately, I mailed it.

Firkusny's manager at CAMI, the personable one, called me. "Why would you write a letter like that? Why would you blast me like that to the big boss?"

"Because it was so unfair! How can you boycott my orchestra!"

"CAMI management called a meeting about your letter and asked me if what you wrote was true," he said. "I've never been so humiliated in all my life."

I wonder what he said to the bosses, about whether or not my letter was true. His name was Ronald Wilford. I should have humiliated somebody else. It wasn't the worst of times yet, but they were coming.

In the spring, the chamber symphony did a transcontinental tour. We performed in Los Angeles and then traveled north into Canada. We played in Vancouver, Calgary, and Edmonton. It was in Winnipeg that the police caught up with us.

I learned that gambling was not the only vice we brought along, and that the wise conductor does pay close attention to the reputations and lifestyles of the candidates who audition. Two of our players had left a stash of marijuana behind in Los Angeles, and U.S. and Canadian police had been on our tail ever since.

An orchestra of three dozen can't perform with two of its members behind bars. Nat pled our case before the judge—would he really deprive the citizens of Winnipeg of a wonderful concert? No, the judge was a nice guy and he wouldn't do that. The offenders agreed to return to Canada after the tour to face charges.

On that long tour, I was also slow to catch onto the method behind the hotel accommodations our tour manager Sam Hollingsworth made. Usually they were rather crummy. Yet often he would say to *me*, "You're getting a suite."

I never asked for one, but okay. Sam himself, I noticed, always had a pretty nice room too. And he had his own room, while the others shared.

Nat and I did a little detective work and figured out that Sam, instead of using our large-group reservation as a way to get a quantity discount, was using it as a way to get perks, like a free room for himself and the suites for me.

He continued as principal bassist for us, but we relieved him of tour management responsibilities.

The first season of the Chamber Orchestra was a wonderful year of my life. My decision to cast away a secure career as a violinist for the utter uncertainty of conducting looked okay. Great, in fact. I even received an honorary doctorate from Capitol University in Columbus, Ohio.

Conducting is a misunderstood profession: you wave your hands and the orchestra plays. Of course, you *can* just do that, and most musicians will keep playing. But it is hard on them.

In order to do their job, they need something from you. Your personal interpretation, in fact your personality, needs to come through all your expressions and movements. You have to communicate with them in a hundred ways, not just with your stick.

And then—just as important—you have to get out of the way and let musicians run. Sound is best when an instrument vibrates maximally, which happens when the musician is relaxed. It doesn't happen when you terrorize your players. The heavy-handed conductor may get perfection without getting any real music.

One dilemma I faced is known to all conductors: Music, like any art, will wither unless it has a feeding stream of new thought. And yet, audiences often would prefer to listen to what they've heard before. Or perhaps a "new" piece by a dead composer whose work they know quite well.

Conductors do it anyway. We perform the work of contemporary composers.

During the short life of the Chamber Symphony, I commissioned several new works. Benjamin Lees wrote for us his Concerto for Chamber Orchestra. I liked Ben's music, even if I did once tell him he wrote as if he were limping. It was a challenge to convey his constantly changing rhythms through the baton. I would remind myself of the promise I had made to Stravinsky a few years earlier. I was determined to be equally faithful to Ben's music. It wasn't the kind of music you could conduct from memory. You had to have 100 percent of your brain concentrating every second.

So why would one of my players want to slip into my score of the Benjamin Lees concerto a provocative nude photo? Here I am waving my stick, and I turn a page and instead of a new time signature for the next phrase, I confront a woman in her simplest form.

I think I got it flipped over before anyone in the overhanging balconies saw it.

No one asked for the photo back.

We gave twenty-nine performances of that work. The funds to pay the composers what they deserved weren't sitting on the table, but there was another way to compensate them: if we could guarantee that number of performances, the composer received royalties from the American Society of Composers, Authors and Publishers.

We also gave twenty-nine performances of Richard Yardumian's *Cantus animae et cordis* for string orchestra, as well as the world premiere of his mass in English, *Come, Creator Spirit*. Other composers we commissioned and premiered works from were David Sheinfeld, Wilfred Josephs, and Rod Levitt.

Some complaints were reaching me that placed me in a painful corner. My brother's remarkable and original clarinet playing was proving an annoyance to others, especially his wind colleagues.

I could have set their objections aside in favor of Nat's artistry. But it was not they who brought the complaint. It was the other principals—representing the whole chamber symphony. "How can he lead the wind section," they said, "when he's not even a team player?"

They had a point. His imaginative style did have a way of undermining our unity.

And yet it had never sounded to me like a significant flaw. Ormandy had always valued that fine individual quality in each player, and I wanted to do the same. However, I was persuaded to set Nat back to second clarinet and hire a new principal.

It was a decision I was to regret. The new player was fine, though he never brought the spark of personal musicianship to the section. Explaining it to Nat was a task I strove to do for the rest of his life, without ever bringing him enough comfort.

By the time our second thirty-four-week season started, we had 122 concerts scheduled. To my delight, soloists like bass baritone Jerome Hines and violinists Jaime Laredo and Henryk Szerying were eager to perform with us. Harry Beall was energetic and thorough at managing our out-of-town concerts. Requests came from around the country, more than we could accept.

The summer ahead, 1968, was also taking shape. Temple University was planning a summer concert space just north of Philadelphia in Ambler. Would the Chamber Symphony of Philadelphia like to be their resident orchestra? Yes, we would!

In New York, I reserved Carnegie Hall for our second season instead of Philharmonic Hall. Our first performance of the season was to be the comic opera, *The Good Soldier Schweik,* written by the young American Robert Kurka, who had died of leukemia in 1957. It was influenced by the Czech folk music of his upbringing and threaded through with anti-war themes. We did it with partial staging and with Norman Kelly singing the title role.

I can't forget what happened right before the performance, though it was unrelated. The conductor's dressing room at Carnegie Hall is large with its own sitting room around the corner. I was getting my music in order and changing clothes when two gentlemen knocked on my door.

"We know you have a concert, but could we have a private meeting in your sitting room?" one said. "We don't have anywhere to go." The other one , who was quiet, had white hair that bounced off his forehead. He looked vaguely familiar to me.

"Sure." I was in nice-guy mode. I stepped back into my inner room to give them some privacy.

I allotted them fifteen minutes, and cut them slack to the half-hour mark, and begrudged them a further half-hour.

Then I said, "I'm really sorry, but I need to be able to prepare for the concert."

"Oh, we're sorry! Have a wonderful concert. You'll have great success!"

Sam Flor saw them walking away and popped his head in my door. "I didn't know you knew Herbert Von Karajan."

So that's who the white-haired guy was. I had seen him greeting Szell backstage in Vienna. Von Karajan was one of the top conductors of the twentieth century—and also the musical darling of Nazi Germany. Most of the best musicians left Germany as Hitler's anti-Semitism came to the fore, but Von Karajan was happy to stay and conduct. I wasn't sorry that my encounter with him took the form of an expulsion.

My workload was spinning out of control all that year, especially as Nat and I picked up Sam Flor's task of travel arrangements. Marilyn remembers me flopping into a chair muttering, "It'll get better. I know it will. It better get better."

If only our financial success could have kept pace with our artistic success. The board of directors was finding it difficult to secure new donors. Since we had the support of the Pitcairn family, many Philadelphians seemed to assume we didn't need any more funding. That was far from true. Even when every seat in the concert hall is filled, the ticket revenue covers only a fraction of the cost of the concert. Every week our brave accountant Ann Tigue worked to make ends meet.

The National Endowment for the Arts had been born the previous year and gave grants to the Boston Symphony Orchestra and the Denver Symphony. I read the application and noticed this requirement: organizations had to be in existence for three years before they were eligible. We petitioned them to make an exception for us. What if we needed them in order to stay in existence for a third year?

They did not make an exception.

We went forward, performing for grateful audiences and with reviews we were all proud to read. On tour, the phone in my hotel room would ring.

"Anshel? I'm not sure what to do here." It would be Ann, trying to keep the lid on some creditor. I would put my assistant conductor in charge and fly back to Philadelphia to ask a donor for a rescue gift or to reassure someone that a bill would be paid.

One day we were performing in North Dakota when Ann called. I explained to the local contact that my assistant conductor was going to do the concert.

"If you don't conduct, we'll cancel," he said.

I stayed to conduct and then got right into my rental car to head for my hotel, which was about thirty miles down the road.

It was an autumn night. Rain splashed suddenly out of nowhere. I slowed down to make sure I wouldn't get lost, or go sliding into a field of wheat. The darkness was close around me and I tried to peer through it for lights. Not much is out there in North Dakota. Farms were miles apart. My gas dipped to a quarter tank.

I was lost. I didn't want to turn into a farm that was completely dark and bang on the house door. A big sign by the road looked significant, but wasn't lit, and my headlights didn't illuminate it. Or maybe my windshield wipers couldn't go fast enough to clear the window in that downpour.

I got out of the car and got my umbrella up, though not before I was soaked, and went closer to the sign. "Welcome to South Dakota."

I somehow found my way back to North Dakota, to my hotel, and into bed around 2:00 a.m. After a few hours, I got a morning flight back to Philadelphia to face the atonal music.

That was one of the times when Harry Beall kindly had the Judson agency cover bills for us until we could pay them back.

Once we had a day off in Bemidji, up in northern Minnesota. Stuart Canin and Nat and I went to a drive-in movie theater to see *Casablanca*. Two other carloads of brave people had the same idea.

I kept the car running for the heater while we waited for the movie to start. Finally Humphrey Bogart appeared and I turned the car off so we could hear that ironic voice of his.

The screen got fuzzy, almost like the TV when it went off the air at midnight. This was real snow, though, falling thick and fast. Then the sound cut out. Now we couldn't hear Bogart, and here came Ingrid Bergman, maybe, behind all those snowflakes, and she was silent too.

"I'm freezing!" Nat said. "Are we nuts?"

Stuart and I were shaking with the cold too.

Just then they turned the movie off. We laughed all the way back to the hotel. Somehow it was emblematic of our lives, devoted to musical perfection and trying to bring it to audiences across our country, against all odds.

The financial basis for the chamber symphony did not solidify, and a number of our players found secure jobs in major orchestras. They were doing what made sense for them and their families. Playing with the chamber symphony was a nice addition to their resumes, and I was glad of that.

But Nat and I had constantly to search for and hire musicians to replace them, especially with our commitment to Temple University. The musicians who signed on in 1968 jumped into our spring engagements and could look ahead to all the summer concerts. But after that a lot of uncertainty faced us all.

Temple University's band shell in Ambler was ready for us on schedule. At our first performance, Van Cliburn played the Beethoven Piano Concerto No. 4. Van was always a joy to work with.

The Ambler Festival was conceived as a mixed offering, and I was thrilled to have my entry into jazz guided by Ella Fitzgerald. We were as new to her as she was to us, both virginal in the other's musical world. Rehearsal was common ground and, of course, she arrived on time. She brought with her several musicians who knew her repertoire.

After we were introduced, this is what she asked me: "Have you ever heard me sing?"

Had I ever heard Ella sing. Was I a living, breathing American?

I wasn't about to ask if she'd heard my symphony play.

"I'm a little nervous," she said. "I've never sung with this many players."

She didn't seem to have any trouble. Later, in the early 1970s, Ella would begin to sing with orchestras frequently.

Her drummer made it easy for us, giving us all the tempo variations. We got to "Sweet Georgia Brown" in the rehearsal, and she gave me a heads up: "I'm gonna take off on this one." Then she ran through the tune by herself before we started.

"I don't think I'm following what you're doing in the middle part," I said. I had to figure out what my players should be doing.

"Honey, you just keep on going and I'll find you." She looked at me from below those beautiful curved eyebrows.

The audience was packed in for the performance. On stage, each of us was startled and thrilled at the experience of her vocal notes dancing over the surface of our sound. She could hear harmonic lines like no one else. When the standing ovation came, we stood with the audience.

Friends told me that Ormandy was often heard referring to our summer concerts as "the so-called Ambler Festival." Oh, well.

One last avenue held out some hope to us—benefit concerts. If I could get a celebrity to help us bring in revenue on the front end of the third season, then we would be able to go ahead.

I tried Bob Hope. His agents suggested that I just ask him to emcee, but I didn't think that would bring the crowds.

Danny Kaye didn't respond.

Jack Benny wrote back, regretting he didn't have any available time that season.

Ethel Merman was a major draw at that time. Her managers listed her requirements, on top of an outrageous fee: personal hairdresser, manicurist, masseuse, private transportation, etc.

Pearl Bailey was gracious. Her fee was $25,000, with $12,000 in advance. We paid the advance and planned the event at the brand-new Spectrum arena, home to the Philadelphia basketball and hockey teams. Configured for concerts it could hold up to 10,000 people. Ms. Bailey threw in radio ads for us and did them with flair.

With our hopes pinned on that benefit concert, we began our third season, playing a concert in Philadelphia and a second one nearby in Allentown. The University of Maine invited us to perform in Orono. My players did an outstanding job on Vivaldi's *Gloria*. Shortly afterwards, the university administration offered me a position. David and Jennie were nearing college age, and a professorship was tempting. Marilyn and I considered it seriously, but in the end, I felt I wasn't ready to leave the concert stage.

And then Ann Tigue, our accountant sat me down. "We can pay the taxes," she said. "That's all." You're done, Ann meant. The Chamber Symphony must close its doors.

We asked for our advance money back from Pearl Bailey's managers, but of course that wasn't going to happen. I signed the check for the taxes and called Marilyn to say I'd be home early.

My son David had gotten a sort of sympathy card for me. "Some day your ship will come in" read the front. Inside it said, "With your luck you'll be at the airport." On my desk, the *Philadelphia Inquirer* was laid open to the classified employment section.

The newspapers and music magazines covered our demise quite gently. One said the chamber symphony had not failed, but the city of Philadelphia had—by failing to support a fine new kind of musical offering.[4] Another said local government had given grants to many arts organizations but not the chamber symphony because the Pitcairn family was too Republican.[5] I'd rather not give credence to the notion that anyone is capable of seeing blue or red in

---

4. James Felton, "Philadelphians Flunked, Not Chamber Symphony," *The Philadelphia Sunday Bulletin*, June 30, 1968.

5. Nancy Love, "Brusilow: After the Fall," *Spectacle*, winter 1968–69, 29–37.

musical notes. That we had a big enemy in town was known to all, but Ormandy's objection wasn't political.

The players did well at finding positions. They had hundreds more concerts under their belt, greatly increased repertoire, and some prestigious recordings. It wasn't long before Ormandy hired William Stokking back for a position he well deserved—principal cellist.

As for the personable manager in New York at CAMI, Ronald Wilford was ascending the ranks toward the pinnacle.

I had a lot of time to think that year. This thinking had to be financed, and selling my Guarnerius del Gesù took care of that.

Quantifying Theo Pitcairn's generosity to me is impossible. Besides the violin and the financial support, he encouraged me personally. He often made time for lunch with me—he always ordered the little-neck clams at the Bellevue-Stratford.

Once we were walking through his gardens in Bryn Athyn, and I asked him the dumb question, what it felt like to have so much money.

"It brings responsibilities," he said. "But one thing is certain, you can suffer in comfort."

In my loss of the Chamber Symphony of Philadelphia, after more than 240 concerts, my real comfort was and continues to be its lasting legacy. There were the five albums recorded by RCA Red Seal Victor. Beyond that, our venture had the happy effect of encouraging the formation of other permanent chamber orchestras.

As I parted also with my beloved instrument, I reflected on how good the violin had been to me. When I played—maybe this is why I didn't suffer from nerves—whether I was playing a concerto with a world-class orchestra or the "Hatikvah" for Edwin A. Fleisher, it was always just me and the violin.

And yet, I gave the music only a small part of myself when I played violin. It couldn't satisfy my appetite, no matter how well I played. On the conducting podium, it was different. A flick of the little finger could draw out a phrase just the way I wanted it, just the way I felt the music inside myself. Something happened between me and the players. A kind of creation, a magical making of something. The satisfaction it gives is like nothing in the world.

Selling my violin both expressed and confirmed what I really wanted to do. It has been difficult for many of my friends and colleagues to understand this.

That same fall, 1968, I got a phone call one day from Carlos Moseley. He was president of the New York Philharmonic's symphony association. "Anshel," he said, "hold on a minute. I've got another friend of yours on the line."

Next came the familiar voice of Zubin Mehta. "Anshela!" He always called me by this affectionate Yiddish diminutive of my name. "I want you to come and be my concertmaster. You can conduct, I don't care, anywhere, as much as you want, Anshela. Just be my concertmaster."

"Oh, Zubin—"

Another voice broke in—it was now a full-on conference call, Lenny Bernstein chiming in too. "Take it, Anshel. Take it!"

My chamber symphony had just folded. We were broke and I had a family to feed. But even with three against one, I couldn't say yes. "I sold it, you know. I sold my del Gesù because that's not what I want to do."

I was not going back to being a concertmaster, not anywhere. That part of my life was over.

Chapter 8

INTO THE WILD WEST

WHERE TO BEGIN ABOUT THE Dallas Symphony Orchestra? Those three years, 1970–73, are a complicated story. In my life, I was fired only once. But the memory of it splinters into arrows coming from different directions at different times.

It was because of the pops concerts. Who did I think I was, bringing Sonny and Cher onto the same stage with the Dallas Symphony Orchestra?

No, it was because of the factions. Some board members didn't like other board members. Some who particularly *did* like me died, or resigned, or were called aside by family matters.

Or was it the critic?

Oh, surely it all came down to money and attendance. Not enough Dallasites chose classical concerts over TV, and I did not change that.

All I can do is lay out what it looked like from the podium, from my office, and from inside my head. If it's a mess, forgive me. Everyone in Dallas musical circles knows what happened, but no one seems to know why.

I will start with music. Music is not a mess. And it is the point. The Cherubini Symphony, the lovely version edited by Arturo

Toscanini, is what my Chamber Symphony of Philadelphia performed at North Texas State University, near Dallas. I didn't know who was on the other side of the footlights, in that Texan audience, but one man was listening with both ears, and soon I was going to know him, for the rest of his life.

To back up a little: In 1968, some while after the Chamber Symphony's last curtain call, Jerome Hines called. Everyone knew him as a baritone, but he was also a composer. He invited me to conduct his opera, I Am the Way. I always loved working with Jerry. While I was conducting his opera in various cities from 1968–70, my antennae were up for a podium to come available at a city orchestra, but I was at a disadvantage without a manager. Arthur Judson, while he headed CAMI, had managed the top American conductors for decades. Now CAMI had a new head: Ronald Wilford.

This was the same Ronald Wilford I complained about, back when he was a mid-level manager, because he wouldn't let his soloists perform with the Chamber Symphony. I had humiliated Wilford in front of his CAMI superiors. He now managed Ormandy and most of the top conductors. I had double toxicity, lacking the support of both the great Eugene Ormandy and the head of CAMI. Harry Beall had represented my symphony, but to represent me personally as a conductor was impossible in that climate.

Seiji Ozawa called. Would I like to be his assistant conductor at the San Francisco Symphony?

Well, maybe.

And concertmaster? Please, Anshel?

No. No thanks.

To Marilyn I said, "I could always drive a cab for awhile."

"How would you find your way out of the driveway?" she asked. "I think I might be more gifted than you in some areas. Some remunerative areas."

She did not throw in my face the offers I'd turned down.

I was optimistic any time the phone rang. One day—not just any day, but exactly one year after the Chamber Symphony had shut down—Carlton Cooley called. He had been principal violist under Toscanini, and then played in the Philadelphia Orchestra with me for several years. I had brought him on as principal violist in the Chamber Symphony of Philadelphia.

"Stay by the phone," Carlton said. "You're about to get a call from an old friend of mine in Dallas."

Not five minutes later, the phone rang again. It was David Stretch, president of the Dallas Symphony Association.

"We're looking for a resident conductor for next season, and Carlton tells me you might be available."

His warm personality came right over the phone. We talked about Carlton and the Chamber Symphony. David Stretch was the person listening so closely when we played the Cherubini Symphony at North Texas State University more than a year earlier. He was also curious about my experience learning conducting under Pierre Monteux.

"Why don't you fly down and check us out?" he suggested.

Some weeks later, David met my plane in Dallas and took me to his house. His wife Mary was an accomplished pianist and wanted to play piano-and-violin sonatas with me.

"I don't play violin anymore."

"Not even with me?" This was a subject she would not let die.

I did let it die, however, each time it surfaced.

The next morning David took me to listen surreptitiously to a rehearsal. Several of the players had been in my Chamber Symphony, and he wanted to keep them in the dark in case I was going to say no.

The Dallas Symphony Orchestra had a mutually beneficial relationship with Southern Methodist University and was rehearsing in McFarlin Auditorium on the campus of SMU, their usual performance venue. It was very cold in there. We dodged our way along back halls and up stairways until we were in the top balcony, too far away to be recognized.

Some of the players were looking at small things they held in their hands. I couldn't tell what they were. They put the objects away when it was time to play. I listened to them and heard the potential to create a fine sound.

Dinner was at the home of another major player on the DSO board, Ralph B. Rogers and his wife Mary Nell Rogers. Ralph had led the development of Texas Industries into a major commercial enterprise. No one said he ran it with a velvet glove. In fact, people who had seen his temper were afraid of him.

He had become interested in the symphony in the 1960s when it was in danger of extinction, and had devoted himself to building a strong lay board. Generous himself, he was also an ingenious fundraiser. He did it his own way. If he thought a corporate contribution was too small, he mailed the check back. Often, he got a bigger check a few days later. When I arrived, he was chairman of the board and had turned over the presidency of the Symphony Association to David Stretch.

David Stretch was a lawyer, and his job was providing legal counsel to Texas Industries. It was nearly impossible for David not to take orders from Rogers—his boss *and* the previous president of the Symphony.

I signed a one-year contract, aware that they were conducting a worldwide search for a conductor. Many candidates were already slated to guest conduct. The arrangement suited me because I would not have to move my family to Dallas during the trial year. I could do much of the work from home in Philadelphia, such as engaging soloists, programming the concerts, and preparing the music.

My third trip to Dallas was to focus on the business side of things. I would stay two nights. I checked in at the Hilton and then spent the evening with David and Mary Stretch.

The next morning, I dressed and opened my hotel room door to go have breakfast.

A man stood there, blocking my doorway. He introduced himself as a detective for the Dallas Police. "We're sorry, sir, but we have to ask you to stay in your room."

"What for?"

He ignored my question. "We'll let you know as soon as you can leave."

I didn't think I was being arrested, though I did spend those minutes dredging up instances of substandard behavior on my part. My room had a door into an adjoining room, which I assumed was locked. This didn't seem like the time to try it.

Finally the police knocked, and I opened the door.

"What did you hear?" they asked.

"Nothing," I said. "May I go?"

"But you have a connecting door. Are you sure you didn't hear anything during the night?"

"Not a thing. What's the problem?"

"There was a problem next door. We need to know what you heard."

"I didn't hear anything. Can't you tell me what happened?"

"A man was murdered," they finally said. "A university professor."

They let me go and, as I passed the open door of the next room, I looked in. The sheets were soaked in blood.

I drove my rental car through the streets of what appeared to be a calm, civilized city. At the orchestra office, I spent the day familiarizing myself with ticket sales, programs, and publicity. The Dallas Symphony had earned only half its operating budget in the previous season—that would bear some hard thinking.

I also found time to change my flight so I could leave that night. The news had covered the murder at the hotel. The professor was visiting from out of state. He had gone down to the hotel bar and met someone who turned out to be mentally unstable. I simply could not return to that hotel.

During the summer, we drove to see Marilyn's family in California. On the way, we would find a place in Dallas for me to rent. We also stopped in New Orleans and took the children to the famous Brennan's restaurant for dinner—crisp white tablecloths and glittering hanging lights. A pair of musicians with a violin and guitar were wandering around playing nice tunes.

The thing is, when you're driving cross-country with your family, you feel a little fancy-free. Nobody knows who you are, and you can act a little crazy.

A few days later, Paul Crume's "Big D" column on the front page of the *Dallas Morning News* reported what happened at Brennan's:

> They came up to Brusilow's table and asked what his party would like to hear.
>
> "Brahms's' Violin Concerto," suggested Brusilow with tongue in cheek. It didn't go well with the performers.
>
> "Okay, wise guy," snapped the violinist snapped. "*You* play it."
>
> Brusilow rose, bowed, accepted the violin, and played the Brahms concerto.[1]

How did Paul Crume hear about it so fast? I never did find out. Well, it was friendly coverage, so I say thanks to Paul.

When I first started playing, there was a hush, and everyone turned my way. But the food at Brennan's is really delicious, so people started eating again, and I enjoyed the quiet percussive silverware against china in the background.

My kids said, "We can't go anywhere with him!"

Of course I had begun thinking about soloists right after I was hired. My first thought for my opening concert in the subscription series was pianist Rudi Serkin. Even back at Curtis when I was one

---

1. Paul Crume, "Big D," *Dallas Morning News*, August 23, 1970.

of the young musical kids and Rudi was teaching piano, he had been very kind to me. And we saw each other frequently during my Cleveland and Philadelphia days. I shot a letter off to him. Rudi was hopeless at answering letters, so I was prepared for a wait.

The other soloists I invited responded promptly and I scheduled pianist Rudolf Firkusny, cellist Pierre Fournier, and others.

Also on my mind was how to reach a broader audience in Dallas. The board wanted attendance and civic support. I thought back to the Gershwin orchestra I played in, and also the theatre of St. John Terrell's Music Circus. They drew a different audience. I began to think of ways to combine orchestral and more popular kinds of music.

"Listen to this, Dad," my son David sometimes said. And then I might hear a song as unforgettable as "Something." Clearly George Harrison and the other Beatles were forces to be reckoned with. David had a knack for finding songs that would speak across age and cultural differences.

That music was written for guitars, drums, and voice—not for orchestra. But I knew a talented arranger, Bill Holcombe. He could listen to a recorded song with a vocalist and arrange it exactly for orchestra, including the vocal line played by an instrument. It was incredible. He arranged whatever songs I asked for.

One day the name *Dallasound* occurred to me. It was natural, after being a part of the Philadelphia Sound. And yet in Dallas I planned to invest the term with a completely new meaning—the orchestra's other side, its performance of popular music. I wanted to find a way to present current pop material in an authentic way, without sentimentalizing it.

The DSO had wonderful traditions that I stepped into. My very first performance was in the free city park series, in a Hispanic neighborhood, so I had the orchestra rehearse the Mexican national anthem as an opener. We played music from the Spanish-influenced opera *Carmen* and, at the end of the concert, several contemporary songs—which the audience cheered as soon as we started.

The DSO's most beloved tradition occurred every fall. At the Texas State Fair, we were to play Tchaikovsky's *1812 Overture* in the Cotton Bowl, and twelve cannons would be brought in to fire (blanks, of course). Tchaikovsky was deeply moved by the story of Moscow burning, although it had occurred decades before he was born. He wrote the overture so that no one would forget that terrible day. Dallas would remember it in 1970 by projecting above the symphony the silhouette of Moscow on fire, as it had appeared in 1812. As I learned about this local tradition, I felt glad to be in a place that honored one of my favorite composers as well as my Russian heritage.

My visits became pleasant. Instead of sleeping in a hotel next to a murder in progress, I had a townhouse near Southern Methodist University, where we rehearsed and performed. The members of the board welcomed me. I heard some rumors of discord, especially over their previous conductor, Donald Johanos, but that was in the past, and I had no wish to explore old wounds. The president, David Stretch, was excited to have me in Dallas, and so was Ralph Rogers.

David was my favorite kind of person—someone you could seriously goof around with. He loved golf, and I loved playing with him. You should, anyway, always play golf with someone who is worse than you are. If David looked up during a swing, the ball could go anywhere.

"Where did it go?" he said after a particularly distracted swing.

I was standing directly behind him. "It's right here, David. By this tree."

He turned around and looked toward me. Sure enough, there lay a ball at the foot of a live oak.

"That's not my ball."

"It's your ball."

It had risen straight up in the air and come down behind him and rolled to the tree.

We also connected over football. Or disconnected, since he, a Naval Academy graduate, cheered for the Navy, and I cheered for the Army.

One of my first challenges was assessing the players. I was very pleased with almost all of them. Demoting a principal player is painful, but it is what a conductor must be willing to do. The principal flute, I felt, needed to be replaced.

I asked him to meet with me and our personnel manager Wilfred Roberts, who is still principal bassoonist at the time of this writing.

"I am going to need to find a new principal flute," I said to the flutist. "I would like you to stay in the position until I find someone, and then remain in the flute section."

I cushioned the blow as much as possible, and he listened stoically.

Then he stood and said, "Goodbye."

He told Will Roberts that we would not see him again, and he left immediately. He was a warm, sociable person and was missed by the players and also by board members that he knew well.

Finding a principal in any instrument for a large city's orchestra was not going to happen overnight. I called in the assistant principal flute to ask him to fill in. Usually such an opportunity thrills a musician, but this man really felt he was not prepared for such an exposed position.

"I think you can do it," I said. "I trust you. And I'd love to see you try."

My formal debut, before the devoted symphony-going public, was in early October. Violinist Itzhak Perlman was our soloist and I couldn't have been happier when he chose to play the Tchaikovsky Violin Concerto. After Perlman, we played Richard Strauss's *Rosenkavalier Suite*. I love this music from the opera *Der Rosenkavalier*. Strauss did not make this arrangement himself;

conductor Artur Rodzinski arranged it with Strauss's permission. Ormandy made his own changes to it. I had both played and conducted Ormandy's version many times, so it was a comfortable beginning for me.

With the players, I was extremely pleased. They saw how much I loved the Strauss and responded with a new enthusiasm themselves. Some said to me, "We've played this with a guest conductor, but it wasn't like playing it with you." Clifford Spohr, our principal bassist, remembers that when I urged them to hear it as romantic, and even sexy, they all became much more expressive with the piece.

A great surprise was in store for me after that first performance. Three members of the board, David Stretch, Ralph Rogers, and Gertrude Shelburne sought me out backstage to tell me that the board had already reached agreement informally. I was to be their conductor. They did not want to make a public decision yet because so many guest conductors were slated for the season, but they wanted to get my commitment right away.

I didn't have to think twice. Marilyn was thrilled, too, and we began talking about buying a house in Dallas.

The *Dallas Morning News* music critic, however, was unimpressed with my debut. He found the playing "rough." We were "matter of fact." We "failed to build." He also had many things to say about the *Rosenkavalier Suite*—mainly that he thought Strauss just threw something together so orchestras could play some of the music from his great opera and he could profit.[2]

This was new territory for me. By the time I took the Dallas position, I had been reviewed perhaps a hundred times as a violinist and several hundred times as a conductor. I was so nearly virginal in the matter of bad reviews that I couldn't imagine such a thing affecting me. I had been spoiled.

---

2. John Ardoin, "Music: Perlman Returns to DSO," *Dallas Morning News*, October 9, 1970.

Some musician friends in Philadelphia and New York had said, "Dallas? I refuse concertizing invitations from Dallas. There's a music critic there who ruins careers."

I turned a deaf ear. Like a teenager, I believed in my invincibility. The orchestra was responsive and promising.

I have not indulged in quoting from reviews throughout this memoir. It would have been unseemly. But at this juncture, I will do so occasionally—no one will accuse me of bragging. The records are public.

The critic my friends referred to was the late John Ardoin. After my hiring as resident conductor was announced, but before I had taken up duties, he campaigned in the *Dallas Morning News* for Charles Mackerras to be named the next DSO conductor. He dismissed all the other candidates including me and devoted six paragraphs to Mackerras.[3]

North Texas had rainy weather that fall. The symphony always played a number of outdoor concerts at the State Fair in October. Several times when we were slated to play, it rained the whole day.

Each time, general manager Howard Jarratt would assemble the orchestra as if the concert were going to go ahead. Of course there was no audience. Who comes to outdoor concerts in the rain? For some reason, Howard could not make up his mind to cancel and get the necessary board approval in a timely way, but rather let the players stand watching the rain fall.

The orchestra members grew irritated as this scenario was repeated. On the Thursday when the "Spectacular" was scheduled, the weather was so miserable that the Fair management postponed it until Sunday.

Then the rain blew away. What blew it away was a cold front, of course. Clear skies, though. On Sunday afternoon, the Marines had brought in the twelve howitzers for the *1812 Overture* and

---

3. John Ardoin, "DSO at Crossroads as Era Ends," *Dallas Morning News*, May 17, 1970.

positioned them on the other side of the football field. They were ready to fire at a signal from the orchestra's percussion section. The Dallas Ballet would also be performing parts of *The Nutcracker Suite*, and we would play Tchaikovsky's music for them. An army band was scheduled too.

As conductor, I could have initiated the process and requested that the concert be canceled. However, it didn't occur to me. In New Orleans, Cleveland, Philadelphia, and other places, I had often had the experience of our outdoor concerts being canceled because of rain or snow. As for temperature, I had both played and conducted in very hot or cold weather (not just outdoors—sometimes performance halls are poorly heated), but we never had contract protection for this. Generally, our concerts were only canceled if it were so cold that no audience would come.

But the musicians in the DSO had very particular circumstances. In McFarlin Hall, they rehearsed in a frigid atmosphere day after day. It seemed that in winter, the heat was inadequate and in summer the air-conditioning was hyperactive. After many complaints, they had managed to have their contract amended so that they would not be required to play in any venue where the temperature was below 68 degrees.

However, I didn't know about it.

It *was* cold that day. But Texans had come to their fair anyway. They milled around the fifty-foot figure of Big Tex, eating the famous corny dogs and deep-fat-fried whatever. Country and Western music was the norm, along with rock, but Dallasites also loved to hear the orchestra every year at the fair. And this year, because of the rain, they'd had precious little of us.

I felt that we were sufficiently ready with the pieces by Berlioz, Borodin, Sibelius and, of course, the *1812 Overture*, as well as the *Nutcracker* music. To shorten the musicians' time in the cold, I canceled our afternoon rehearsal. Low temperatures also are not good for the instruments, particularly the woodwinds, and our sound would be compromised.

People were streaming into the Cotton Bowl when I arrived for the evening performance. A strange process was going forward on stage. Several of the musicians were crossing back and forth staring at something in their hands. It reminded me of the very first time I'd seen them rehearse, watching from an upper balcony in McFarlin.

This time someone told me what they were looking at: thermometers. And they were registering 59 degrees. It was at that moment that I learned about the clause in the DSO players' contract that excused them from playing if it was less than 68 degrees, whether they were inside or out. Their frustrations had been further primed by the last-minute rain cancellations.

Meanwhile, at least 4,000 people had assembled in front of us. David Stretch and Ralph Rogers both came to the stage area to try to persuade the players to go ahead and play. The musicians wanted to discuss it among themselves. They called a union meeting, which of course no one else was allowed to attend. It was a "closed door" meeting, but as we were on a football field, they had to hold it in open air, between the goal posts.

The amusement editor of the *Dallas Morning News* had been around as we were setting up. He was John Ardoin's boss, and I was rather glad he was covering the event and not Ardoin.

But then I saw something that was out of order. This editor, William Payne, emerged from within the musicians' gathering. No one except union members should have been allowed to listen.

"What were you doing in that meeting?" I asked him.

He said, "I was invited," and started walking away.

"Mr. Payne," I called after him, "I'd like you to get your boy off my back."

He didn't feel a need to answer.

The trouble with spoken words is that even though they're invisible they hang around and can't be sucked back in. I don't think those words endeared me to Bill Payne.

The orchestra musicians decided not to play. No one could persuade them otherwise.

The performance went ahead without us. The ballet danced to taped music. The Fourth U.S. Army Band stood in for us and played Tchaikovsky's *1812 Overture,* and the guns were fired. I suppose the silhouette of Moscow in 1812 was projected.

Having no control over the situation, I left with my orchestra. No one was happy.

Soon I was happy, though, because I always flew back to my family when I had a few consecutive days without a rehearsal or performance. I was unaware of the public response for days.

Back in Dallas, the players took a lot of heat for that missed performance. The dynamics of how concerts get canceled and by whom, let alone the ways various instruments respond to temperature, were not generally understood by the public. It looked to the average Texas State Fair attendee as if the musicians just didn't feel like putting on their jackets and playing with chilly fingers.

The powerful Ralph Rogers, who should have known better, demanded that the players offer a public apology for refusing to play . . . "or else I'll resign." He was planning a campaign to raise $450,000 for the orchestra. He said that, under the circumstances, he didn't feel he could approach donors and ask them to contribute.

As the brouhaha boiled over, I was summoned back to Dallas. I tried suggesting that we offer a free concert, but perhaps the atmosphere between the musicians and the board was too toxic for that to be realistic. It was a toxicity with a history.

And a future.

The musicians had voted to refrain from making public statements, so their first communication was a letter to Ralph Rogers. They wrote that they did regret disappointing the audience. They also expressed regret at the "humiliation and animosity" that they themselves had suffered.[4] They stuck to their guns about the terms of their contract, however. It wasn't their responsibility to cancel concerts in a timely fashion, but rather the board's.

---

4. "Rogers Rejects Letter of Symphony Members," *Dallas Morning News,* October 23, 1970.

Rogers upped the ante. Their letter, he said, was not really an apology. He painted himself into a corner.

If only he had not issued the threat, or if he had accepted the musicians' apology, things might have calmed down. Will Roberts pleaded with him not to resign. But Rogers felt he had to keep his word—or, rather, carry out his threat.

The board accepted his resignation. (His energies after that would be poured into saving public TV from the axe Richard Nixon held poised over its neck. Rogers won that one.)

His departure meant a loss of leadership and fund-raising prowess to the symphony, and a personal loss to me. As he watched events unfold over the next two years, Rogers came to regret deeply his sudden resignation. He was the one to offer an apology, to me privately and also publicly. "My wife told me I was wrong," Rogers said, "and looking back, I guess I was."[5]

At the time, I remained an optimist. Ralph Rogers was one man, after all. I didn't see any reason we couldn't all survive his leaving. The president of the board was my great friend, and I was getting to know several other board members. Marilyn and I loved playing bridge with Margaret McDermott and Gertrude Shelburne. Sarah Massey and Sis Carr always cheered me on. Just seeing Sis Carr gave anyone a lift, with her infinite varieties of yellow clothing, yellow accoutrements, and even yellow vehicles. Plack Carr, her husband, dressed beautifully too. Once at a dinner party, I admired his ruffled tuxedo shirt, and the next day a messenger brought it to my house all freshly washed and ironed.

Also, after one of my early concerts, a familiar face approached me backstage to reintroduce himself. Ken Cuthbert was a friend from Monteux's conducting school when I was young, often eating dinner with Harold Glick and me and asking us questions about conducting. Now he was Dean of the School of Music at North Texas State University and had been present when the Chamber

---

5. John Merwin, "High Culture, Low Politics: The Death of the Dallas Symphony," *D Magazine*, November 1, 1974.

Symphony of Philadelphia had played there, in Denton. He also served on the DSO board, and he had immediately felt I was the right man for Dallas.

In early October the board had told me of their informal decision to keep me. I don't know when they ratified that by vote. But some time in November, they announced publicly that I was to be the conductor and executive director of the Dallas Symphony Orchestra.

General manager Howard Jarratt had been let go. Someone had to run things, and I rather liked the idea of filling both roles. Ormandy had done both and done them well . . . mainly by always making it appear that decisions had been made by someone else. I should have watched more closely.

Alternatively, I could have said a sensible "no" to the politicking side of the job. The music is enough for one person. Someone else can run the organization and pay the bills, but only the conductor can plan the programs, train the players, and perform the music. I saw immediately how much I had to rob Peter of hours in order to pay Paul. I was not so quick to realize how ill-suited I was for the political side of the job.

Our family was delighted to make Dallas our new home. Marilyn and I found just the right house. She and the children stayed in Philadelphia till school ended, and I bounced around the empty house.

The symphony, I felt, was sounding better all the time. The principal flutist did well in his new role. Even so, he was relieved when I found Jean Larson (now Jean Larson Garver) to be our principal. She would begin in the fall of 1971. She pleased me and, apparently, every conductor since my time, as she continued as principal flutist until her recent retirement.

Musicians, like most people, do their best when they feel confident. Yet it's in the nature of group rehearsals that, while everyone is learning to play a piece together and according to the conductor's plan, every player will occasionally play something wrong. My past orchestra experiences sometimes provided anec-dotes to help us over rough spots.

One morning in rehearsal, a musician made a loud mistake. The man—you could see it on his face—felt terrible. I told them all about Herbie Pierson in the Philadelphia Orchestra, the fourth hornist with the black shoe polish on his leg under the tear in his pants. Once Ormandy had assigned a single important note to Herbie alone. We were performing Dvořák's "New World" Symphony in Carnegie Hall. Dvořák has an E natural in the fifth bar that is for two horns. But Ormandy liked it better played by just one horn so, at this performance anyway, he gave it to Herbie. It was all his. But poor Herbie played every note his horn offered before he landed on the E natural.

Afterwards, he sat slumped on the stairway up to the dressing rooms. "Anshel," he said, "do you think anyone heard it?"

Laughter is good for musicality.

In December 1970, Rudolf Firkusny came to play Beethoven's Piano Concerto No. 3. The visiting soloists, when they were old friends, were a touch of home to me.

In the *Dallas Morning News*, Ardoin savaged Firkusny's playing and our accompaniment. Of Dvořák's "New World" Symphony, he asserted that it "underwent some rough handling Thursday, which left many of its tunes bruised by exaggeration and coarseness."[6]

That review brought out the first reader response to Ardoin's coverage of us.

Dallas Morning News: Letters from Readers, Dec. 27, 1970

[As] an orchestra buff of many years. . . . the Symphony "From the New World" was simply magnificent! This I have surely heard more than 100 times and this is the first time I would have said this

---

6. John Ardoin, "Erratic Night with DSO," *Dallas Morning News,* December 11, 1970.

is great music. I can only suspect that the kind of criticism Ardoin
has been putting forth must be distorted by a bitter prejudice. I, for
one, am most grateful that we now have a conductor who inspires
in our orchestra enthusiastic response, and I look forward to the
time when Brusilow will be conducting most of the concerts.

> Elsbeth Chadwick
> Dallas

Dallas had two newspapers. At the *Dallas Times Herald*, we got
fair-minded reviews, written by Olin Chism, Don Safran, or Bob
Porter.

Dallas had its core constituency of classical music lovers, but most
people were tuning their car radios to rock. The financial pressure
on the symphony continued unrelieved. At the series concerts on
Thursdays, Fridays, and Saturdays, we played only classical music.
Also the school and youth and the area tour concerts were all classical. But we had been including a "Dallasound" section of popular
tunes in our park concerts and a few of our special concerts. Now
I brought an idea to David Stretch, while surpassing his drives on
the fairway at the golf course. Why not bring in popular performers
to play with the orchestra? We could do blended concerts with part
of the night given to a big name popular musician with orchestra
accompaniments, and part given to classical music. The audience,
I hoped, would be drawn by the big names but enjoy both—and
come back later for more classical.

David Stretch loved the idea. It made sense.

At least it seemed to.

As for the big-name popular performers, I'd never run in those
circles. But I began to work with the William Morris Agency that
managed most of them. The agents were accommodating, even
sometimes procuring the orchestra arrangements I needed.

The *Dallas Times Herald* sponsored our first all-Dallasound
concert. We reserved the Apparel Mart for January 9, 1971.

Only in Dallas would a major concert be performed in a venue with a name like that. The city wanted to compete with New York in the fashion industry, and an enormous, sharply angular building was built to attract the industry giants. Oscar de la Renta, Pierre Cardin, Bill Blass, and other designers showed their creations in Dallas.

The plain exterior didn't prepare visitors for the Grand Hall inside the Apparel Mart, with its three curving balconies, terra cotta mosaics, and skylights. An audience of thousands could fit into that space.

But would they come?

Getting pop stars on the schedule would take a while, but for this first concert I had added a few special musicians, including drummer Paul Guerrero, bass guitarist Al Wesar, and guitarist Jack Peterson. They helped us get the authentic rhythm and feel of the music we were performing.

It was 1970 when we were laying these plans. The Beatles and all the music that sprang up in their wake had lodged in the minds of adults as well as teenagers. You could find yourself humming "Yesterday" and not even know where you'd heard it. But it was still young people's music, and hardly anyone was mixing it with adult forms.

Asking my orchestra players to go along with this new direction was a stretch, and an uncomfortable one for some. Musicians trained classically at that time usually felt that popular music was beneath them. A purist approach still seemed possible, I guess you could say, whereas today musicians play whatever they must in order to keep a symphony alive.

And no doubt it was hard for them that the melody lines went to the guitars. Sometimes the arrangements had the strings playing long series of whole notes in the background. These notes the players dubbed—not fondly—"footballs." Worse, arrangers referred to strings as the "sweeteners."

At times, the popular music really did challenge their skills in a different way, requiring a completely different kind of musical expressiveness. Some of the orchestra players liked it better than others.

Backstage at the Apparel Mart, I got nervous.

Philip Ruder, the concertmaster, was peeking through the curtain.

"Are there any people out there?" I asked him.

"Yeah, quite a few."

When it was time, I walked out onto the stage. The hall was packed. Some of the younger people were perched on steps and railings. I think the orchestra felt that excitement, even if they would rather have played Mozart. We had to turn away more than a thousand people.[7] The ones who got in loved the music.

Things seemed to be settling down in the spring of 1971. The orchestra, I felt, was getting better and better, both at performing symphonies and at accompanying our guest artists. One weekend we had the thrill of performing with an unusual piano duo: Gina Bachauer and her protégée, Princess Irene of Greece. Princess Irene was more than just a pretty face—she did her part creditably next to her phenomenal teacher.

I saw that Rudi Serkin was scheduled for a special solo recital here, listed on the DSO spring schedule, and yet not playing with us. He never had answered my letter inviting him to solo with us. On the day before his performance, the sound of his practicing upstairs in McFarlin Auditorium reached me, and I went up to greet him.

He jumped up from his seat and hugged me. "Anshel! I never wrote back. I didn't know what to say. I told Ormandy you'd invited me. He looked at me and just didn't say anything. He started walking out. But he turned back and said, 'Do what you want.' And then he left."

I'd heard those same words. Ormandy had bullied a musician so harshly that the players came to me and asked me not to stand when Ormandy came onstage at the next performance—so they wouldn't

---

7. Marilyn Schwartz, "Fans Dig Food, Bach, Rock," *Dallas Morning News*, January 12, 1971.

have to follow my lead. I took the matter to Ormandy and got that same curt "Do what you want." I knew what it was: a threat.

Ormandy and Rudi were close. But friendship would not prevent Ormandy from shutting Rudi out of soloing with the Philadelphia Orchestra. I wouldn't want to have any part of damaging Rudi's well-deserved success.

Mel Tormé sang with us in March. He was a singer with an unusual degree of musicality. With Mel, it was always song, never just notes, and somehow his own song. I had gone to Los Angeles myself to make the arrangements with him and, during the course of an afternoon at his house, learned that he loved the music of Frederick Delius. We planned a concert that included some Strauss and Tchaikovsky, then Tormé conducting Delius's Prelude to *Irmelin,* and finally Tormé singing several contemporary pieces.

Dallasound was generating a lot of excitement, and that first year we released a record of our best contemporary music, all arranged by Bill Holcombe. The musicians were paid extra for it, and the orchestra made money.

Andrew Lloyd Webber had composed something called a "rock opera," with lyrics by Tim Rice. It topped the charts when it came out in London as an album called *Jesus Christ Superstar.* Lots of groups wanted to perform the work on the stage, but no one could get permission since it hadn't yet come out on Broadway.

But maybe it could be performed concert style?

David Stretch, being a lawyer, assessed the permissions situation for me. "Let's do it!" he said. "We need a big venue."

Dave Brubeck's son got the music for me and lined up a narrator and four singers. Each would stand on a spotlighted pedestal, with the orchestra below them, miked. Our principal bassist Clifford Spohr was delighted to switch to electric bass.

We reserved the Dallas Memorial Auditorium (now the Dallas Convention Center). The orchestra parts arrived in the mail, with a note saying that changes to the music would follow.

As always, we sold the tickets from our offices in McFarlin Hall at SMU. I looked out the window and saw a double line of people stretching around the corner. The line circled the building. We sold 10,000 tickets in one day.

My secretary, Vicki Rapp, called me to the phone to take a special call.

"Hello, Mr. Brusilow. This is Greer Garson. Would you have two tickets to this *Jesus Christ Superstar* show?"

Yes, I did. I wasn't about to ask her to stand in line.

On the morning of the performance, a lot needed to happen. The singers arrived and their voices were wonderful and well suited to their roles. A couple of guitarists came along too. They were awfully good.

"Did you go to music school?" I asked them.

"Yeah," one said. "We went to Juilliard. I studied oboe, and he studied clarinet."

There's always something to create performance anxiety—the orchestra parts were still not finished! But soon everything fell into place.

Watching 10,000 people assemble was exciting. Audiences at concerts like that one behave differently from Brahms audiences. Where was the respectful hush that falls over the concert hall before we begin? During *Jesus Christ Superstar,* anytime we looked out over the footlights, we saw people wandering around eating popcorn and hotdogs. Some of the players had a hard time with that, and some loved it. It's an alternate way of enjoying music.

In the summer, my family joined me. Marilyn adjusted to the more southern culture of Texas with ease. David was ready to start his freshman year at Southern Methodist University, Jennie would be a junior in high school, and Mindy would be a second grader at the elementary school near our house.

Year Two in Dallas had a troubled start as the musicians struggled to work out their contract with the board. The early subscription concerts were canceled, but agreements were in place in time for the opera season. I hired my friend Earl Murray—our matchmaker in San Francisco—as assistant conductor. I needed a lot of help with the crazy workload of both conducting and managing.

I knew there was disagreement among board members about the Dallasound direction and other things. Board members generally do feel free to make their concerns known to conductors, which is only fair since they give so much of their time and money to the symphony. It is best to answer thoughtfully and respectfully.

Sometimes it was difficult to know what to say.

For example, one of our programs opened with Bach. When it was over, the trombones came out and took their seats to join us for the second piece. At intermission, I normally try to disappear to rest a little, but on this occasion three board members sought me out. If it were just one board member, I might have been tempted to slip behind a curtain. But three? I made myself available.

"Maestro Brusilow," they said. "The Bach sounded very nice. But you let the trombones off."

"I'm sorry?"

"You didn't make the trombones play."

"There's nothing for them to play. Bach didn't write them into the piece because there weren't any trombones when he was composing."

"Are those players being paid for this whole concert?"

"Yes. I mean I didn't dock their salaries."

"Then surely you could have written something for them to play."

Ah, yes, I suppose I could have written trombones into Bach.

A fragment of overheard conversation was even more alarming. My publicity director, Sarah Mitchell, had stopped in at the *Dallas Morning News* to deliver some press releases. When she came back, she was unusually quiet.

"Something wrong, Sarah?"

She shook her head.

The following day she still seemed discouraged, so I asked again. She looked up. I could tell she was torn about something.

"I'm going to tell you," she finally said. "At the newspaper office yesterday, I heard something you wouldn't like."

"Maybe not, but I still want to know."

"There were three men in the room. They saw me, I thought. It was the amusements editor, the music critic, and somebody else."

So, Bill Payne, John Ardoin, and a third person. I had to prod her forward.

"Okay, what they said was, 'We'll get rid of Brusilow by the end of his contract.'"

A few successful performances were what we needed, I thought. Boards respect profits. And my work with the William Morris Agency was about to bear fruit. On November 20, we played with the Fifth Dimension in Memorial Auditorium. Using Holcombe arrangements, the orchestra added its own dimension to their songs "Aquarius," "Never My Love," "Stone Soul Picnic," and others. The *Dallas Morning News* gave us a beautiful review. The reviewer was not given a byline.

A few days later, the orchestra played for the Dallas Civic Opera. This time John Ardoin was the reviewer. He found the musicians wanting and blamed it on their having played a Dallasound concert so recently.[8] Apparently the experience of thrilling 6,000 listeners in blue jeans rendered them unable to play Beethoven's *Fidelio*.

The large audiences attending the popular music concerts were not buying into the subscription concerts. That disappointed board members who hoped the symphony could raise the tastes of the Dallas populace. It disappointed me too. How much do I love Beethoven? And yet, I love "Light My Fire" too.

I do love Beethoven more.

---

8. "Concert: Dimension, DSO a Good Blend," *Dallas Morning News*, November 23, 1971; and John Ardoin, "High Note Will Close 1971 DCO," *Dallas Morning News*, November 28, 1971.

Some board members strongly encouraged me to give it more time. I often discussed my plans with David Stretch. He knew my responsibilities were excessive. It was a relief to me when two more people were hired, Ken Meine as general manager and also a development person. Now I could devote the necessary time to programming and conducting.

Sonny and Cher drew a huge crowd. Also Lou Rawls, Doc Severinsen, Victor Borge, Curtis Mayfield. We had to hold some concerts in the 10,000-seat Memorial Auditorium. We made money.

But it was the wrong color of money—the Dallasound color, not classical.

We offered a rich variety of classical music at the series concerts. Concert after concert, the audiences loved our music. And Ardoin found our playing "shoddy in ensemble, weak in balance, and coarse in sound" and, in that case, went on to denigrate our soloist Jerome Hines.[9]

Another of his bleak reviews was of a concert that included Tchaikovsky's tone poem *Francesca da Rimini*. For the clarinet solo, I showed Ross Powell, who was substituting for our principal clarinetist, the way I had conceived for my brother Nat to play it long ago. Ross loved it and was able to stretch his breathing long enough to do it very nicely. It was the one thing in the performance that John Ardoin praised. Ross couldn't swallow the injustice of it and wrote Ardoin to give credit for my direction of the clarinet solo.

Ardoin was gentle, however, with Van Cliburn in 1971 and 1972 playing Grieg, Tchaikovsky, and Rachmaninoff. For the rest of the concert Ardoin took off his gloves and said things like "The evening opened with an empty performance of the Symphony No. 41 of Mozart. And I mean literally empty. We got the shell of the work without its filling."[10]

---

9. John Ardoin, "DSO Opens 71-72 on a Low Note," *Dallas Morning News,* December 10, 1971.

10. John Ardoin, "Cliburn Performs Grieg Concerto," *Dallas Morning News,* May 13, 1971.

The *Dallas Times Herald* listened with a more balanced ear, usually with Olin Chism reviewing us. And I also got relief when I left to guest conduct elsewhere. Whether I conducted in nearby San Antonio or in Glendale, California, the newspapers always reassured me that I still knew what music was.

Once when I guest conducted in Fort Worth, Van Cliburn was in the audience, and he invited some of us to his house afterwards for dinner. It was very informal—in fact, we just raided the kitchen for vast amounts of food. Van's mother, who was his first teacher and still advised him, joined in the fun. In the midst of it all, Van told the story of when he lost his place in a Brahms concerto with the Philadelphia Orchestra and floundered around adding notes until he remembered how to get back. Afterwards, he said, he came backstage and overheard me saying, "What the f*** was that kid doing out there? Composing?"

"No!" I said. "I really don't think I said that."

"Anshel, I was walking past your dressing room. I know your voice."

"So you didn't actually see me?"

"I didn't have to."

"Yes, you did. Or you can't really be sure I said that."

I'd like to think I didn't say it. But I can't go so far as to say I wouldn't have.

In the spring of 1972, the city of Dallas was about to suffer a great loss. One day in March, David Stretch collapsed in his office. In an instant, a massive heart attack took away a fine man, a generous philanthropist, a real friend.

News like that sends chills down your spine. The board members were in shock, the orchestra was in shock, all who knew him mourned.

The board had to scramble itself to replace him. Later I heard the process described as "an upheaval" and "jockeying." Jack Vandagriff emerged as the new president.

We played *in memoriam* to David Stretch music that he would have loved to hear. Tenor Richard Tucker and the Grand Chorus from North Texas State University joined us for Beethoven's 9th Symphony.

Within weeks of David's death, there was some discussion or movement on the board that was not in my favor. I don't even remember it, but on April 17, 1972, the players' committee wrote a letter to the board saying that they wanted to go on record as wanting to keep me in place. I was given a copy of the letter. Apparently that calmed things for a time.

Of course the symphony went on, with the series concerts and the special concerts. Phyllis Diller came. She surprised me by approaching the piano with desire and fortitude. Hard work was no stranger to her, though she lightened it with hilarious self-deprecating jokes at her own mistakes. She gave a delightful performance of the first movement of Beethoven's Piano Concerto No. 1, two Bach compositions, and several songs from musical theater.

Not long after, she invited me to conduct for her a similar program with an orchestra in Hartford, Connecticut. She was great fun to be around.

At a later concert with us, Phyllis Diller was playing arrangements of Tom Jones tunes. His concerts generated huge publicity because of the articles of clothing that used to greet him as he arrived on stage—unmentionables, we used to call them. Tom Jones was present in the spirit of his music, it seemed to me, and I let it be known that if any women in the audience wanted to contribute lingerie—or even keys to their apartments—to the stage, I would . . . oh, who knows what I promised. I can't remember.

What I do remember is a set of keys landing at my feet with a clatter. They looked familiar.

The keys to my own house. Marilyn was sitting near the front and, apparently, was not amused. She has a good throwing arm.

Don Safran, amusements editor of the *Dallas Times Herald*, became a good friend of mine. One day I mentioned in passing that it would be amazing if we could ever get Elvis Presley to sing with the DSO.

"Let's go," Don said.

"Where?"

"To Vegas. He's there now doing his show. Let's see what he says."

I just shook my head, which was less than a definitive refusal, and on the strength of that Don got us rooms as the Sands Hotel and tickets to Elvis the night we arrived.

By this time, of course, we're talking about the older version of Elvis. The mostly female audience displayed no age prejudice whatsoever.

Actually, that's hard to prove since they began to scream *before* he set foot on stage. I hope they weren't taken aback by the real thing.

His performance was impressive. Not something one would forget.

"Now," Don said, "we're going to go see him. Or at least Colonel Parker."

"Who's that?"

"His manager. Or confidant. Anyway he makes the arrangements for Elvis."

Elvis was staying at the Sands, too. We took the elevator up to the top floor and walked toward the door that had to be his suite. Two enormous men appeared.

"Can we help you with something?"

"We'd like to speak with Mr. Presley about performing in Dallas."

"He doesn't talk to people about that. We'll see if Colonel Parker has time to see you."

Enough time passed for us to be grateful that the hallway offered a bench for the likes of us.

"This way," the big pair finally said. It seemed to take both of them to usher us into the large office where the colonel was enjoying a cigar at his desk.

"Delighted!" he said when Don introduced me as the conductor of the Dallas Symphony Orchestra. That got my hopes up.

"We would like to have Elvis perform with the symphony in Dallas," I said.

The colonel felt no need to pretend to consider my proposal. He burst out laughing. "Can your symphony play 'Hound Dog'?"

"We can."

But his amusement continued. "But you can't pay."

"We've got a venue for 10,000," Don said. "What do you charge?"

"Seventy-five."

If Elvis was our entertainment that night, we were Colonel Parker's. The price was out of our league.

On Easter Sunday we kicked off the free concerts in Lee Park to a crowd of thousands. The atmosphere was full of joy—adults relaxing and children playing. They responded with the same enthusiasm to Wagner and Rimsky-Korsakov as to popular songs. Since it was Easter, the music we played from *Jesus Christ Superstar* hit the perfect note.

In June 1972, John Ardoin pulled out the big guns. In an article titled, "Quo Vadis DSO? The Choice Is up to the Trustees," he called on the board to fire me. He compared his experience at the whole season of our concerts to visiting a sick person in the hospital.

> The DSO is now on the critical list and a review of its case is imperative. . . . The disease to which the orchestra has fallen prey is one of complacency. The board-of-trustees of the symphony has either forgotten what constitutes a major orchestra . . . or else it no longer cares . . . and it is the board that bears the responsibility for the gradual illness which has beset the orchestra. After having missed the possibilities of men such as . . . Charles Mackerras to lead the DSO, it appointed Anshel Brusilow. . . . Brusilow's contract expires at the end of the

1971–72 season, and the board must seriously and without emotion or personal consideration review. . . .[11]

Etc., etc., you get the point. At least the newspaper was still willing to give voice to its readers:

Dallas Morning News: Letters from Readers, July 4, 1972:

Fanning the Flames of Controversy?

As a member of the Dallas Symphony Association I would like to address this letter to the misinformation written by John Ardoin June 25. . . .

It is a known fact that, with the exception of two, all of the Dallasound concerts, including Jesus Christ Superstar last year and continuing through the Fifth Dimension, Phyllis Diller, and Sonny and Cher, have been near to or total sellouts of 10,000 at Memorial Auditorium—hardly the "lack of interest" that Ardoin points out. . . .

Ardoin himself has a great part to play in the lack of substantial audiences when his critiques have consistently been so scathing on the orchestra and particularly on the personalities of the conductor and the associate that the lay person reading his columns and not knowing better would easily be turned away from attendance. . . .

Mrs. Richard C. Bower
Dallas

The DSO was doing something right, because we attracted the attention of Hope Somoza in Nicaragua. A cultivated American woman and a lover of classical music, she had married in 1950 her cousin Anastasio Somoza, a younger son of the president. By 1967, her husband was president of Nicaragua and Hope was first lady.

11. John Ardoin, "Quo Vadis, DSO? Choice for Future Up to Trustees," *Dallas Morning News*, June 25, 1972.

She fostered the arts and had the Rubén Darío National Theater built for concerts and other performances.

The DSO was invited to perform in Managua. However, even with the cost of airfare and accommodations for the musicians and guests paid, it seemed like a lot of fuss for two performances. I explored the possibility of Nicaragua hosting DSO for a visit to several other countries.

They were happy to do that.

The musicians were excited—the DSO had never toured Central and South America. I engaged pianist Susan Starr to travel with us. Board president Jack Vandagriff was suddenly very friendly, and so was Mayor Wes Wise. They both came on the trip, along with other board members and spouses. President Nixon telegraphed his pleasure that we were "sharing a vital part of our American heritage with friends in other lands."

We landed in San Salvador, El Salvador, on a humid afternoon in the middle of a tropical downpour.

The weather was no deterrent to the locals. At the concert we began with the Salvadoran national anthem, followed by our own. Thunder reverberated against the mountains and lightning flashed as Susan Starr played Rachmaninoff's *Rhapsody on a Theme of Paganini* to a packed house. We also gave them Berlioz, Tchaikovsky, and Creston. It was a thrilling start to see the audience's wild enthusiasm for Susan and for the orchestra.

At the end of every concert, I addressed those warm audiences in their own language, though I claim no command of Spanish. I had a few sentences I could say about sharing music with them, and I meant it.

In each city, Mayor Wes Wise expressed the hope that many of them would visit us when the international airport in Dallas opened. He brought keys to the city of Dallas, American flags, and other gifts for the government officials of each country.

Next we flew to Colombia. Deep in a valley in the Andes Mountains is tucked the city of Medellín. A plane must spiral downward for some minutes before it can touch ground. We were relieved when it came safely to a halt at the bottom.

Our hotel, the Intercontinental, was a semi-circle carved out of a mountainside with a stunning view of the terrain. All eighty-five musicians and our staff and guests had reservations at the Intercontinental. And yet when we arrived, there was no room for a large number of our party. They were sent off on a bus to search for another hotel that could accommodate them.

As we approached the concert hall that evening, we had to walk between parallel lines of soldiers, heavily armed and wearing helmets. We had no idea what was going on. South of the border, it seemed, information was rarely available when you wanted it.

We assembled on stage, ready to begin Stravinsky's *Firebird* Suite. Then I received a signal to wait. Even though it was time for the concert to begin and the hall was packed?

Yes, I was signaled by an official to wait. For forty-five minutes, we sat on the stage.

It turned out that Hope and General Somoza (this being the period between his two presidencies of Nicaragua) had flown into Medellín to meet us there. The military display at the entrance was an honor guard for him. Also, the top two floors of the Intercontinental Hotel were needed for his retinue. Hence the displacement of so many of our musicians to another hotel.

We played two concerts in Medellín. The audiences were stomping with excitement. After the second one, they insisted on three encores. One woman asked one of the players, "What have we done to deserve such beauty?"[12]

The next day, our plane circled its way up and over the Andes. With the Pacific Ocean on our left and the Caribbean Sea on our right, we flew to Panama City. The temperature and humidity hung together just below 100 as we deplaned. Nevertheless, costumed dancers swirled across the pavement right up to the plane,

---

12. John Neville, "Good Will Greets Symphony Tour," *Dallas Morning News*, September 18, 1972.

followed by musicians and drummers. They escorted us to a nearby pavilion and onto the dance floor. Each of us received a small bottle of rum.

Our performance that evening was in a school gymnasium that was open to the weather. This was not an advantage. The stage was a raised platform similar to a boxing ring, and two thousand people were seated on three sides of us. Most of them, and all of us, were sweating. The men's bathroom served as my dressing room. I have performed in heat and in cold, but I believe the circumstances of that performance were the most trying of any. However, my musicians gave the Panamanians a whole-hearted performance of Wagner's Overture to *Die Meistersinger* and Vaughan Williams's Symphony No. 6.

The plan had begun in Managua, in the imagination of Hope Somoza, and now we were finally going there, our last stop. The acoustics in the Rubén Darío National Theater there reward every ounce of effort the musician gives. It was patterned after the great concert halls of Europe, not deep but circular and many-storied.

The *Dallas Morning News* had sent critic John Neville with us, and the *Dallas Times Herald* had sent Bob Porter. Both sent wonderful reviews back to Dallas every day. When we got home Bob Porter heard us play some of the same pieces in McFarlin Hall that he had heard us play in Rubén Darío. He wrote, "Oh, if only all Dallas could hear that magnificent, stunning sound in Managua."[13]

Tours are filled with dinners and receptions for conductors, soloists, board members, and politicians, while the musicians go find dinner where they can. But General Somoza and his wife invited the entire orchestra to a reception at their home.

The orchestra was housed at the nicest hotels in Managua. At mine, our concierge told us that the top floor was restricted. Naturally that aroused curiosity, and sooner or later someone ferreted out who was there: Howard Hughes. One intrepid woman traveling with us pushed the button and rode the elevator up.

---

13. Bob Porter, "For DSO; Both a Beginning and an End," *Dallas Times Herald,* September 22, 1972.

It stopped at the top, and the door opened. There stood two burly men in suits.

She said, "Excuse me," and pushed the Close Door button.

One group of our musicians arrived at their hotel in Managua to find a flustered concierge. There had been some mistake, apparently, and they didn't have all the necessary rooms available. Realizing that we were the guests of General Somoza, the concierge turned white. The musicians sat in the lobby and watched hotel employees bringing many suitcases down to the desk area. Tourists came into the lobby and asked for their keys only to be handed their suitcases. The concierge had dispatched an army of maids to clear out rooms and ready them for the DSO party. He did not want to find out what would happen if General Somoza's guests were not accommodated.

Of course, Somoza was not a nice man. The Nicaraguan people suffered under him. Hope did too, I imagine. She moved to London and divorced him. He was assassinated in Paraguay eight years after our visit.

We were on a high when we got back. Adulation goes to your head. The board members were very warm to me. Jack Vandagriff, since he had gone on the tour and seen the response, had to offer the same congratulations and praise for the orchestra's work as everyone else. The *Dallas Times Herald* published a cartoon of a press conference: me conducting the reporters with a baton. I loved it.

John Ardoin wasn't at that imaginary press conference. He did give a glowing review of our next performance—but then added, "which should be the norm instead of a welcome and stimulating exception."[14] I was used to that by now.

Mostly, things were looking up.

Yet there was a niggling worry behind my confidence. The orchestra had a new manager. He had come along on the Central

---

14. John Ardoin, "DSO Returns Home in Superb Form," *Dallas Morning News*, September 22, 1972, 14A.

and South American tour, had seen the undeniable success, and yet had no interest in getting to know me. I couldn't help wondering if he knew something I didn't.

The city of Dallas was renovating a charming old performance space, Fair Park Music Hall. Our acoustics were poor at McFarlin Hall, but the music hall had even worse acoustics. Nothing in the renovation plan would address that problem, and it may have been impossible to fix. I had gone on record saying that the project was a waste of public funds.

Me and my big mouth. The city could not at that time have built something like our current Meyerson Symphony Center.

An opportunity for a relaxing little family vacation presented itself when the Honolulu Symphony invited me to guest conduct in November. I took Marilyn and our little Mindy along for a week of Pacific sun.

At the concert, Michael Ries of CAMI was present as the agent of our soloist, and he approached me. After very kind words about my conducting, he asked, "Who manages you?"

I admitted that I had no manager, and that this was a problem.

"I'm going to talk to Ron about that," he said. "You need to be with us."

He meant Ronald Wilford, who reigned at CAMI.

"Well, you go ahead and try," I said.

When we got home from Hawaii, Jack Vandagriff called to arrange a meeting. I was feeling especially warm toward our board president. At a recent concert, he had come on stage to address the audience. Referring to our Central and South American tour, he said, "The thing was—the extraordinary account that Conductor Brusilow and the musicians made for themselves. We are extremely pleased."[15]

---

15. Bob Porter, "For DSO; Both a Beginning and an End," *Dallas Times Herald,* September 22, 1972.

I looked forward to a meeting with him. "Sure, Jack. Why don't you come to the house?"

When he arrived, I brought him into our comfortable family room, where he sat on the leather sofa facing the hearth and our coffee table made from driftwood.

I wondered what he had to say. It was possible that he just wanted to congratulate me on my success in Hawaii. Or talk about the tour again—he and Mrs. Vandagriff had such a nice time. It was also possible—I knew the board was still divided—that he was going to shorten my next contract to two years instead of three.

But none of those were on his mind. What he came to say was this: "While you were in Honolulu, the board voted not to renew your contract."

Not renew. *Not renew*. As in, You can leave our city.

My mind felt fuzzy. What did he mean?

But there could be no question. There was nothing fuzzy about it. It was just a new experience.

Ormandy's worst fury at me was because I *left* his orchestra. "This is the best job in the world! Why would you want to quit?" he had said.

Memories tumbled through my mind. Szell's face hanging out of his office door—"You're not going anywhere!"

Being locked into Hilsberg's office. "Sign that contract, Anshel!"

Nothing prepared me for this.

Jack Vandagriff said, "You can choose to leave. You can resign and make the announcement yourself. You're still the conductor through May."

I said what a fired person can say, something like, "I see," though one is blinded with the shock and cannot see. We were polite, and I saw Jack to the door and closed it quietly behind him, and kept my feet moving, back down the hall, through the family room into the kitchen where Marilyn was, so that I could get it over with, the necessary saying out loud of the new Fact, the purpose of Jack Vandagriff's visit.

She said what a wife can say, something like, "Oh, honey, I'm so sorry." I was looking at my shoes, and they continued their monotonous motion down the hall.

Marilyn called to me that she would be back in a few minutes. The door to the garage closed.

My shoes took me into the bedroom, which for some reason I needed to visit. There stood the bed, where sleep always refreshed me and presumably would again. I walked around it and looked in my closet, which contained many more pieces of black and white clothing than a man in another profession would need.

I slammed my hand against the wall. As if waiting for that signal, pain tore across my chest. Not a heart attack, I knew, just physical grief.

It subsided.

My feet took me back toward the center of the house, now silent with no one home but me. I had come to the living room.

The living room felt white. The carpet was very nearly white, the upholstered sofa and chairs were creamy yellows. Sheer curtains on the bay window washed the late sun to white as it fell into the room.

The grand piano was black. And the music stand was black except at the battered corners, where the bare metal was exposed. I stood before my black things, to be in their presence.

Jack had not said the word *fired*. But that was the word that language offered up to me, if I let language into my mind at all. I closed my eyes and rested my left hand on the top of the piano. My fingers noted the texture of the runner of intricate Asian embroidery that Marilyn had laid there.

Of course, there was music driving through my head. It had started in the bedroom, while my chest burned. Now I named it to myself. Beethoven's *Eroica* Symphony, the second movement—the funeral march. In the wake of the oboe and strings, pulsed all of Beethoven's personal agonies. He invites every person who has ever grieved to feel the agonies with him. In the silence of the living room, I heard the funeral dirge in my head, just as Beethoven had to listen to it in his head, unable to hear real instruments playing anymore.

Whenever I began to prepare a piece, I would set the score up here on the piano and transpose each instrument so that I could play its part in concert pitch. I would make up my mind about particulars and stop to jot notes on the score.

I didn't go get the *Eroica* score in my study. I just sat at the blank piano began to pick out the oboe line: G — G G — ^{D}C B♮ C and then a rise that felt like a heart-pinch, up to D E♭ — C.

That melody, known to me since childhood, said the thing that my heart wanted to say, if I had been able to think in words. Thinking in notes was just easier.

Words might have formed a question: *Why did I ever come here?* It was a real question that I would wrestle with in the coming months.

But on this day I had only notes as thoughts, and they offered a simple and true answer to that question before it ever found language.

I came for the music, and it was inside me, safe and secure.

Marilyn came back, sensible and comforting. I knew she would have had a good cry in some parking lot. Her words were measured to the capacity of my state. She would have realized that the smart thing to do was take Jack up on the offer to resign. And she would have realized the pointlessness of trying to convince me of that.

Michael Ries, the CAMI agent I met in Hawaii, thought he could get me onto the CAMI roster. Maybe he would get me a manager.

I was struggling to get my mind around the fact that DSO wanted me to go away. I convinced myself, that I probably could turn this around. I did not resign, and the news of the board's decision leaked out—I don't know how—and was confirmed. The newspapers announced it. William Payne got first crack at it in the *Dallas Morning News*. After his boss, John Ardoin got to write about it too, trying hard to keep his glee in check. Local television got in on the act, and I was invited to be interviewed.

I've always done better at expressing myself with a violin bow or a conductor's baton, but at that interview I had neither. So when I was asked on TV, "Maestro Brusilow, how do you think the public will react to this news?" I had to use my mouth.

I opened it and said, "The public may respond to this and really let the board know what they think." I didn't understand how Dallas works. In Dallas, the powers that be settle their differences in private, not necessarily politely, but always privately. Then the public is told how the land lies. The public is not invited to participate in the dispute.

But I had invited them in, and some wrote letters to the editors of the newspapers, which were comforting to me but couldn't really change the situation.

The symphony board was deeply divided over my position. But finally I had given them something to agree on. I had invited the public to rise up in revolt. It was as if I had invited lepers to sit in the first violin section . . . and caught leprosy myself.

The public response was not large, but sometimes quite articulate.

Dallas Morning News: Letters from Readers, December 4, 1972

Dallas Deserves Brusilow's Talent

It was with great distress that I read of the dismissal of Anshel Brusilow as director of the Dallas Symphony. As a native Dallasite and a former season ticket holder for many years, I attended innumerable DSO concerts, and never have I been more impressed with the orchestra's precision and sound or with the sensitive musical interpretation. . . .

Is it possible that the people of Dallas can be misled by a petty, spiteful critic who could and did review the Bach A minor Violin Concerto when the piece actually performed was the Bach

E Major? Mr. Menuhin is still telling that story. I had two people ask me about it during my last trip to Europe. If, as the critic wrote in his audacious defense, "our mind wanders," then I must ask why the Symphony Board patently ignores the profound damage done to Dallas' entire musical climate not by the conductor of its orchestra, but by a twisted, poisonous pen? . . .

S. P. Dalton

New York, NY

Once I got over the reality hump—yes, the conductor who can't sell the symphony gets replaced—there was a lot to think about. First, I was going to acquit myself with excellence for the remaining concerts with DSO. And we had a lot to look forward to on the schedule.

Second, the orchestra moved. We gave our first performance in Fair Park Music Hall on December 14. Visually, it was very pretty, and we did our best to project from the stage to the audience. General Somoza and his wife flew up from Nicaragua for the opening. I was all done complaining about the acoustics in our renovated hall. Still, how embarrassing, after playing in the acoustically perfect Rubén Darío performance space in Managua!

Third—that question. Had it been a mistake to come here? David still had two years at SMU, and Jennie was now at the University of Texas. Mindy was happy at her elementary school. Marilyn liked it in Dallas. Also, she really believed that something good was going to happen. She thought I had some gifts in the realm of music and somehow they would be called upon.

On January 9, 1973, the CAMI agent I had met in Hawaii, Michael Ries, wrote to me, and I still have the letter:

Dear Anshel,

I finally had a moment to speak quietly to Ronald Wilford about you and I am afraid it will not work. He feels rather strongly about the Johanos affair, which I must say I knew nothing about.

Apparently this is something which is still pending and which he feels you had a major hand in and naturally this has turned him against you.

Sorry, but I tried.

With warmest wishes,
Michael

The poor man had been made to feel embarrassed for even asking. CAMI had managed Donald Johanos, so Ronald Wilford had access to the inside story of whatever happened. The departure of Johanos was planned before I was even on the Dallas radar screen, and it had nothing whatsoever to do with me.

It was kind of Michael Ries to plead my case.

I saw plenty of kindness. Princess Irene of Greece and pianist Gina Bachauer wrote to protest and to say they loved my accompaniment. Violinist Henryk Szeryng wrote in dismay to board member Gertrude Shelburne. Gertrude was upset herself on my behalf and wrote a long letter to Eugene Ormandy, because she knew that he would hear a skewed version of what went down, and that I was still very fond of him.

Leonard Rose performed with us in February, playing Bloch's "Schelomo: A Hebrew Rhapsody for Cello and Orchestra." This was shortly after his mother had died. Rose's cello seemed to be drawing the grief out and conveying it through Bloch's deeply emotional music.

Besides the cello, the piece has some nice work for the principal bassoonist. Our Wilfred Roberts played the bassoon part with such authentic feeling that I had to ask him if he was Jewish. I think he was flattered. He should be.

That spring the Dallas Symphony Orchestra toured west from Texas and up the California coast, twenty-one cities in three weeks. Arthur Whittemore and Jack Lowe came along as our soloists, and they brought their own grand pianos along, in specially built cases.

You know it's worth the trouble when you hear them play Poulenc's Double Concerto for Two Pianos. We were also giving our audiences Beethoven's Seventh Symphony and works by Berlioz, Wagner, Mendelssohn, and others. The reviews polished the image of Dallas.

Reno, Nevada, was one of our stops, and there I got a surprising phone call in my hotel room.

"Anshel?" It was Efrem Zimbalist, Sr., my violin teacher at Curtis. He was living in Reno with his daughter and had seen a notice of our concert. "Would you have time to come and see me?"

No, of course not . . . but yes, of course! Old age hadn't robbed Zimmy of any charm. He still practiced violin daily and even gave me a little performance. His daughter said he shouldn't go out that evening to our concert. Three weeks later he sent me a memento of his affection, a photograph of himself with a warm inscription. I was touched and a little surprised, not because I knew of any hostility between us, but because it seemed imperative to him to communicate good will toward me.

I am still thinking about it, as I recently saw my records from Curtis and learned that it was his decision that I not be allowed to return to Curtis after my "homesickness" in Maine. His reason may certainly have rested in my indifferent commitment to the violin in my early teens; I cannot have been among their most promising students. Whatever the reason, Zimmy's late show of kindness comforted something that was long buried in me, and yet still smarting.

In May we performed Yardumian's Mass, *Come, Creator Spirit*, again with Lili Chookasian. Theo Pitcairn generously financed the productions with the Maryville College Choir in Tennessee and then in Dallas with North Texas State University's Grand Chorus. It's hard to describe what a conductor experiences when a multitude of fine voices joins the orchestral instruments under your baton. I can't imagine being more alive.

My final concert at Fair Park Music Hall was all Brahms, and I felt so sad. British pianist John Ogdon played the Piano Concerto

No. 2, and we played Brahms's First Symphony. After a number of curtain calls, I thanked the audience and told them how much I appreciated working with their orchestra. "The symphony belongs to you and to Dallas, and it deserves your support," I told them. "Music doesn't stop with the comings and goings of musicians."

Dallas Morning News: Letters from Readers, June 3, 1973:

Good Show

. . . I have noticed, too, that John Ardoin seldom has a good word to say about the DSO and I was disappointed in his review of the final performance, in which he grudgingly (it seemed to me) wrote a few words of praise for the performance.

He said nothing about the spontaneous and prolonged standing ovation given Mr. Brusilow and the orchestra for a job well done and a thoroughly delightful evening for those who were there to enjoy the music—not to criticize.

Mae Martin
Dallas

I loved conducting the DSO. But if you choose the artistic life, you must choose it for love of the art and nothing else. In this city in this decade, and in that city at another time, a form of artistic expression will find itself in a dark place, a haunted alley. It doesn't last forever, and even if it dampens a few careers, the arts rebound. That's what they do, waking up all over again in younger hearts.

Music won't go away. It's an antidote to the turmoil of the age, to all the anxieties we're surrounded with, the materialism, the pragmatism. It quiets the fretting baby. It effervesces into dance. It opens the doors of grief and then soothes the mourning. Music can't be stolen from you or devalued. It can be owned fully by millions of people at the same time.

And you don't have to know much about techniques to enjoy it. Some people go to a concert clutching scores and trying to catch the mistakes. Well, good luck to them. The expert in chord structure isn't always the one who gets the most out of the highly evolved orchestral sound.

Two years after I was fired, Don Safran wrote an article for the *Dallas Times Herald*: "Who gunned down Brusilow at the DSO Corral?"[16] I'd come a long way from the young musician planning a book called *Shoot the Conductor*. Back then I was mad! How dare the Monteuxs try to prevent my marriage? And Szell, yes, we all wanted revenge. And Ormandy, who was so fatherly and then barred soloists from playing under me. In my youth, I could imagine letting a slender arrow fly off my bow towards my giant conductors.

But now we were in Texas. Here they talk about gunning conductors down. At least it's still metaphorical.

A last word on Jack Vandagriff. I never was naturally savvy about how people wielded power or ran orchestra boards, but even I could tell that Jack was carrying out plans that weren't his own. I don't know any more than that. Some people have used the term *figurehead* of his presidency.

In the 1980s, we were both at the same party once and, as it got later, I saw Jack come weaving toward Marilyn and me on the dance floor. It was all so long ago by then, I couldn't imagine what he wanted to talk about. He leaned heavily on my shoulder.

"Anshel. I gotta say this tonight. I owe you an apology. A terrible thing, back then."

He seemed to feel better after that, and he went on his way.

So did I.

---

16. November 30, 1975, 1–J.

Chapter 9

THE LESS WILD WEST

AT TIMES LIKE THAT, YOU JUST DO THE NEXT THING, live from today to tomorrow, fulfill your engagements. I conducted the Bournemouth Symphony in England in some all-Russian concerts, and we recorded an album for EMI—Rimsky-Korsakov's *Skazka*, Balakirev's *Grand Fantasy on Russian Folk Songs*, and Borodin's Symphony No. 2. It was beautiful and gave me comfort.

A surprise awaited me at home: Ken Cuthbert asked me to teach conducting and lead the orchestra at North Texas State University, where he was Dean of the School of Music. I was scheduled to guest conduct in Marseilles and then Mexico City in October. In November I was to conduct Yardumian's *Abraham* in Philadelphia. Ken said they could work around my plans.

Sammy Mayes, principal cellist in the Philadelphia Orchestra, urged me to consider Phoenix, a smaller orchestra with a season of only twenty weeks. I didn't want to move the family, so I didn't apply.

On August 24, 1973, Eugene McDermott died. His wife Margaret asked me to plan the music for the funeral and to play violin. I wasn't performing anymore then, but for Margaret, I did. She always kept out of the political side of the board's affairs, but she was broken-hearted about my firing.

At the funeral, it was quite an experience to see how beloved Gene was not only by his friends in charitable work but also by the hundreds of people he employed at Texas Instruments.

I chose Tchaikovsky's *Serenade for Strings* for the ensemble to play—the first movement as people entered the church, and the final movement at the conclusion. During the service I played the Sarabande from Bach's Partita in D Minor for solo violin. One-hundred years old at the time of this writing, Margaret still remembers how the music helped her to heal after the loss of Gene.

North Texas State University already had a prestigious and well-developed jazz program. Now they wanted to raise the classical music program to a similar level. I would be conducting the orchestra and chamber orchestra, and selecting and teaching the students in the Master of Music in Conducting program. The richness of being at a music school that embraced more than one kind of music was not lost on me. Do we really need demilitarized zones between music styles? I hear rock rhythms in the march in Wagner's Overture to *Rienzi*. In "Something," the Beatles combined a melodic line with a middle section that develops a rock beat, which influenced many other rock composers.

I wasn't sure what to expect in myself as a teacher. When Joe Gingold set me up with a couple of violin students in Cleveland, I didn't last long. My students at Temple University, though—they were full of excitement in the classroom. They had assembled at my house after I conducted *The Rite of Spring*. When I hired a fifty-year-old musician, I got what I got. But when I worked with young people, I sometimes said hello to an awkward player and just a few years later launched an artist into a strong career.

I checked out the forty or so kids in the orchestra. Their faces were so fresh! But after that, I noticed how half the violinists couldn't reach the G string because their wrists were plastered to the necks of their fiddles. Bewildering varieties of rhythm emerged from them.

My students weren't sure what to expect of me either. At least one student caught his first glimpse of me on local TV, emerging from the stage door of Fair Park Music Hall, wearing a shocked expression. It was all over the news that I had been fired from the DSO.

I held auditions to add to the orchestra. At 9:00 a.m. I began listening to students, and thirteen hours later I finished. Every student who wanted to audition should have the experience, it seemed to me. I doubled instruments wherever possible to give more students orchestra experience.

Congeniality is nice, but I was sure of one thing: in music there is only one contest that matters, and it's the beauty contest—of sound. For admission into the orchestra, I insisted on a meritocracy of tone production.

Every year the September auditions were a big deal. The next day my assistant conductor would post the list, and everyone crowded around it in the hallway.

Then I might get some visits.

"Maestro Brusilow, why am I the fourth viola?"

"That's because I really need strength in the middle there. Can you help me by making sure your intonation is perfect, so it will help the others around you?"

They always bought it.

Once in a while I would hear, "Maestro, my name's not there! It's not on the list."

"Really? I must have made a mistake. I think I meant to put you in. Yes, you're in the back of the cellos."

My student orchestra was *almost* a meritocracy. One young man auditioned with his violin, and I said to him on the spot, "I'm so sorry. I don't think you would make it."

"Please," he said. "I'll work hard."

I put him in the back of the second violins, and I will say that his hard work boosted the morale of others to whom the music came more easily.

Years later I was recruiting in another city, and that former student sought me out. "I teach violin in a junior high school," he said. "I love my job! I love it!"

Somehow, students come to college having years and years of instrument lessons, and having played in their high school orchestras, and yet never having heard some of our most gorgeous music.

"Open Beethoven's Fifth now."

A rustling of papers. Students checking to see if their entrance is soon or a page away. At the downbeat, the strings all play. As the first four notes bounce out, their faces show stunned recognition. They can't look up, the music is too challenging, but I see the thrill in their energetic playing, never mind the mistakes. I get to see them hearing Beethoven, experiencing Beethoven, for the first time. I am back with Mr. Happich, with the Symphony Club, and with my mother.

Sometimes my students were shy of the music. I had to tell them, "If you're going to make a mistake, make it a big one."

For years, our performance hall was too small, seating 450–500, and the fire marshal felt it necessary to keep an eye on us. College kids folded themselves into the tiniest places along aisles and in corners. It was a delight, always playing to a packed house. Of course the price was right: free.

That first year, 1973, a shy girl came to audition, held her violin correctly, and pulled some gorgeous notes off the strings. She was Elisabeth Adkins, a freshman. Before long, I made her concertmaster, and she raised the level of the whole orchestra. She had a tough mother who had made her practice every day.

From the start, I explained to the students that there's *practice*, which the musician does alone, and there's *rehearsal*, which is with the orchestra, under the conductor. Practice prevents the playing of wrong notes in rehearsal. Most of them still needed to work on their intonation—hitting the note exactly—that I understood. But notes that were completely wrong were unacceptable.

"If you don't practice," I said, "I won't rehearse you."

Sometimes they didn't. So I went back to my office. My assistant would finish the rehearsal. If the students didn't learn that much from me, they wouldn't get very far in a professional orchestra. I owed something to their tough mothers, and it wasn't coddling their darlings. They had pushed their kids, and I would too.

The conductor's authority was a new concept to some. Joe Gingold ridiculed Szell with doublespeak but Joe, even with all his talent and originality as a violinist, would never challenge Szell's musical choices. Concertmasters *lead* the players in *following* the conductor. Individuality is what soloists are allowed, not orchestra members.

One year, my two best players were violinists. But these boys cut up during practice and didn't take the work or my direction seriously. I could see it affecting the motivation of the other students, so I dropped them from the orchestra. I missed their fine playing, but all the others played better without them.

I used the music faculty as soloists at most of our concerts. For students, I held a concerto competition for each section. The winners soloed the following year in a concert, under the baton of one of the conducting students.

Composer Martin Mailman was on our faculty, and I loved showcasing him and other composers at UNT. Some student compositions also were performed, either by the full student orchestra or our smaller chamber orchestra.

I had a three-day teaching schedule, with conducting classes and orchestra rehearsals on Monday, Wednesday, and Friday. A curious pattern emerged. After working on a program for a number of rehearsals, the orchestra would peak. Then it would go downhill! They were bored with the repetition. So I mixed other music into rehearsals, either for future programs, or just for fun.

My second boredom tonic I used sparingly.

"I think I already told you about when Ormandy heard *The Pines of Rome* on the car radio," I might say.

"No, you haven't!" They'd lay their bows across the music stands or set their horns in their laps and sit back. They thought they were getting away with something, distracting the conductor from the hard work. But it was what their brains needed, five music-free minutes when they reverted to the world of words.

"Okay, let's start the second movement again." And they would sound so much better.

The sweet center of a professor's life is influencing how students see themselves and music. The kids started coming into my office to hang around and talk. I had a couple of chairs, and other kids would sit on the floor. Often I had ten or a dozen crowded around my desk.

"Did Pierre Monteux talk about the riot over *The Rite of Spring?*"

"What was it like to play under Stravinsky?"

One young man wanted to become one of my conducting students, and I told him I didn't think he had what it took. He felt so lost. He went to law school and has since argued before the Supreme Court. He contacted me recently and said that my decision had saved his life, by allowing him to find his area of giftedness.

It was a long time before I stopped wishing for the miracle of another major city orchestra. But after some years, I looked around at where I found myself, a full professor with tenure. What was it like to wave the baton over students instead of professionals? They paid for the privilege and appreciated it. My colleagues, the other professors, were dedicated, talented musicians.

A few members of the faculty had opposed my hiring and gave me a cool reception. They knew all about me from the local news—what a troublemaker I was. George Papich felt that way, and so did Martin Mailman.

We started playing golf together. The need for players in this sport has been the downfall of many animosities. That's not my fault. Martin was a poor golfer. So was George. So was I. We *had* to be friends.

At least I identified the problem with Martin's golf stroke. "You're hitting the ball from the wrong side!"

He claimed being left-handed as an excuse.

University politics can be bruising, and we all got some elbow jabs. No puncture wounds, no blood flow. I liked that, after the armed conflicts of the professional music world. And my schedule was fantastic.

Once on the way to lunch, Martin delivered some good news to George and me: the university was considering going to a four-day week.

"Over my dead body!" I said. "I'm not teaching a fourth day."

They called me the Part-Time Professor.

In the beginning I wondered how I was going to teach conducting. NTSU was one of the earliest schools to offer a degree in it. In most schools of music at that time, conducting was just a course offering, and I knew how it was usually done: the professor maintained a syllabus of conducting scores, and he took the class through each one, pointing out all the pitfalls.

Monteux, with only a month to teach us each year, did better than that. He had us sing the melody line to him and conduct an imaginary orchestra, or two pianists representing an orchestra. Later, as more students came to Maine, we had a small orchestra.

I accepted six students each year to work towards a master's degree. They couldn't really be beginners. They had to at least demonstrate a flair for it, a natural grace of movement, balletic without being theatrical. I took my first cue from Monteux, but I taught my students for nine months, not just August. I had them learn whatever scores I was working with at the time.

In our conducting class, they conducted with the other students singing the parts to represent the instruments. If a rhythm was sung incorrectly, I would ask the student who was conducting to explain the correct rhythm. Sometimes the student couldn't do it, but another student could. As I watched them, their mistakes were evident to me, and it was not difficult to help them improve.

In the orchestra rehearsals, which they attended, I set Fridays as the day they would be called on to conduct at some point. They liked that, and wished I would stick to it. But I found that if I sometimes asked them to conduct on a Monday or a Wednesday, the latent terror served as a good motivator to hard work. It took a thick skin to graduate from my program, but the graduates needed it for the careers they hoped to pursue.

My emphasis was always this: Know what you want the players to do, give them every cue they need. Then step back to leave space for their own instincts. They are artists, and they must have some freedom of interpretation.

Never, I told them, try to entertain the audience at your back.

It shouldn't be necessary to say that. When you raise your baton, you suck in your breath, and then comes an incomparable thrill. Music, big music, comes out of the players and you have the privilege of controlling it. The privilege is almost too much. One feels unworthy. I can't imagine, as the music washes over me like a gift from the players, turning my mind to the people just sitting there in the audience. Aren't they, like me, just wanting to hear what the musicians are offering? If I am really in the score, directing every instrument and melding the sounds into a whole, how could I possibly at the same time do a little dance for the audience?

And yet, one sees it done. I didn't want any of my conducting students to minor in dance.

In the process of teaching conducting, I had to become aware of what I was doing in order to explain it to them. Why did I never conduct a piece of music exactly the same way twice? The best music offers more possibilities, I realized, than I could see in one performance. Some new dimension would suggest itself in a score, and I would want to bring it out.

Students noticed that my physical movements are those of a violinist. My accent gestures are diagonal from top left to lower right. That's like bowing a violin, of course. The motion begins in my right foot with a slight lift in preparation for the swing to the left. I didn't teach a specific set of movements. Each conductor has to find his or her own way to communicate the music all the way to the back of the orchestra.

Stylistically, I tend toward the romantic, a more subjective approach. But no one could learn under George Szell and not also appreciate objective precision. These two are supposed to be incompatible, but I try to grab both.

In order for my students to be accepted at doctoral programs in conducting, they needed competency in reading orchestral scores, interpreting music, transposing, and planning programs that audiences would enjoy. I would give them an imaginary orchestra of eighty players and a budget. They would plan rehearsal space and its cost, work out the details of how to audition players, establish salary levels, and plan classical programs of not more than eighty-five minutes. They also had to audition players and plan the logistics of running an orchestra. Their finals were real performances: our children's concerts, one pops concert each year, and the concerts with the student soloists who had won the concerto competition in their sections.

One day my daughter Mindy informed me that she and I were playing our violins for an assembly at her elementary school. I asked what the pay was.

She rolled her eyes. "We're playing 'Twinkle, Twinkle, Little Star.'"

"Good! I know that one."

"Dad," she said, "we have to play it from the music." She set it on the old music stand by the piano in our living room.

We played through it, and I mostly stuck to the music.

"No, Dad. We have to play it the way it is on the paper. We have to practice."

We did, every day. When it was time to go out on stage, she gave me a solemn order: "No fooling around!"

I didn't dare.

I had more freedom in my paying job. As the years went by, the NTSU orchestra produced fine, expressive music. At Curtis or Juilliard, the conductor has an uphill battle making the students play together. Each one wants to solo. But an orchestra sounds best when players share the spotlight and are willing to recede. These students could take direction from a conductor. Seeing them thrill to their collective sound—which was much better than they thought they were capable of—took me right back to my own youth. I wish everyone could know what it is to be ravished by music. I felt it again every time I saw a student feel it.

When we performed Béla Bartók's riveting Concerto for Two Pianos and Percussion, Marilyn said on the way home, "How do you think the percussionists played?"

"They were fantastic!"

"Hmm," she said. "And yet you didn't have them take solo bows."

I sent a congratulations/I'm sorry telegram to Doug Walter, the principal percussionist, and he sent copies immediately to the others.

Once a recording of the NTSU Orchestra was taken from a concert performance of Strauss's *Till Eulenspiegel's Merry Pranks*. Like most musicians, I prefer not to record concerts because it's not easy to correct the inevitable mistakes. But that night we played *Till Eulenspiegel* perfectly and were pleased to have the proof on vinyl.

A fine cellist named Christopher came along in the early years. He had a mother enforcing his practice too. In fact, it was the same mother who had made my concertmaster practice—he was Elisabeth Adkins's brother. And I had only begun to tap the pipeline of Adkins talent. Clare, Anthony, Alexandra, and Madeline followed. The boys played cello and the girls played violin. The Adkins family raised the quality of our strings sections for many years, and the law of diminishing returns never applied to them. Both parents were musicologists teaching at NTSU.

The university orchestra was integral to both the opera and conducting programs. We played the doctoral recitals for conducting students. For the opera program, we played Mozart's *Marriage of Figaro*, Tchaikovksy's *The Queen of Spades*, Leoncavallo's *Pagliacci*, and others.

I had some goals for the school: a university orchestra that could play on a professional level, conducting students that were qualified to take on good orchestras, and a Doctor of Musical Arts program in place for conducting students. We attracted talented students, and the orchestra program was heading in exactly the direction I wanted. I wasn't interested when Southern Methodist University offered me a similar job, but with higher pay and a shorter commute.

NTSU was chosen to play in San Antonio for the Texas Music Educators Association, a great honor. The incomparable choral conductor Robert Shaw would be there to conduct Brahms's great choral piece, *A German Requiem*. Bob Shaw and I were friends from Cleveland days when he was Szell's assistant conductor. He requested that I be the one to prepare the orchestra for him to conduct at the performance. I was glad to, especially with my granddaughter singing in the chorus.

Our orchestra also played Strauss's *Also Sprach Zarathustra*, an extremely difficult tone poem. The students knew it from the movie *2001: A Space Odyssey*. I declined the opportunity to have it recorded and have regretted it ever since. How was I to know that this would be one of the most beautifully perfect performances I would ever conduct?

Much as I loved teaching, I did want a bit of additional income, and it came from a surprising direction.

A man named Phil Kelly called because he needed a violinist. Of course, I told him I didn't play anymore. He was a composer of commercial music.

"You can find lots of violinists," I reassured him.

"But what I need is a little Jewish hora. You know that dance thing. Solo violin."

"You can find lots of Jewish violinists."

Pretty soon it came out that this was to be an ad for some jewelry. I was as open to jewelry music as I had been to playing lunch music for the Curtis faculty. I told him again to find someone else.

"Musicians are so hard to work with," he complained. "They want it always to be Mozart. And they have trouble with the electronic timing systems."

I didn't know what he was talking about. Also, I wanted it always to be Mozart.

"I'm going to pay you, you know. This is good money."

That gave me pause. David and Jennie were both in college.

"Okay. When do I show up?"

No one would be there except Phil and one engineer. The other musicians had already done their parts and were on the tape.

Phil was providing the violin, and he handed me the case when I arrived at the studio. When I opened it and looked in, my instinct was to blow. A cloud of rosin dust billowed off the instrument. The bow had a bushy tuft of horsehair hanging off the end. But it tightened up okay.

The problem I encountered was not, actually, with the violin. It was my fingers. They were perfectly functional when holding a baton or, in the case of the left hand, directing players on its own. But on the neck of the violin, and moving a bow, my fingers felt like cement. They didn't want to flex. It took forever to get them moving at a reasonable speed. I tried some scales, and by the third scale my fingers and my bow arm felt perfectly natural again. I started playing scales as fast as I could.

Phil came running out of the booth and said, "It sounds fantastic! Let's do it!"

He says my warmup took thirty seconds, but it seemed like a whole five minutes to me.

"Put on these earphones, Anshel, and I'll get the click track ready. You'll hear four clicks and then you start playing."

I heard the clicks and played his music.

Phil came out to stop me. "You have to stick to it," he said. "You don't get to zoom off on your own. The other instruments are on the same tape, and this is how we make them work together."

I needed to adjust my thinking. All my life I had driven my music from inside my head. Even under Szell, I had more freedom than the click track was going to give me. I learned it, and Phil was right about the money.

I had my mother send me a good violin I had left at my parents' house. Once again, the violin came to my rescue, if in a different way.

The biggest surprise was that I was having fun. I said yes when other arrangers called. Instead of just an engineer, I found other string players there—mostly members of the Dallas Symphony Orchestra. We worked well together, and pretty soon I simplified the process by conducting from my chair. Then I became the contractor and organized a string section of very compatible players. We did commercial work, studio work with artists on major labels, television work like the Wishbone PBS series, and a couple of movies. Working with composers like Phil Kelly, Dave Zoller, and Don Zimmers was eye-opening. They jotted down musical notations and rhythms as they heard them, transposed music for various instruments on the spot, and switched between styles of music as easily as changing hats.

Sometimes I worked with the enormously talented Tom Merriman. He grew up in Dallas and came back after studying music at Indiana University and Juilliard. Once he was running late to one of our sessions, and told us he'd finished the composition while stopped at red lights.

All these producers were willing to work around my university schedule. Classical music was always central, and occasionally I brought it into the commercial sphere. For a Honda TV ad, I picked my own music. The excerpt from Paganini's 24th Caprice in A Minor alone (as it was written) seemed perfect, with a few revisions to make it fit the time slot. Since my regular union players were busy, I played it with a group of talented UNT students who were thrilled to get the chance to record a jingle for real money. I even had a line in that commercial: at the end, I said, "It's simple."

The benefits worked both ways between commercial and classical settings. In the 1980s, Jerome Hines wanted to record a version of I Am the Way with the Luxembourg Symphony. My skills with the click track technology enabled Jerry and me to fly over without bringing along any soloists or assembling a choir there. As I conducted the symphony's parts in the opera, I wore headphones to hear the click track and think of the arias the singers would be doing. When I wanted a singer to hold a certain note, I counted the length on a separate conducting track.

Back in New York, the choral conductor used the track with my counting on it to conduct the chorus so that they fit perfectly with the Luxembourg Symphony. The soloists also sang their parts while listening to my track, which told them when to come in, how long to hold notes, etc.

In the early 1980s, administrative changes at NTSU brought a change in priorities that neither Dean Blocker nor I could do anything about. Funding for the orchestra was pared back. We were asked to mimeograph our concert programs. That blurry purple ink!

I was courted again by Eugene Bonelli, Dean of the Meadows School of the Arts at Southern Methodist University. University president Donald Shields also weighed in. I said yes to a new challenge, and for some years had a budget that could attract students from New York and Philadelphia. We could offer generous financial aid.

Football fans will remember the fate of SMU in the mid-1980s. Their recruiting practices came under scrutiny, and the usual stonewalling worked for a while. But the NCAA kept uncovering unpleasant facts about payments to players that went beyond normal student aid. Finally the newly enacted "death penalty" was handed down, shutting the university out from football for 1985 and 1986. Resignations were inevitable: the football coach, the Athletic Director, and eventually the university president.

The repercussions of the demise of football at SMU affected every aspect of the school, including the orchestral program. Scholarship funding shriveled. Music Division chairmen succeeded one another before I had time to get to know them. The new president had far less interest in music than Donald Shields.

I had accomplished what I intended, however, and developed an orchestra program that was a credit to the school.

On the other hand, NTSU, renamed as the University of North Texas (UNT), got serious about the orchestral program again. When Dean Blocker made me a tempting offer in 1989, I decided to come back. It was difficult, though, to leave some of my SMU students in the midst of their doctoral studies.

My student Gabriella Diaz-Alatriste followed me from SMU to UNT. She became the first woman to be named conductor of one of Mexico's big five symphonies, the Orquesta Sinfonia del Instituto Politécnico Naciònal de México.

The students in the orchestra say even today that I somehow made them play "better than they had any right to."[1] Yes, I hope so. There was plenty of talent, though. My return was rewarded by several more musical Adkins kids coming along.

---

1. From conversations with Irene Mitchell, Doug Walter, Arturo Ortega, and other former students.

My doctoral students, if you talk to them today, say that I wasn't always nice.

No, I suppose not. Any time a student claimed to have a score memorized, I said, "Great! Write it out." Just as Monteux had asked of me.

Arturo Ortega remembers this from his student days: He was conducting the UNT Symphony Orchestra's final dress rehearsal of Dvořák's Cello Concerto. I came up to the stage and pulled on his pant leg to get his attention.

"Yes, Maestro?"

"Arturo, I think you should tell the piccolo to tone it down."

"There's no piccolo in this section," he said.

Well, I did the simplest thing. I looked between Arturo's legs at the girl playing the piccolo and motioned for her to lower the volume. She nodded.

It was a little hard on Arturo, with the whole orchestra watching. He was an excellent student and normally was aware of every instrument he was guiding. Particularly by the time dress rehearsals rolled around. Today he oversees acquisitions for the world-class music library at UNT and guest conducts many orchestras. I am confident that he maintains a special awareness of piccolo parts.

In January of 2000, our orchestra suffered a loss none of us can forget. Concertmaster Lucyane Guedes, principal bass Simon Lim, and principal viola Herbert Wentz were driving to a performance and never arrived. Their car crashed, killing all three. Our memorial concert included music loved by each of them. The students and I felt that we could not fill their first chair seats that season— no one would have wanted to be chosen. I just brought three roses to each rehearsal and laid them on their chairs.

My UNT students inspired me with their talent and dedication. Many came from humble circumstances to this public university, just as my brother and I had gone to Curtis. We continued to attract top-notch talent, especially as our graduates were landing prominent positions. Just from the Adkins family, Rostropovich hired

Elisabeth as associate concertmaster of the National Symphony Orchestra when she was only twenty-five; Christopher became principal cello in the Dallas Symphony Orchestra; and Madeline became associate concertmaster of the Baltimore Symphony Orchestra. My conducting student Hector Guzman conducts two orchestras. The list goes on.

I found time to conduct for the Dallas Ballet during those years, and also to conduct the Richardson Symphony Orchestra. With so many friends in the business, I had no trouble getting soloists for Richardson. If only Theo Pitcairn had lived to hear his granddaughter Elizabeth Pitcairn playing Sibelius and other concertos with us on her famous Red Mendelssohn violin. I recently passed the orchestra on to my assistant, the promising young conductor Clay Couturiaux, and I expect it to have a bright future.

Dallas was good to me in the end, a hospitable city for my family to live in, and a place where I could make a musical contribution that still bears fruit. I was appreciated by the universities and received many awards. In retirement, I am honored by the chair that has been established in my name at the University of North Texas with a grant from Sue and Christopher Bancroft.

Chapter 10

IN GOOD COMPANY

JOE GINGOLD, IT TURNED OUT, WAS RIGHT. I needed to be teaching. Working with young people is a salve for some of the grief that awaits the long-lived. We lose people.

Joe Gingold died in 1995. He had left the Cleveland Orchestra the year after I did. He loved teaching and did not love Szell, so he took a position at the Indiana University School of Music. After the funeral, his children gave me two of Joe's violin bows. Then they handed me a photo. Across a corner was written, "To Joe Gingold," and it was signed by David Arben.

"Dad meant to give this picture to the soloist," Joe's son said, pointing to the violinist standing next to Joe. David Arben, of course, after playing the Mendelssohn Violin Concerto, Robert Shaw conducting. Joe knew what the picture would mean to David, who had survived the concentration camps by virtue of his violin playing and lived by it ever since. "Do you think you could get the picture to him, Anshel?"

"Sure," I told Joe's son. "I'll find out where he is now." Arben had stayed with the Philadelphia Orchestra, moving forward from the fifth stand until he was assistant concertmaster. He had recently retired. I hoped I would get around to it quickly, but I didn't.

An event in the early 1980s still knocks around in my head like an annoying ghost, so I will backtrack further to air it, and maybe then it will go quiet.

I got a phone call one day. It was Stephen Sell, executive director of the Philadelphia Orchestra.

"A new hotel is opening across the street from the Academy of Music." He referred to the Hershey Hotel. "We're planning the dedication ceremony for their Eugene Ormandy Ballroom."

"I'm happy to hear it. But—excuse me—why are you calling?"

"To invite you, of course. And Mrs. Brusilow."

"Thank you. I—" My feelings were all jumbled. I still loved Ormandy—a part of me could never let go of the father-son relationship we had. The trouble was, the warm and cold of my concertmaster years seemed to have frozen to ice when I turned maestro. I had seen only the spiteful Mr. Hyde version of Ormandy since then.

However, now I was a professor and no threat to him, so maybe a melting was in progress.

"Well," I said to Mr. Sell, "I just would like to make sure Mr. Ormandy really meant for me to be on the guest list. Are you certain of that?"

"Yes. Absolutely."

A little bit of elation leaked in. I told him I'd check our schedule and call back.

Oh, what a pained look Marilyn gave me. "Please, Anshel. Put it out of your mind."

A few days later, an engraved invitation arrived in the mail. Marilyn was convinced it was a mistake or—worse—a prank. "I'll go with you if you want to be there," she said.

When I called to R.S.V.P., Mr. Sell was pleased and said he would make the arrangements for our room at the Hershey Hotel.

So we flew out to Philly and checked in. Having some free time, we took the elevator down to the lobby to check out the ballroom.

As soon as we turned the corner and entered the room, a mural of the orchestra faced us, and it was full of all my old friends—there sat my assistant concertmaster Dave Madison; Veda Reynolds of the candy wrappers; David Arben in the back of the violins, Herbie Pierson with no visible tear in his pants; John de Lancie—and here came the A of his oboe in my head; Sammy Mayes, who shared my Ginastera concerto secret. For some reason, the painter had used a photograph of the orchestra that must have been from the mid-1960s.

Only one head was an unrecognizable blur. Mine, right in front. My left foot was sticking out as usual, though. No one familiar with the orchestra would fail to recognize that. It struck us funny and we stood there laughing.

"Oh, Mar, I see we shouldn't have come," I said. "But here we are, and we'll go to the dinner and see what happens."

In the lobby, we felt at sea. The hors d'oeuvres were coming out, and the room was filling up, but we didn't know anyone.

Then Lenny Rose, my favorite cellist, appeared. "Anshel, did you see the mural? I've never seen you looking better!"

We were so glad to see him—somebody to laugh over old memories with. Like the time he was rehearsing for a performance with the Philadelphia Orchestra and Ormandy bent toward the cello section to instruct them. This meant his backside was facing Lenny and me. Nobody but Lenny Rose would even think of using his cello bow to goose the great Eugene Ormandy. Ormandy flipped around, and Lenny gave him an engaging smile.

The same bow, we remembered, that I used to bat out of his hand.

By this time the Ormandy Ballroom was packed. "Who are all these people?" I asked him. "I don't know a soul."

"Neither do I," he said. "And my wife couldn't come. They must be donors or something. The latest crop of board members?" He didn't know why he was invited either.

Ormandy came in and, before long, saw me. The expression that came over his face was one I knew. It was the look he got when he was conducting a work from memory and his mind went blank.

He turned away.

I felt awful. He hadn't expected me. None of the other players from the orchestra were there, and not even soloists I knew, except Lenny. The event seemed to be for the development community, not the musical community. If Mr. Sell had made a mistake in inviting me, Ormandy could be imagining that I had come to ruin his evening.

I couldn't stand that thought. The mural was nothing to me, but Ormandy himself—at that moment I saw him as a fixture in my life, something that I would always be moored to because of his role in my early musical life.

We sat for dinner at our assigned place in a back corner. When I saw Ormandy not crowded around by others, I got up.

"What are you doing?" Marilyn said.

"I have to."

"I wish you wouldn't."

I crossed the room to where he stood and said, "Mr. Ormandy." It sounded odd, but I couldn't say, "Boss."

"What are you doing here?"

"I was invited and I came to honor you."

He walked away.

In March of 1985, when the news reached me that Ormandy had died, I could only think of dear Dr. Jekyll. In the car on the way to New York, he would turn to ask Gretel in the backseat, "What did you get for sweets?" I could still hear his pleased chuckle as she pulled out a box of apricot *hamentashen*.

In May of 2013, I returned to Philadelphia to address the alumni of the Philadelphia Orchestra, so many friends gathered together. One of the alumni who lives in Philadelphia never misses this annual event—David Arben. He has retired as associate concertmaster. Before I left I tucked the old photograph into my suitcase. In the lobby of the Rittenhouse Hotel, I saw him. He has grown old, as I have, too. What a beautiful smile broke over his face when I handed him the photo. There stood the young David Arben with his violin, Joe Gingold sitting nearby, and Robert Shaw with the baton. Just looking at it made Mendelssohn float through my mind, and I'm sure David heard it too.

These are the years for looking back, and I do. If I could take back that phone call to Ronald Wilford's boss at CAMI to complain about him? Yeah, I would.

If I could go back and please the Monteuxs and have a concertizing career? Sorry, no can do. I was made to have a family. That choice left me positioned as the perfect candidate for Ormandy's concertmaster—someone who just missed a concertizing career. That was a great job, and a lot of people think I should have kept it.

I have already confessed that musical greed sucked me into conducting. I did my penance during those three years with the Dallas Symphony Orchestra. Except I forgot to repent. I love conducting, both professional and university orchestras.

I even loved teaching conducting. Instead of getting another big city orchestra of my own, I was drafted into the honorable company of the giants of my youth. Mr. Happich took on a kid who didn't want to play the music of anybody who scowled like Beethoven. Mr. Zimbalist accepted an eleven-year-old who told the Curtis faculty to finish their lunches first and then listen up. Jani Szanto refined the playing of a teenager as far as it could go on the mediocre violin his family could afford, and then lent me one of his own.

I have the pleasure that must have been theirs, too, of being counted among the mentors of conductors, players, and teachers of music all over the world.

I've been a little promiscuous about music, quick to enjoy tunes that make me want to dance or sing along. Almost any type of music can make me feel happy or sad. But it is classical music, with its intricacy and large structure, that plumbs the depths of human feeling. It's not a pretty house—it's monumental architecture. The shortsighted are always saying classical music is dying. It won't. It will never be set aside or forgotten. We will die, and a new generation of music lovers in another corner of the globe will discover it again and add to its canon.

Forgive me. I get carried away.

No. I'm right. Music connects everyone listening. Even more, it connects those making the music with one another. How can I forget playing with Joe Gingold, sharing the music stand, looking at the same page? The notes in front of us weren't music. They were only instructions. The music that we created—sound vibrations—connected us, though we couldn't touch it with our hands. The cloud of vibrations that is music has held me aloft all my life.

Inside my head, I will admit, I hear music all the time. A day can begin with playing Beethoven's "Pastoral" under George Szell in Basel, Switzerland, every note not merely perfect but also beautiful.

More often I'm conducting. It might be the sacrificial dance at the end of *The Rite of Spring*, the percussive music making you picture the ballet, that chosen girl who must not stop, must dance herself to death. My arms, no, my whole body tries to capture Stravinsky's wildness and infuse the orchestra with it, to make it burst out of them as one fury. . . .

But this makes my arms twitch. It's after midnight, and Marilyn sleeps next to me. That's what I want to do—sleep. And I don't want to wake her. She can always tell when I'm conducting in my head. She knows the little jerks of the shoulder and arms, movements of the head. Imaginary violin playing is a bit less disruptive than conducting.

Some nights I can just turn off the music and find a normal dream. Other nights I turn off a symphony only to find that a concerto has sneaked in, and my Guarnerius del Gesù is in my hands.

The best is when I have company, the company of some friend now gone.

Anshel, Anshel.

I cannot switch it off. It's Leonard Rose.

I'll see you in the coda! he says.

Yes, absolutely, I wouldn't miss it for anything. Lenny's playing the Dvořák Cello Concerto in Philadelphia again. There's that place in the finale where his cello is joined by my solo violin, and we look at each other, breathe, and play.

Index